ESCAPE & EVASION

If you can quit the compound undetected,
    And clear your tracks, nor leave the smallest trace,
And carry out the programme you've selected,
    Nor lose your grasp of distance, time and space...

If you can walk all night by compass bearing,
    Or move discreetly in the light of day,
And temper your elusiveness with daring,
    Trusting that sometimes bluff will find a way...

If you can swallow sudden sour frustration,
    And gaze unmoved at failure's ugly shape,
Remembering for further inspiration
    It is your constant duty to escape...

If you can keep the little bastard's guessing
    With explanations only partly true,
And leave them in their heart of hearts confessing
    They didn't get the whole truth out of you...

If you can have the patience to think clearly
    Of planning methods wiser than before,
And treat your past miscalculations merely
    As hints let fall by Fate to teach you more...

If you can scheme with patience and precision
    (It wasn't in a day they builded Rome)
And make escape your single sole ambition
    The next time you attempt it – you'll get home!

Parody of Kipling's poem '*If*'
found in one of MI9's E Group files

ESCAPE & EVASION

POW Breakouts in World War II

IAN DEAR

RIGEL

Rigel Publications
A division of the Orion Publishing Group Ltd.
5 Upper St Martin's Lane
London WC2H 9EA

First published by Arms and Armour 1997
Cassell Military Paperbacks edition 2000
This edition published in 2004

British Library Cataloguing-in-Publication Data
A catalogue record for this book is available from the
British Library

ISBN 1-898-79983-0

Printed and bound within the European Union

CONTENTS

ACKNOWLEDGEMENTS

I should like to take this opportunity of thanking the staff of the Library service of the London Borough of Merton who over the years have been unfailingly courteous and helpful, as have been the staff of the London Library and those of the Imperial War Museum's departments of Documents and Books. The Keeper of the Department of Documents allowed me access to material from the following documents for chapter seven: P132 and 132A, 91/14/1, 90/2/1, 87/25/1 con shelf, 82/24/1, and 92/14/1. These contain the quotes I used from manuscripts by R. Edwardes-Ker, D. C. Robinson, Gerald Scott (courtesy Mrs Scott), J. O. Dykes, Bill Reynolds, and L. E. C. Davies. Where possible, I have tried to trace the copyright holders of this material and would like to thank those who have contacted me and given me permission to use it. I should also like to thank Fay Martin for her help with chapter thirteen, and Helen Long for lending photographs from her book, *Safe Houses Are Dangerous*, a seminal work for anyone interested in the subject of escape and evasion. I have tried to trace the copyright holders of the uncredited photographs, but without success. Crown copyright material is reproduced with the permission of the Controller of HMSO.

INTRODUCTION

Escape and evasion have always been a part of warfare. The authors of *MI9: Escape and Evasion 1939–45* suggested that Saint Joseph, who organised the escape from Herod into Egypt for his wife and the infant Jesus, could justifiably be called the patron saint of evaders and escapers. They then go on to list other historical figures, such as the Empress Matilda who 'did a model midwinter passage through her enemies' lines around Oxford castle in 1142, wrapped in a sheet to hide herself in the snow', and Charles II who hid in an oak tree after his army's defeat at Worcester in 1651.

The list is endless, but the Napoleonic Wars were probably the first conflicts in which prisoners were held in any number; towards their end the committee that managed relief funds for British prisoners had about 16,000 names on record, and the British were holding some 80,000 French prisoners, most of them soldiers. The majority of British prisoners were naval, though the number of soldier prisoners increased after the Peninsular War had begun in 1808. Napoleon's escape from Elba in 1815 was, of course, the best known instance of escape and evasion at this time, but in 1812 the French government published a list of 355 British prisoners who had escaped.

In his introduction to Captain Hewson's narrative of his escape from the French during the Napoleonic Wars, published for the first time in 1981, Antony Brett-James makes the interesting point that the more senior the officer the less likely he was to escape. Admittedly, senior officers were more likely to be exchanged and many of them were on parole and refused to break their word of honour, but Brett-James gives the telling statistic that of more than a hundred naval officers who made successful escapes, about 90 per cent of them were midshipmen. This was by no means the case during the Second World War when even the most elderly British officers participated fully in escapes from POW camps.

The literature on escapes by prisoners during these early conflicts is sparse, though Donat Henchy O'Brien's *My Adventures in the Late War*, published in 1814, and Captain Edward Boys' *Narrative of a Captivity, Escape and Adventure in France and Flanders during the War*, published in 1817, were both republished in Victorian times and showed that even that long ago escape books were popular with the reading public.

Certainly the story of Winston Churchill's escape in November 1899 during the Boer War was rapturously received, and made the young journalist famous. Churchill loathed his time in captivity which is doubtless why, when he was prime minister during the Second World War, he never forgot the thousands of prisoners of war incarcerated in enemy territory and did everything he could to alleviate their misery.

Intent on regaining his freedom, Churchill did what hundreds of others were to do in both world wars: he seized his opportunity when two of the guards turned their backs to him and began to chat, and scrambled over the wall of the school where he was imprisoned. But, as others were to find, escape from prison was one thing, to get clear away was quite another. 'The town was picketed, the country was patrolled, the trains were searched, the line was guarded,' he wrote in *My Early Life*. '... how was I to get food or direction? ... But when hope had departed, fear had gone as well ... I looked at the stars. Orion shone brightly. Scarcely a year before he had guided me when lost in the desert to the banks of the Nile. He had given me water. Now he should lead to freedom. I could not endure the want of either.'

Orion led Churchill to the railway line where he again did what many others were later to do. He managed to climb aboard a train, hide himself, then jump off before he was discovered, and finally throw himself on the mercy of a member of the local populace who did not betray him, and he eventually reached British lines.

Churchill was lucky, because he had forgotten to take with him some of the essential tools of the escaper. His mistake was latched on to during the Second World War by the British escape and evasion organisation, MI9, which used it as a warning to all would-be escapers not to forget their escape kits.

'He dropped into the garden and crept into some bushes,' ran the prefix to MI9's escape Bible used by all intelligence officers. 'To his horror he realised that he had left his food tablets, maps and compass on the wrong side of the wall, as a result of which he later suffered considerably.

'This prisoner, who escaped in the Boer War, is now the BRITISH PRIME MINISTER

BUT THE MORAL IS STILL THE SAME.

ALWAYS CARRY YOUR ESCAPE AIDS WITH YOU'

Churchill's escape, as one of his many biographers has remarked, 'contains all the necessary ingredients of an adventure saga of high quality', but it was the escape literature of the First World War which catapulted the genre to the popularity it retains today (one need look no further for confirmation of this than Andy McNab's phenomenally successful *Bravo Two Zero* which is largely about the author's evasion of Iraqi forces during the Gulf War in 1991). Such titles as *The Road to En-Dor* by E. H. Jones, *The Escaping Club* by A. J. Evans, *The Tunnellers of Holzminden* by H. G. Durnford, and *Within Four Walls* by M. C. C. Harrison and H. A. Cartwright, were all best-sellers between the wars, and the date stamps of my copies from the London Library show that they still have, quite rightly, a substantial readership. In them can be found some of the early methods of communicating with prisoners of war,* and of escape techniques such as forgery, tunnel digging and deception, which were of inestimable value to those captured during the Second World War, and which is why two of the authors, A. J. Evans and M. C. C. Harrison, were employed by MI9.

Although, as I have intimated, the history of escape and evasion is long and varied, I have chosen to confine my book to the period of the Second World War and its immediate aftermath, because it was during those years that escape and evasion reached, among the Allied nations at least, a pinnacle of efficiency and ingenuity, and therefore is of the greatest interest.

Nor have I chosen to write about the legendary escapes of the Second World War on which such best-sellers as *The Wooden Horse*, *The Great Escape*, and *Colditz* were based, preferring rather to concentrate on the escape organisations that worked for the freedom of all Allied escapers and evaders and to give examples of escapes by those on the Axis side.

The chapters on escapes by German and Japanese POW speak for themselves, but a further word of explanation is needed about why I have also chosen to write about Allied escape and evasion organisations, the escape lines they spawned, and those who used them. It is this. In all the extensive Second World War literature on the subject published during the immediate post-war period, very few of the authors seem to have realised that those who helped them in enemy occupied territory were not just individuals working on their own – though a few were – but were part of an organised, secret network.

Time and again one reads in these books that the escaper or evader happened to fall in with 'someone in the Resistance' or 'a brave and patriotic family who sheltered us', or something similar, and it wasn't until Airey Neave published his book *Saturday at MI9* in 1969 that the public began to have a clear idea of how the clandestine networks operated to extract escapers and evaders from enemy occupied territory, even though biographies of some of the principal organisers had been published before then.

Colonel Ride's book on the British Army Aid Group based in China was a similar revelation when it was published in 1981; and precious little was known of the American escape and evasion organisation MIS-X until some mention of it was made by M. R. D. Foot and J. M. Langley in *MI9: Escape and Evasion 1939–45*, first published in 1979, information which was amplified as late as 1990 by Lloyd R. Shoemaker's *The Escape Factory*. And it was not until 1995 that some of the official documents and reports on the cross-Channel sea escape routes, and those between Gibraltar and southern France, were made public for the first time in Brooks Richards' official history, *Secret Flotillas*.

Even when the escape lines became public knowledge, it took George Watt, as he describes in his memoir, *The Comet Connection*, until 1985 to discover which

---

*Coded letters from families, rather less sophisticated than those used in the Second World War, fed information about the progress of the war to prisoners. One particularly amusing example of this comes from *The Road to En-Dor*: 'The news that somebody's father's trousers had come down was, I remember, the occasion of a very merry evening, for it meant that Dad's Bags (or Baghdad) had fallen at last.'

organisation had helped him after his Flying Fortress had been shot down over Belgium in November 1943. At the time intelligence briefings given to airmen hinted that escape organisations existed but gave the cover story that they were ones left over from the First World War.

Except for the Vatican ratlines, where a cover-up must be suspected, the reason for such tardiness is, of course, security. During the war ordinary potential escapers and evaders could never be told about these organisations, and for many years after the war details about them continued to be withheld from public scrutiny in case they were needed again (as indeed they were during the Korean War).

In one or two instances – the files of MIS-X, for example – they were withheld forever, having been destroyed, but during the early 1970s most of MI9's files were at last released. Equally importantly, what remain of the files of the Special Operations Executive (SOE), which formed its own escape lines, are now in the process of being made available to the public. Luckily for me, the relevant SOE file on the Indragiri River Escape Line was one of them, as are what SOE files remain relating to MI9's E Group in the Far East.

Finally, it is necessary to emphasise that the escape lines – or ratlines as they had come to be called by 1944 – mentioned in this book are just a few of the better known ones. There were many more, some of which have left no trace of their existence except for a passing mention in official reports.

1

CROCKATT'S SECRET EMPIRE

In 1917 a small sub-branch of the British War Office's Intelligence Directorate was opened to investigate the possibilities of obtaining intelligence from German prisoners of war (POW) and from British personnel who had escaped from German POW camps or who had managed to evade capture. One of its successes was to organise coded communications with those incarcerated in camps in Germany. Called MI1, it was resurrected again in August 1939 and Lieutenant-Colonel Gerald (later Field Marshal Sir Gerald) Templar was given command of it.

When war was declared Templar joined the British Expeditionary Force to France, leaving Captain A. R. Rawlinson in charge of the unit, but on 28 September 1939 Templar found time to write to the Director of Military Intelligence (DMI) on his ideas for communicating with POW by code. Coincidentally, one of the authors of a famous First World War escape book, *Within Four Walls*, M. C. C. Harrison, contacted the DMI to suggest that an inter-service department be established whose task it would be to help POW to escape.

The DMI sought the advice of Major J. C. F. Holland, then head of an obscure branch of the War Office called MIR which was soon to become one of the founding elements of the British sabotage and subversion organisation, Special Operations Executive (SOE). Holland wrote a paper supporting the proposal and it was accepted by the Joint Intelligence Committee (JIC).

The JIC suggested that this new secret branch, to be known as MI9, be run by someone who had been an escapee in the previous war. Holland disagreed. He argued that the ideas and actions of anyone who had been an escapee would be coloured by their experiences. Instead, he proposed an old friend of his, Major Norman Richard Crockatt, who was working with him in MIR. Crockatt, then 45 years old, was a regular officer in the Royal Scots. He had a distinguished record as a fighting soldier, having been awarded the DSO and the MC during the First World War in which he had been severely wounded. 'He was also clear-headed, quick-witted, a good organiser,' noted the writers of the history of MI9, 'a good judge of men and no respecter of red tape: excellent qualities for his early struggles in the War Office.'

The charter of the new organisation was issued on 23 December 1939. Crockatt's initial aim to fulfil it was encompassed in five brief paragraphs which he later listed in a survey of his wartime work:

1. To facilitate escapes of British prisoners of war, thereby getting back service personnel and containing additional enemy manpower on guard duties.

11

2. To facilitate the return to the United Kingdom of those who succeeded in evading capture in enemy occupied territory.

3. To collect and distribute information.

4. To assist in the denial of information to the enemy.

5. To maintain morale of British prisoners in POW camps.

In April 1940 MI9 took over the section of MI1 responsible for obtaining information from enemy POW and renamed it MI9(a). Crockatt put Rawlinson in charge of it, and interrogation centres for German POW were opened at Cockfosters and Marylebone. The section of MI9 which dealt with British POW and internees in enemy and neutral countries, and the intelligence to be gleaned from those who were repatriated, was designated MI9(b).

MI9 was originally allotted room 424 in the Metropole Hotel in Northumberland Avenue, but in September 1940 it was moved to Wilton Park, a country house near Beaconsfield, and given the cover name of Camp 20. Among Crockatt's staff officers were Rawlinson, Clayton Hutton, who was in charge of producing escape devices (see Chapter Two), and 'Johnnie' Evans, author of *The Escaping Club*, one of the best books on escaping to have come out of the First World War.

Unlike many military bureaucrats, Crockatt worked with as small a team as possible, but it was inevitable that during the course of the war MI9 expanded considerably. In August 1940 it formed a section in the Middle East which was part of Colonel Dudley Clarke's secret deception unit known as 'A' Force. Clarke had considerable knowledge of escape and evasion, and with his encouragement the section, known as N Section, grew rapidly and under various cover names eventually operated throughout the Mediterranean theatre where it was known to escapers and evaders simply as 'A' Force. N Section was commanded first by M. C. C. Harrison and then from September 1941 by Lieutenant-Colonel A. C. Simonds. In September 1943 it became a joint venture between MI9 and MI9's American equivalent, MIS-X (see Chapter Six).

MI9 was also at work in the Far East and in October 1941 it set up an advance base in India. Initially part of the New Delhi Intelligence Directorate GS I(d), in May 1942 it became an independent section, designated GS I(e), under Lieutenant-Colonel Robin Ridgway who became the outside link between New Delhi and the British Army Aid Group (see Chapter Nine). When Mountbatten's South-East Asia Command was formed in the autumn of 1943, GS I(e) was renamed E Group and in June 1944 Ridgway moved to another appointment and was replaced by Lieutenant-Colonel R. C. Jackman. In July 1944 a directive was issued which resulted in E Group's working closely with Force 136, SOE's organisation in India.

The nature of the war in the Far East and the huge distances involved precluded Ridgway and Jackman from operating as MI9 and its branches did elsewhere. Contact with POW in Japanese camps was almost impossible, though reports in recently released SOE files show that it did occur towards the end of the war when POW working on the notorious Burma–Thailand railway had messages smuggled to them. Escapes were also rare, though again they sometimes did take place. In one operation, 'PARTERRE', E Group managed to exfiltrate by air three British servicemen from Thailand who had escaped from a Japanese POW camp there in December 1944, and during the previous month five RAF evaders whose aircraft had been forced down in Thailand were hidden in a civilian internment camp by the pro-Allied Free Siamese Movement.

However, for most of the war the Group's activities were virtually restricted to making up evasion kits, running two schools for jungle training, air reconnaissance, and lecturing on evasion. It also made emergency food and medical supply dumps on strategically placed islands in the Indian Ocean for the use of downed air crews. Its single operation was launched when the Dutch East Indies fell to the Japanese in the spring of 1942. Ridgway dispatched a small reconnaissance party to discover what had happened to the large number of POW and civilian internees trapped on Sumatra. It was put ashore by submarine but was never seen or heard of again.

In Europe the *Blitzkrieg* of May 1940, which had overrun the Low Countries and much of France, resulted in thousands of Allied escapers and evaders. Most of these gravitated to the southern part of France which, after the Franco–German armistice of June 1940, had remained under the nominal control of a collaborationist French government based at Vichy.

In an army training memo of 31 July 1940, at least partly based on the interrogation of those who had escaped or evaded after the Fall of France, the importance of escaping quickly, while still in the hands of troops not accustomed to guarding prisoners, was emphasised, as was the need for escapers and evaders to acquire civilian clothes and the fact that any help they received from a civilian put that individual's life at risk.

'The following points as noted by an escaper from France in civilian clothes illustrate', said the memo, 'the importance of conforming to the habits of the country from which a prisoner is attempting to break out: 1. Do not march in a military fashion, but adopt a tired slouch. 2. Try to "collect" a bicycle. They proved invaluable to several escapers. 3. Do not wear a wrist watch. Carry it in your pocket. 4. Sling your haversack: French peasants commonly carry one in this way, but never as a pack on their backs. 5. Do not use a cane or walking-stick: it is a British custom. 6. Get rid of Army boots and adopt a pair of rope-soled shoes as worn by peasants, if procurable. 7. French peasants are generally clean-shaven, though a slight growth of beard is not uncommon. 8. A beret is a very effective disguise. 9. Village priests are likely to be helpful. Care should be exercised in approaching them and one should avoid being seen talking to them.'

At the end of 1941 Crockatt was promoted colonel and made a Deputy Director of Military Intelligence (Prisoners of War). From 1 January 1942 Rawlinson's MI9(a) became MI19 and MI9(b) was now given the task of dealing with general questions, co-ordination, distribution of information, and liaison with other services and government departments, and overseas commands. A new section (d) was also created to train combatant personnel of the three services in the UK, and to issue evasion and escape equipment and information to units at home and MI9 organisations overseas.

At the same time the cover name Intelligence School 9, or IS9, was created as an umbrella for sections which carried out MI9's executive work. IS9(W) interrogated escapers, evaders and repatriated service personnel; IS9(X) dealt with escape and evasion planning, the preparation of escape maps, and the location of POW camps and the dispatch of escape material to them; IS9(Y) prepared code messages with which to communicate with POW camps; and IS9(Z) dealt with the production of escape and evasion equipment and the experimental work associated with it. But the most important section was IS9(d) which, guided by the Secret Intelligence Service (MI6), employed and trained agents who were dispatched into the enemy occupied countries of western Europe to help establish escape lines (see Map 1). To those who worked in this secret department it was known as Room 900, the room allotted to it at the War Office.

In September 1943, when planning for the Normandy landings of June 1944 was already well under way, an MI9 unit, known as IS9(WEA), was formed to work as part of Eisenhower's Supreme Headquarters (SHAEF); and in August 1944 N Section, which had been divided between the eastern and central Mediterranean in December 1943, became IS9(ME) and IS9(CMF). The duty of all these sections was the rescue and protection of POW in enemy occupied territory.

Finally, there was IS9(AB) which, when the time came, interviewed helpers of British and American escapers and evaders in France, Belgium, Holland and Denmark with a view to investigating and settling financial claims and recommending awards.

MI9(d)'s training school in North London was attended by intelligence officers of all three services who learnt how to lecture service personnel on the art of escape and evasion. Advice was given as to whom to approach, and when, and that once in hiding patience was important. On no account were escapers or evaders to attempt to make their own way to safety, but were to wait until a member of the escape line contacted them. When in the hands of the escape line they were to obey instructions to the letter. They were not to start friendly conversations with unknown persons nor were they to offer cigarettes or chocolate. (Several escapers were betrayed by the nicotine stains on their forefingers, and chocolate was unknown in Germany and in occupied countries.) To add realism to the lectures, successful escapers and evaders were encouraged to lecture on their own experiences and the difficulties encountered.

To enliven these lectures amusing stories were often related to hold the attention of the audience. One never failed to amuse, though it was probably apocryphal. A sergeant pilot was shot down near a French convent and before the

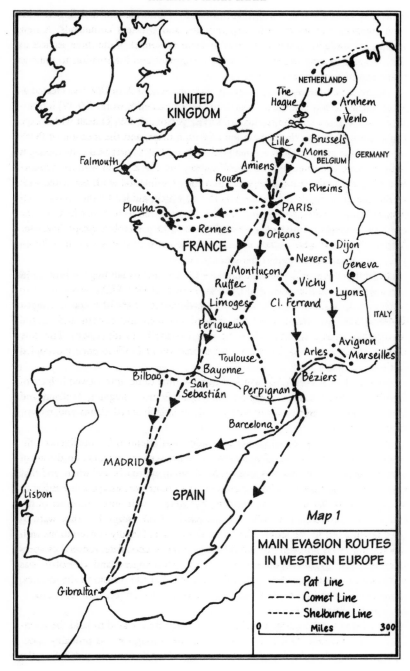

Map 1

MAIN EVASION ROUTES
IN WESTERN EUROPE

——— Pat Line
- - - Comet Line
······ Shelburne Line

0 Miles 300

Germans could close in on him he was whisked away by some of the occupants and dressed in the habit of the Order. The next day he found himself in the garden alongside a truly beautiful nun but his tentative advances were brushed aside when she turned and, in a masculine voice, said sharply: 'Don't be a bloody fool, I've been here since Dunkirk.'

Lectures also drummed into service personnel that being a prisoner was not a disgrace, it was just another posting. The individual remained on active service and his duty remained as clear as when he had been fighting with his unit: to escape as quickly as possible to rejoin those fighting for his country and in the meantime to make himself, within reason, as much a nuisance as possible to his captors while he remained under their control. 'Goon baiting', the taunting of guards who were known to all POW as 'Goons', was a particularly popular way of doing this, but a more serious method for a POW to make a nuisance of himself was to escape, even if this inevitably meant recapture.

One mass escape, made from *Oflag VIIB* at Eichstatt in Bavaria in June 1943, showed just how much German manpower could be diverted. All the escapers were recaptured but during the two weeks the 65 men were at liberty no fewer than 50,000 German personnel – police, troops, home guard and members of the *Hitlerjugend* – were deployed to find them.

Emphasis was also placed by MI9 lecturers on a POW's demeanour and how he should behave towards his captors. Concrete evidence of German reaction to the general bearing of POW was naturally hard to obtain, but a captured SS secret report on internal security in Germany, dated 12 August 1943, did show that the attitude of Allied POW was having a deleterious effect on morale in Germany. It commented on the self-possessed bearing of British POW and on the fact that the scruffy, hangdog look of those captured in 1940 had completely disappeared. Instead, the Germans now found themselves guarding men who were dressed in far better quality uniforms than those of the *Wehrmacht*, and who were well fed and confident, and that the manner in which they distributed chocolates and ciga-rettes to any ordinary German they met had a deplorable effect on civilian morale. To Crockatt, POW who behaved in such a manner were all part of the Allied propaganda machine which was slowly grinding down German morale.

During the course of the war MI9(d) lectures on escape and evasion were given to more than 600,000 British and Commonwealth servicemen, but another, equally important, aspect of MI9's work was its communications with those already incarcerated in POW camps. These camps were organised along military lines, the Senior British Officer (SBO) or Senior American Officer (SAO) taking the position of commanding officer who had under him, among others, an intel-ligence officer and an escape committee.

It was important for MI9 to maintain contact with POW camps so that intel-ligence could be gleaned from those in them and information passed to them. The most common form of communication was by coded letter. MI9 lecturers chose the most security-conscious and level-headed members of their audiences to be code users – CUs in MIS-X parlance. Statistically, this amounted to 1 per cent of army and navy personnel, most fighter pilots, and 6 per cent of other aircrew.

MI9's code section invented numerous characters and firms to correspond with prisoners in special codes. The section did not have a large staff and there was always the danger that the same member would write coded letters to different prisoners in the same camp, and that the handwriting would be recognised by the German censors. This led to outsiders being employed to write letters of great intimacy or obscure business policy to prisoners they did not know, though the earliest communications in code were between husbands and wives who had pre-arranged their own in case the husband was captured. These were known to MI9 as 'dotty' codes, not because the organisation had doubts about the sanity of the correspondents using them but because dots were commonly used to show when a message in code began and ended.

One of the first 'dotty' codes to prove its worth was the one employed between a Captain Rupert Barry and his wife. When Barry was captured he asked his wife to contact the War Office. MI9 then requested Barry's wife to encode the message that her husband was to wash half-a-dozen handkerchiefs to arrive in his next Red Cross parcel. These revealed the details of an MI9 code which Barry then used during the four years he acted as the coding officer in Colditz Castle, the notorious POW camp for those who were persistent escapers.

During 1940 a code, designated by the initials 'HK', was developed by MI9 officers with the help of an expert from the Foreign Office. It was simple to use and difficult to detect, much less to decode. The manner in which the date of the letter was written indicated whether there was a hidden message in its contents. This established, the writer would then indicate in his opening words which part of the code he was using.

Radio messages sent out by the BBC were also used in conjunction with coded letters because most POW camps had hidden receivers that had been smuggled in or constructed by the prisoners. One of the BBC programmes Crockatt used was the immensely popular – some seven million are said to have listened to it – Wednesday evening broadcast by the Radio Padre on the Forces programme. If the Padre, the Very Reverend Dr. R. Selby, began by saying 'Good evening, forces', those listening in POW camps knew there would be a coded message for them in his text, and it was taken down in shorthand and the message decoded from it. A few camps also had transmitters but Crockatt gave strict orders that they were to be used only in a dire emergency which, luckily, never arose.

By the beginning of 1942 communications in code had been established with every officer POW camp (*Oflag*) in Germany. As the war progressed more codes were invented and were employed with greater frequency. In April and May 1943 two successive records were set when 367 and then 413 messages in code were received at Wilton Park. Of those received in May 47 acknowledged receipt of escape kits hidden in parcels, but possibly the majority contained intelligence matters because a camp's intelligence officer would always interrogate newcomers as to how, why and where they had been made POW, as were unsuccessful escapers who had been returned to the camp. These interrogations could produce important data re such matters as German fighter tactics and potential targets for Allied targets. One outstanding example of intelligence being passed in code occurred in 1942 when a captured British radar expert was able to send some important information regarding German night-fighter radar to MI6's scientific expert, R. V. Jones.

But coded letters were primarily used by POW requesting items that would help them to escape (the earliest successful escape came in March 1941 when a private in the Army Dental Corps, L. A. Coe, managed to reach Switzerland). The replies would tell the POW how to identify the parcel containing what they required, and it was up to the POW to make sure that it was not opened and searched by the Germans. The parcel offices at POW camps were almost always manned by prisoners under the command of a camp guard, who was rarely incorruptible. If the guard proved obdurate prisoners were adept at making sure the marked parcels were not searched. Occasionally, the marked parcels could be lifted straight from the parcels office by bribing the soldier guarding it with tobacco or coffee.

One of Crockatt's policies was never to use Red Cross parcels to smuggle in forbidden items, for the Red Cross had given the Germans an undertaking that they would not allow themselves to be used in this way. Parcels containing escape equipment or clothes were often dispatched via the Red Cross, but then the Red Cross was merely the deliverer of them and bore no responsibility for what was in them. (Neither side apparently infringed Red Cross neutrality with parcels – it would have been counter-productive to do so – but Donald Darling, MI6's representative in Gibraltar, certainly infringed it by using the Swedish captain of a Red Cross ship to transmit written messages.)

There were many ways of secreting vital escape equipment in a prisoner's parcel. The handle of a cricket bat could contain a screwdriver; a hacksaw blade could be hidden in a comb or toothbrush. But not only smuggled items in parcels were of use to would-be escapees; the parcels themselves produced invaluable material as did some of the disposable contents. Those sent by the Red Cross were made of strong thick cardboard, or plywood, which proved useful for lining escape tunnels; empty tins joined together formed ventilation ducts for the tunnels.

In 1941–2 as many as 1,642 'special' parcels, as they were called, were dispatched with escape equipment hidden in their contents, and 5,173 ordinary parcels, many of which were full of tobacco or coffee, useful material with which to bribe the guards. The parcels were always packed by MI9 and purported to come from such fictitious organisations as the Prisoners' Leisure Hours Fund and the Welsh Provident Society. Great care was taken to ensure that the postmarks were authentic and that the newspaper used for wrapping the contents came from the locality of the alleged sender.

At first MI9 came under the aegis of MI6 which until the Second World War had held exclusive sway in running agents in occupied countries. It was headed by Major-General Stewart Menzies, known as 'C', but it was his formidable deputy, Claude Dansey, who closely supervised the operations of MI9 in occupied Europe to ensure that the junior organisation did not impede the intelligence gathering which was MI6's primary task (new recruits into MI9 were often lectured by Menzies on the unfortunate fact that Nurse Cavell had been shot by the Germans during the First World War for helping escapers although her primary task had been intelligence gathering). MI6 had a say in the running of escape lines in much of Europe, though MI9 had outright control in other combat theatres until the USA began setting up MIS-X after entering the war in December 1941.

During much of the early part of the war, MI9 was the Cinderella of the secret services and was treated with such indifference that for some time it was impossible even to create a proper wireless network with its agents in occupied territory. The three armed services were no better. They disliked all secret services on principle and regarded MI9 with suspicion, even hostility. There were many chairbound officers in Whitehall who were averse to encouraging servicemen to think about the possibility of captivity at all.

It was Menzies, for higher political reasons of his own – almost certainly connected with the formation of SOE, a potential rival of MI6 – who offered to help form the first escape line for Crockatt: from Marseilles to Barcelona, and thence to Gibraltar or Lisbon. Crockatt accepted and in July 1940 a young trilingual MI6 agent, Donald Darling, who worked under the code-name 'Sunday', was dispatched to Spain to establish what later became known as the PAT Line (see Chapter Three).

Darling was able to contact Captain Ian Garrow of the Seaforth Highlanders, the leader of the many escapers and evaders in Marseilles who had been gathered from all over France by the Vichy government and interned. By the spring of 1941, when he was obliged to move to Lisbon (and then Gibraltar), Darling had established a courier service between Marseilles and Barcelona which had also passed along it a number of evaders. Communications to and from this embryo escape line were, in those early days, weak. No trained wireless operators were available to MI9 and this made efficient co-ordination difficult if not impossible, but Darling saw that Garrow was at least adequately funded.

Another member of the newly fledged escape organisation – recruited on the hunting field and given the code-name 'Orchid' – was Nubar Gulbenkian, the son of the Armenian oil multi-millionaire, Calouste Gulbenkian ('Mr Five Per Cent'). Gulbenkian senior was living temporarily in Vichy after fleeing from Paris, and because Nubar was a member of the neutral Iranian legation in London, which entitled him to a diplomatic passport, he had little trouble visiting his family.

On one of his trips Gulbenkian helped arrange a system of guides for those escaping across the Pyrenees into Spain. The deal for supplying guides was struck in a café in Perpignan with a man named Michel Pareyre who owned a garage in the town. Pareyre, Gulbenkian was told, could be identified because he would be reading a French newspaper upside down and answer positively to the question: 'Have you a Parker pen? A Parker Duo-fold?' The price agreed was £20 for other ranks (enlisted men), double that for an officer. Payment was strictly on results and the money was to be paid into a London bank whence Pareyre could extract it after the war.

Gulbenkian rather took to this new and exciting way of life, but after he had been in and out of Vichy France a few times it was explained to him that it was too dangerous for him to continue, and to his great disappointment his role as a secret agent was abruptly curtailed, though his sister in Paris continued to escort escapers and evaders across the city.

An early recruit to MI9 in London was J. M. Langley, a Guards subaltern. In October 1940 Langley had escaped from a hospital in Lille after his left arm had been amputated, and had made his way to Marseilles where, before he was repatriated because of his wounds, he met and worked with Ian Garrow. He arrived home in March 1941 and was immediately interrogated, as were all returning escapers and evaders, by one of Crockatt's Intelligence Officers, H. B. A. de Bruyne.

In his book *Fight Another Day*, Langley gives a number of insights into those connected with MI9 and how the organisation worked. De Bruyne had travelled a long way to join the war; in September 1939 he had been running the family sheep farm in southern Chile. He liked to be called 'Bruno', but because of his agricultural connections, was universally known to his colleagues as 'Bo Peep'. Langley records how de Bruyne knew all about his movements because the censors had intercepted all his letters from Vichy France. He especially wanted detailed information on Garrow's activities.

'"You know all about him then?" I asked.

'"Broadly, yes. The details, no. In his last message he indicated that an officer who had worked with him would be coming straight back to England. We guessed it would be one of the repatriation party which was originally routed through Lisbon. Your arrival at Gibraltar and immediate departure caught us by surprise."

'I laughed. "You were not the only one who was surprised."

'He laughed in turn. "We are slowly learning that escapers usually do the unexpected. I suppose that is why they escape ..."'

After a month's leave Langley reported to his regimental headquarters where his Colonel's opening remarks were far from reassuring about his future.

'"You are well aware of the immense power of the Brigade of Guards in all matters concerning the employment of its officers?"

'I nodded.

'"As a last resort we can always appeal to the Monarch."

'God, I thought, what have I done now that merits possible appeal to His Majesty King George VI.

'"However, in your case," he continued, "we can do nothing and I am further informed that the Monarch would be powerless to intervene."

'Too numbed with shock I could think of no crime where the King could not use his royal prerogative of mercy; my situation could obviously not be worse.

'"It goes without saying that I personally can do no more than give you the orders I received yesterday by telephone."

'"Yes, sir."

'"You will go at 12.30 this afternoon to the Savoy Hotel where in the foyer opposite the restaurant you will see a man dressed in a dark suit, wearing a red carnation, with a folded copy of *The Times* on the table at which he will be seated. You will make yourself known to him."

'There was a silence while I digested these facts.

'"What do you think it all means, sir?" I enquired.

'The Colonel glanced nervously towards the door of his office, which was closed.

'"I think", he said in a whisper, "it must be the Secret Intelligence Service."'

The Colonel was correct for the man Langley met at the Savoy was none other than Colonel Claude Dansey.

'My first impression', Langley wrote later, 'was very much of a benign uncle, with his white hair, blue eyes and general air of benevolence; but this was quickly erased as he looked me sharply up and down and with a grunted "Hm" said, "F. O. L.'s son and wounded. What a bit of luck."

'I merely stared in amazement and he proffered me an explanation. "Your father worked for me in Berne in 1917 and 1918. Some of my young men are finding it difficult to explain to their girl friends why they are not fighting. However, be that as it may, I am going to ask you the same question as I did your father when he joined my staff. What do you want?"

'"I am sorry, sir, I do not quite understand."

'"Surely, I make myself plain. It is always easier if you get what you want before you start working, then you don't spend half your time worrying about your possible award. Now, an MC or an OBE? A DSO is more difficult and you are too young for a CBE. However, there are plenty of foreign decorations available. I am told that the Poles have the nicest ribbons – the Order of Stanislaus, or some such other outlandish name is very much sought after. I call it "Pologna Prostituta" as it is immensely popular with the women. Take your choice but be quick about it."

'I replied that I did not want anything.

'"Just like your father. Well, do not come complaining to me that you have not been properly looked after ..."'

His recruitment thus achieved, Langley reported the following Monday to MI6's headquarters, Broadway Buildings opposite St James's Park underground station. The brass plate outside proclaimed that was the main office of the Minimax Fire Extinguisher Company.

'Uncle Claude, as Colonel Dansey was widely called, wasted no time in getting down to business.

'"Just listen to me and don't ask any damned silly questions," he said. "The likes of you in France and Belgium are causing me considerable trouble, which is being made worse by the apparent inability of the RAF to remain airborne over enemy-occupied territory. My job, and that of my agents, is the collection of information about the Germans' intentions and activities, not to act as nursemaids to people who seem totally incapable of doing much to get back on their own."'

It transpired that an evading RAF pilot was being sheltered by a female MI6 agent in occupied France, an action which, in Dansey's eyes, certainly compromised her reputation and could compromise her work as well. It was Langley's job, Dansey said, to arrange for the pilot's removal immediately because sex could not be allowed to interfere with MI6's work. Theoretically, Dansey told him, Langley was to be on loan from MI9. In practice he was on Dansey's staff and under his orders.

This was a somewhat anomalous situation, but Langley managed to work for both organisations to encourage the formation of escape lines. His section, set up in the War Office's Room 900 in the summer of 1941, was the most highly secret part of Crockatt's organisation. It dealt solely with escape lines from Belgium, France and the Netherlands (see Map 1), including the PAT and COMET (see Chapters Three and Eleven) Lines, and, later, with SHELBURNE (see Chapter Twelve).

The organiser of SHELBURNE was a French-Canadian sergeant-major named Lucien Dumais who had been taken prisoner after the Dieppe raid and later managed to return to Britain via the PAT Line. He was approached with a view to joining MI9 and in due course decided to do so, and later recorded the efficiency with which he was vetted.

Dumais' first interview was in St James's Park, sitting on a bench in the summer sunshine, but his interrogator's initial remarks froze the Canadian to the bone. Did Dumais know what he was letting himself in for? What if things went wrong and he was caught? Dumais supposed he would be shot.

'"Eventually, yes; but only after the Gestapo have finished with you."

'"I understand," I said, and suddenly it seemed as if the day had grown chilly.

'"And there will be nothing we can do for you. Nothing. As far as we are concerned, you will have ceased to exist."

'"Isn't that a bit rough?"

'"It's a rough game, Sergeant-Major. Well?"

'"I've made up my mind. I'm ready to go."

'"Not so fast. First of all, we have to decide whether you can be of use to us."'

The interviews continued during the next two weeks until Dumais realised that his whole past life, every detail of it, was being closely scrutinised, and that what he did each day was also under the microscope. Unaccountable incidents occurred during those weeks. He was approached in pubs by total strangers who pressed drinks on him, and then tried to get him talking about what he did. On one occasion he was picked up by the police on some trumped-up charge. On another, the military police accused Dumais of having a forged pass. They overdid it, Dumais got angry and insisted on laying a charge against them, but when he mentioned the incident to Langley, he told Dumais to forget it. The Canadian soon realised that his reactions were being tested and this put him on his guard, but he still got caught out.

'One morning I was told to report to the Free French HQ and ask for a certain captain. Langley was there and introduced us, then strolled away, leaving us talking. The French captain asked me a number of loaded questions, and then, staring at my chest, snapped: "And may I ask why you are wearing a medal to which you are not entitled?"

'This really got my goat and I lost my temper.

'"If you weren't in uniform", I said, "I'd fill you in" – and a lot more on the same lines. I was seething. The major returned from examining the pictures on the far wall.

'"Cool down, Lucien. I just wanted to find out how good your French is. Now I know." He turned to the captain. "What do you think?"

'"The accent could be that of central France – say the Nivernais. I suggest his background be constructed accordingly."'

Towards the end of the fortnight Langley gave Dumais his let-out. The unit, Langley said, needed a man of Dumais' experience to train the youngsters. In any case, he added, the Canadian was old enough to quit active service. There would be no disgrace in this; on the contrary, Dumais had a decoration which showed he had done his bit. He summed up: "You'd be far more sensible to return to your unit."

Dumais was stunned and bewildered, but also suspicious as he was by now always looking for a new trap into which he could easily fall. Was Langley implying that he had failed in some way, and that he was no longer required? Or was he simply giving me a final opportunity to have second thoughts? Dumais had no means of knowing but he had no intention of backing down, and said so forcibly.

'"Fine," said Major Langley. "Glad to have you with us."

'There was not even a handshake; just a casual sentence, "Glad to have you with us."

'I was "in".'

Once accepted, Dumais trained as a parachutist, received lectures on security, practised throwing off a shadower, learned the art of picking locks, and became a first-class pistol shot on a range beneath Baker Street station in a room 15 feet wide by 30 feet long '... in which stood ten men. When an instructor called your number and a target number you pulled your gun from its shoulder holster, pushed aside the other instructor who had been asking you to light his cigarette, went into a crouch, and weaving in between the others, got six shots off in pairs. The main object was to get the first two shots off fast. With practice we became red-hot at this.'

When Dumais and a fellow agent, Labrosse, were ready to go into the field they were given a number code which was micro-photographed on to cards so small a magnifying glass was needed to read them, and other essential information was also microfilmed. 'At last we were ready to go. In our pockets and distributed about our persons were demob papers, old Metro tickets, French money, two small compasses, road maps, tear-gas fountain pens, wire metal saws (hidden in our trouser turn-ups), escape ropes made up into the soles of house slippers, and so on.' Both agents carried large sums of French currency in money belts, because running an escape line was an expensive business.

The recruitment and training of an MI9 agent varied during the course of the war, but Dumais' experiences were not atypical; and throughout the war an agent was always controlled by Room 900 and the men who ran it. Initially Langley ran it on his own. Then from mid-1942 he had an assistant, Airey Neave, who had escaped from Colditz and travelled down the PAT Line.

Neave's recruitment into MI9 was not dissimilar to Langley's but by this stage of the war MI6 was not as prominent in MI9's affairs, and Crockatt conducted the interview.

'Crockatt was sitting beside the bar,' Neave wrote later. 'He was unlike the father-figure of the standard spy story, but youngish and military. He shook hands, beckoned us to chairs and ordered us his "specials" in one elegant gesture. He had a handsome, kind, intelligent face. Dark hair, with a neat moustache, slim and smart. He was wearing the uniform of the Royal Scots with the DSO and MC. He must have been forty-five, with features of distinction ...'

He asked Neave to tell him about attempted escapes from POW camps and Neave related how, on one occasion, prisoners tunnelling out of their compound had misjudged the distance and had emerged in the Commandant's wine cellar instead of beyond the camp's perimeter fence. They soon saw that the cellar was full of rare and expensive wines, the Commandant being a connoisseur who often gave lavish dinners for the local nobility. To compensate themselves for not having got out, the prisoners drank the contents of more than one hundred bottles, and replaced the corks after having refilled them – and here Neave paused – with an unmentionable liquid. Crockatt laughed and said he must tell the story to Winston Churchill. Then he turned and said seriously: 'You've seen the people who work for us behind the lines. They need money and communications. Do you want to help them?'

Neave said that of course he did, and he stayed with the organisation for the remainder of the war. In September 1943 he took charge of Room 900 when Langley was given joint command of Intelligence School 9 (West European Area), or IS9(WEA), with an American officer, Lieutenant-Colonel Robert J. Nelson. Shortly after the Normandy landings of June 1944, Neave also joined IS9(WEA). He became joint commander of POW rescue operations in western Europe with Major James Thornton as his American opposite number, leaving Room 900 under the command of Donald Darling who had returned from Gibraltar. By now

IS9(WEA) comprised 26 more officers, and 52 other ranks (enlisted men in American parlance) and it was made, in Crockatt's words, responsible 'for the continuation of escape and evasion until the war in the west is over', though Room 900 continued to be involved in the planning of underground escape operations.

The joint commanders of IS9(WEA) were also ordered, once the invasion had taken place, to set up reception and interrogation centres for escapers and evaders behind the battle line and to arrange for the distribution of intelligence gained from interrogations, and for the safe return to Britain of all those passing through the centres. As Langley later pointed out, this 'was not quite such a simple task as it might first appear since the intake could include deserters, traitors, and enemy agents, or indeed anyone who initially claimed that he had at some time or other been a member of the armed forces of any of the nations fighting with the Allies'.

IS9(WEA) was attached to Eisenhower's Supreme Headquarters Allied Expeditionary Force (SHAEF) so that it could establish and maintain a close liaison with all other SHAEF departments and formations whose actions might affect escapers, evaders, or Allied POW. It had its own sign: three witches on a broomstick, a reference to another famous First World War escape book, *The Road to En-Dor* by E. H. Jones. It formed two mobile interrogation teams and four Rescue Teams all of which could be sub-divided or amalgamated as required. Attached to each rescue team were Dutch- or French-speaking men or women known as Retrievers. Their task was to pass through enemy lines to locate and then escort to safety any escapers or evaders known to be in the area in which the team was operating.

These teams worked with such good results that it was reckoned that if an airman survived being shot down unscathed in German-occupied territory he had a fifty-fifty chance of avoiding capture and returning to his unit. The interrogation teams proved their value, too. For example, on one occasion a downed RAF pilot who had escaped from his captors related how his German interrogator had told him of an effective method to deal with the Flying Bombs, the V1s that were then causing such damage in London and the southern counties. This was to fly a fighter in front of them because the fighter's slipstream affected the weapon's stability and caused it to crash – and this proved to be correct.

The fighting in France after the Normandy invasion, and the destruction of railway communications there, had made the continuation of escape lines impossible. Instead, a plan had been made for the establishment of three large camps in remote wooded areas, two in France and one in the Ardennes on the Franco-Belgian border, where escapers and evaders would be well away from the fighting but could be supplied by air and, when the time came, liberated by the advancing Allied armies.

MI9 agents were parachuted into the chosen areas well ahead of the invasion to put this plan into action. Two of the camps, near Rennes and Châteaudun in France, were successfully set up. When Neave arrived at the one near Rennes he found that the evaders had already left of their own accord to reach Allied lines, but he personally escorted back 132 evaders who had been hiding in the camp near Châteaudun. But when he moved north into Belgium he found that no camp had been set up in the Ardennes. Instead, the numerous evaders in the area, encouraged by those operating the 'Comet' Line who had been suspicious of the MI9 agent in charge of the proposed camp, had preferred the high life in Brussels.

Neave was also involved in the last mass rescue operation of evaders in western Europe which took place after the abortive airborne attack on the bridge at Arnhem on 17 September 1944. After the attempt to hold the bridge failed, several hundred paratroopers were left hiding in the area sheltered by local Dutch residents. IS9(WEA)'s initial attempt to rescue them failed after an MI9 agent, who had been sent to organise their extraction, was captured and the family sheltering him was shot.

Shortly afterwards, on the night of 22/23 October, another operation, orchestrated by IS9(WEA), the SAS, the local Dutch Resistance, and American, British and Canadian troops, was mounted some eight miles west of Arnhem. This was completely successful and 138 evaders, most of them paratroopers but including some USAAF and other Allied personnel, were safely ferried across the lower Rhine in assault boats rowed by Royal Canadian engineers.

When Neave heard that there remained about the same number of evaders waiting to be rescued he attempted to repeat the operation the following month. But this was as great a failure as the first had been a success. Only seven of a party of 120 were rescued, the rest having been ambushed and either killed or captured. However, during the winter months IS9(WEA) rescued more than 30 evaders, including the future General Sir John Hackett, who were ferried in ones and twos across the marshes downstream from Arnhem.

The story of these operations, the last carried out by MI9 in western Europe, is well told by Leo Heaps in his book *Grey Goose of Arnhem*. A Canadian paratrooper who dropped at Arnhem, Heaps acted as one of the beachmasters on the northern bank during the first rescue operation and was subsequently recruited by Langley to work for IS9(WEA) in the area.

In conclusion it must be said that throughout the war MI9's work was constrained by certain factors: at home by MI6's distaste for anything that might hinder the work of their own agents; in occupied countries – especially in Germany – by the fear that extremists might use POW as bargaining counters in any showdown. This latter concern made Crockatt wary of doing anything that might, inadvertently, imperil the lives of POW.

Despite these constraints, Neave calculated after the war that 'In western Europe, including Italy, the total number of servicemen from Britain and the Commonwealth who reached the Allied front lines (including Russian), between the outbreak of war and June 1945, was 3,631. For the same period, the number of Americans was 3,415, making a grand total of 7,046. These figures include those who escaped from prison camps or from the battle zone, were brought down escape lines to neutral territory, were evacuated by sea or air, and by operational rescue during the Allied invasion of Europe.'

Neave also calculated that before the Normandy landings of June 1944 (D-Day), some 4,000 British and American escaping or evading servicemen were returned from Belgium, the Netherlands and France. About a thousand of these were British soldiers who had evaded capture after Dunkirk, the remainder being airmen who had been shot down. An additional 500–600 were liberated by Allied forces after D-Day.

2

CLUTTY AND HIS ESCAPE DEVICES

One of the first officers to join the staff of MI9 was Christopher Clayton Hutton, known to his contemporaries as 'Clutty', whose task it was to design aids to help servicemen escape or evade. Hutton's ingenuity became as renowned as his capacity to court trouble; after the war he became involved in a ludicrous legal wrangle with the Air Ministry as to whether he had, or had not, broken the Official Secrets Act.

'This officer is eccentric,' the head of MI9, Colonel Norman Crockatt, wrote to an army provost marshal on one occasion during the war, after Hutton had infringed some regulation. 'He cannot be expected to comply with ordinary service discipline, but he is far too valuable for his services to be lost to this Department.'

Hutton had served in the Army during the First World War before becoming a pilot. He tried to join up again in 1939 but was rejected. Not being the sort of person who gave up easily, he started pestering various departments by sending them telegrams to emphasise the urgency of his request to make use of his talents in whatever capacity.

Eventually he received a reply from a Major Russell at the War Office whose job, he told Hutton, was to try to find square holes into which to put square pegs. He listened politely as Hutton outlined his career in newspapers and in the film industry as a publicist, and then asked if Hutton had always been interested in show business.

'All my life,' Hutton admitted enthusiastically. 'Magicians, illusionists, escapologists in particular – they all fascinate me,' and went on to describe how on one occasion he had challenged the famous escapologist, Houdini, then appearing at the Birmingham Empire, to escape from a wooden box which was to be made on the stage by Hutton and his co-challengers. He still had, he said, a copy of the challenge in his wallet.

To Hutton's surprise Russell asked to see it and after Hutton had described how Houdini had outwitted him – by bribing the carpenter who was one of the co-challengers – Russell told Hutton that he thought he might have a job for him. He took him then and there to see Crockatt, whose secret escape and evasion organisation, MI9, had been recently formed.

Crockatt listened to the Houdini story, and to Hutton's 'forthright views on the psychology of escape', as Hutton described them, and then announced that he was looking for someone who would provide the tools and equipment needed to help escapers and evaders to freedom, and that Hutton seemed just the man for the job.

'Wire-cutters and saws, for instance, would be useful; so would maps and compasses,' Crockatt told him. 'The difficulty is that the obvious escape aids are too big to be hidden. One of your headaches, then, will be concealment. Another will be the invention of new escape material. Other problems will undoubtedly crop up as the scheme develops. Now, do you think you can cope?'

Hutton accepted enthusiastically and Crockatt made him the organisation's technical officer with the rank of lieutenant. Johnnie Evans, one of the few men to have escaped from Germany during the previous war, and the author of *The Escaping Club*, was an MI9 Liaison Officer and he gave Hutton some sound advice. 'Remember this, Clutty,' he said. 'The best time for a man to escape is immediately after capture. There's precious little to be done for him once he's behind the wire. My own view is that every serviceman should be issued with three basic escape aids – a map, a compass, and food in concentrated form – *before* he goes into battle. And if you can think of a way of concealing the map and the compass, so much the better.'

Hutton took Evans' advice about the importance of maps and compasses, but his first move was to acquire a library of escape books and have them summarised. This exercise emphasised the importance of maps to any escaper and he secured all he wanted from the map firm, Bartholomew's. He then worked with a printer to transfer a map of Germany on to a handkerchief-sized piece of white silk. The first attempts were blotched and unreadable, but then Hutton thought of trying pectin – which is used to set jam – to coagulate the ink. He didn't hold out much hope that it would work, but it did, and before long all aircrew possessed the most important of escape devices, an easily concealed map of Germany twenty-one inches square. A later development gave an even better result with Germany being printed on one side and France on the other.

Hutton also had developed from Japanese pulp very fine, but strong, paper on which could be printed maps on both its sides, and which could be soaked in water, screwed up into a small ball without rustling, and then smoothed out with hardly a crease. Another development allowed a map printed on the thin paper to be concealed between two sheets of ordinary brown wrapping paper. This made the map impossible to detect until the brown paper was soaked in water and peeled off to reveal it.

The Germans much admired these maps when they discovered them and a German military report of British escape methods and aids commented that they 'are remarkable for their clarity and completeness'.

But maps were not much use without a compass. Hutton approached an East End firm of instrument-makers who devised numerous types of miniature compass that were easy to conceal about the person. The first was the simplest: a magnetised bar that could be dangled from a thread had two luminous dots at one end to indicate north. Another was a ¼-inch brass cylinder which had a luminous needle balanced within it under a protective transparent cover. It was easily concealed in a small object such as a pipe or a fountain pen, or behind a cap badge. A third type, slightly larger, was disguised as collar studs which were then still commonly used to attach collars to the front and back of shirts. A fourth was disguised as a tunic button; others were made to look like fly buttons or a three-penny coin.

Besides compasses that could be disguised or concealed, objects such as razor blades were turned into magnetised compasses. One of the most ingenious was the pencil clip compass. In those days pencils often had a tin clip at one end so that they could be secured to the lip of a pocket. Hutton had identical clips made of magnetised steel and had a tiny dent punched into them at their point of balance. It was then a simple matter to convert the pencil and clip into a rudimentary compass by taking off the clip and balancing it on the pencil's lead tip. Altogether some 2.3 million miniature compasses were manufactured during the war and distributed by MI9. They were made in large numbers because they were affected by damp and each airman carried several of them. Some were only ⅛-inch in diameter, so small that they could be concealed in a pencil, or, later in the war, in the large signet ring that many American servicemen wore. Hutton even concealed one inside a false gold tooth.

Having dealt with the first two essentials for any escaper, Hutton turned his attention to the third aid which Evans had recommended: concentrated food. Initially, he had given this a lower priority than the other two escape requisites – surely, he thought, any enterprising escaper could live off the land – but Evans quickly disabused him of this notion. 'I can assure you, Clutty,' he said, 'that the escaper's greatest enemy is hunger. When a man is starving, he very soon becomes reckless and insensitive. He takes unnecessary risks. Once a man's belly is empty, he makes a hundred and one mistakes – changes his plans, crosses main roads in daylight, throws himself on the mercy of civilians, ventures into villages, steals, uses violence. You can take it from me, Clutty, that you will be doing a great service for the potential escaper if you provide him with something to sustain him on his long trek.'

This Hutton did by designing a series of emergency food packs which air crew could easily slip into their pockets. His first effort was to buy up 50,000 hip flask-shaped cigarette tins, fill them with concentrated malted milk tablets, benzedrine tablets, chewing-gum, chocolate, water-purifying tablets and a rubber water-bottle, as well as a compass and a map, and seal them with adhesive tape. These proved satisfactory until an airman, who had ditched in the English Channel, found that the tin was not waterproof and that its contents had been ruined. Hutton immediately had the remaining packs sealed with waterproof tape but decided that what he needed was a better container.

He discussed how this could be done with the chairman of the firm of Halex, which made toothbrushes. Their discussion led to the manufacture of a slightly larger case which was not only waterproof but transparent so that the crewman could identify what he needed at a glance. The extra space enabled Hutton to include a tube of condensed milk.

This was a definite improvement, but Hutton was not happy about the rubber water-bottle because it tended to rot and when full was difficult to hide. Also, rubber was in very short supply and Hutton could foresee a time when he would not be able to obtain any. He persuaded Halex to design and manufacture an ingenious circular plastic container with a shallow neck and screw stopper which, when unloaded of its contents, could be used as a water-bottle. It was loaded through an aperture in the side which was then closed by a large screw cap. Inside the transparent stopper was a small compass which could be used for navigating without having to unpack the container, and behind the compass was a watch.

Hutton had now provided servicemen with the basics for evasion that Johnnie Evans had recommended, but he didn't stop there; from his office came a steady stream of inventive ideas to help the evader. For example, he knew that a hacksaw would be an invaluable aid to any escaper, but impossible to smuggle into a POW camp. By chance he mentioned his problem to a friend who promptly told him that what he wanted was the kind of saw surgeons employed in some particularly delicate operations. Called gigli saws, they were made of very strong but fine wire with a serrated edge. They were so slender that they could be easily disguised as a bootlace when covered in cloth, and thousands were hidden in this fashion.

The success of the gigli saw led Hutton to think about modifying an airman's flying-boot to help him escape. 'We were naturally interested,' he wrote later, 'in the stories of airmen who had been compelled to bale out over Occupied Europe and who had managed to find their way back to this country. Factual accounts of their evasions and clandestine journeys helped us tremendously in the preparation of our pre-capture devices. Many a young flier frankly admitted that he would not have got very far without his map, compass and ration pack. Most of them had only one complaint to make – they were handicapped by their flying-boots. In wet weather they became soggy and uncomfortable and tended to slow the wearer down. If the weather were dry, marching for any distance in the fur-lined boots caused feet and legs to swell and eventually produced raw sores. At all times their distinctive appearance attracted immediate attention, thus ruling out any possibility of movement by day.'

Hutton set about the design of a flying-boot that could be adapted to the evaders' needs, and had samples made. At first glance it appeared to be an ordinary fleece-lined flying-boot, but around the ankle was a strip of webbing which, if cut by the wearer with a small knife concealed in the top of the boot, severed the fleece-lined leggings from the rest of the footwear. If the seams of the leggings were then slit open they became two parts of a fleece-lined waistcoat which could be sewn together, and the lower half of the boot was transformed into an ordinary black walking-shoe.

An additional benefit of Hutton's design was that the heels of the shoes were hollow with sufficient space to store several maps, a compass, and currency notes of the countries over which the air crew flew their missions (money was also provided in a separate bag: typically it would contain 1,000 French francs, 350 Belgian francs, and 20 Dutch guilders). Ingenious though these boots were, they were not entirely successful simply because, when airborne, the cold seeped through the webbing and froze the unfortunate airman's feet; and on the ground the shoe became easily water-logged in wet weather.

Providing POW with convincing clothing in which to escape was another problem that exercised Hutton's fertile mind. 'I had to provide would-be escapers with materials from which could be improvised either civilian suits or German service uniforms. To hoodwink the enemy, I arranged for a special RAF pamphlet to be published, announcing that a new mess dress would in future be worn by all personnel as and when supplies became available. This would enable me, when the time was ripe, to furnish captured airmen with outfits that could easily be converted to *Luftwaffe* dress. With the aid of the Wool Association, we saw to it that the correct cloth was employed. Then, attractive wire facing had to be included, so we simply used suitable lengths of wire to bind up our parcels. The prisoners, we knew, had learnt to fashion their own Iron Crosses, but we thought it would help if we sent them packets of handkerchiefs tied up with strips of black and white material, from which the right ribbons could be made.'

This subterfuge worked so well that the Commandant of *Stalag Luft III* commented after the war that 'two of the most ingenious aids that I personally found were the very clever uniforms that came into the camps and quantities of German money skilfully pressed into gramophone records. The uniforms were perfectly made and with very little alteration could be transformed into German military wear.'

Hutton's method of providing an escaper with civilian clothing was to design blankets which had cutting patterns impressed on to them. These only became visible when the blankets had been washed by the recipients, and from these patterns the camp tailor could make a perfectly convincing overcoat or suit. Another method was to smuggle in dyes which would turn Allied uniforms into civilian working clothes. To do this Hutton invented a fountain pen in which the ink bag was divided into three. Two of the compartments carried brown and blue concentrated dye, the third, nearest the nib, carried normal ink.

Having discovered the fountain pen as an efficient escaping aid, Hutton further improved it by magnetising the filling lever, the clip and the nib, so that they could all be used as compasses; he also found room to secrete some aspirin and benzedrine tablets in the barrel of the pen and a miniature compass in the cap; and finally he devised a barrel for the pen with an outer and inner cylinder between which a map could be concealed.

How did the Germans react in the face of such ingenuity allied to the determination of many American and British POW to escape? After the war Hutton was at pains to point out that the German guards were not 'stupid or blind', but for the most part 'intelligent, shrewd and painstaking men, and that *in time* they intercepted nearly all my various gadgets'. If one were discovered the design was either modified or abandoned. For example, when camp guards discovered how Hutton's button compass was concealed they were fooled for a little longer by the manufacture of a button with a left-hand thread instead of a right-hand one, so any attempt to unscrew the button only tightened it further.

Such ingenuity must have been difficult to combat, and it is worth quoting at some length the comments of two Germans who had to prevent escape devices entering their camps. 'It must be remembered,' the Commandant of *Stalag Luft III* wrote after the war, 'that the time soon came when the prisoners far outnumbered the guards, and thus the problem became a nightmare to us. While our guards were naturally "on their toes", so were the prisoners, each and every one of them.

'They were always pitting their brains against our camp systems, more or less on the lines of each man being an individual magician working out a trick to escape. This meant that in the camps we were faced with a lot of brainy young conjurors who had plenty of time in which to work out their various tricks against us ...

'However vigilant our guards were, it was only with the greatest difficulty that many of these schemes were brought to light. It was quite impossible to watch every prisoner night and day. Our work in the camps was made even more arduous owing to the vast quantity of "smuggled" goods introduced into parcels sent from England by the British organisation responsible. I must admit that at no time during the whole war was a parcel from the Red Cross ever found to contain anything other than official items. All the "smuggled" goods were sent to prisoners in what to us appeared to be quite innocent packages, sent in the guise of welfare bundles from various societies and charity funds.'

The evidence of a camp guard from *Oflag VIIC* also underlines the difficulties of those facing such a huge deluge of escape equipment which eager recipients were all too ready to use. 'As the war proceeded,' he wrote, 'incoming prisoners increased all the time and their accommodation became a real problem; naturally the number of parcels arriving increased in proportion. The British prisoners gave us more problems than other nationals, chiefly because the majority were mad on sport and gymnastics (we Germans are the same). On account of this, many of the British devices got through to the British prisoners hidden in sports equipment, before they were discovered.

'When suspicion was aroused, it was only natural to think that much of this contraband was arriving in Red Cross bundles, and much time was wasted in the careful but fruitless examination of large numbers of parcels. Often our examining X-ray apparatus broke down and we were unable to get replacements from Berlin as they were all being sent to the front. The result was that vast numbers of parcels were held up for examination and the prisoners became violently insulting to us all, threatening to report these hold-ups to the Swiss Government. This they did, and we were ordered by our superiors in Berlin to release large blocks of the held-up parcels, which of course were never examined. In such cases much escape material must have reached the prisoners.'

This had an unpleasant sequel, for many of the camp guards were subsequently arrested by the Gestapo for failing to discover the escape aids.

3

THE PAT LINE AND ITS TRAITORS

The PAT-line was the first escape line to be developed and operated by MI9. Code-named ACROPOLIS by the Germans because of the number of couriers it employed who were of Greek origin, it was run by a Belgian Army medical officer, Albert Marie Guérisse.

Guérisse, whose talents were many faceted, escaped to Gibraltar after the fall of France in June 1940. There he met a French naval officer who had commandeered a 270ft French cargo vessel, *Le-Rhin*, and taken her to the British colony, and Guérisse became the ship's First Officer. *Le-Rhin* was taken to England where she was acquired by the Royal Navy and renamed HMS *Fidelity*, though her French crew remained aboard as members of the Royal Navy and were given naval ranks. For security reasons the crew were given assumed names, and Guérisse became Patrick O'Leary with the rank of lieutenant-commander in the Royal Navy.

The ship was subsequently taken over by the Operations Section of the Secret Intelligence Service (MI6) to land SOE and MI6 agents, and to ferry early evaders and escapers from southern France to the safety of Gibraltar. It was on one of these missions that on 21 April 1941 *Fidelity* launched a small fishing-boat under O'Leary's command to collect a party of Polish evaders from the small Mediterranean French port of Cerbère, close to the Spanish border (see Map 2). Things went wrong, the fishing-boat was captured by a Vichy French *chasseur*, and all its crew except one, who leapt overboard and swam to the Spanish shore, were taken prisoner. They all subsequently managed to escape and, except for O'Leary, returned to England.

O'Leary chose to remain because, after escaping from St-Hippolyte-du-Fort near Nîmes – where, from the spring of 1941, the French had begun interning all British personnel – he met a British Army officer, Captain Ian Garrow, who asked O'Leary to join an organisation he was running which helped Allied servicemen escape across the Pyrenees into neutral Spain.

After the fall of France Garrow had evaded capture and had made his way south to Marseilles where he had been helped by the Revd. Donald Caskie. Caskie ran a Seamen's Mission where, despite the vigilance of the Vichy authorities, escapers and evaders were sheltered and fed, and were given the necessary civilian clothes and identity papers to escape into neutral Spain.

But Garrow, while on his way to the frontier, decided to return to Marseilles to organise a proper escape line, and asked Caskie to help him. He already had contacts in northern France who would pass evaders across the demarcation line which now divided occupied France from the southern part ruled by Marshal

Pétain's collaborationist government established at Vichy. What he needed was an organisation in the south which would hide evaders until they were passed on to a guide who would take them across the Pyrenees.

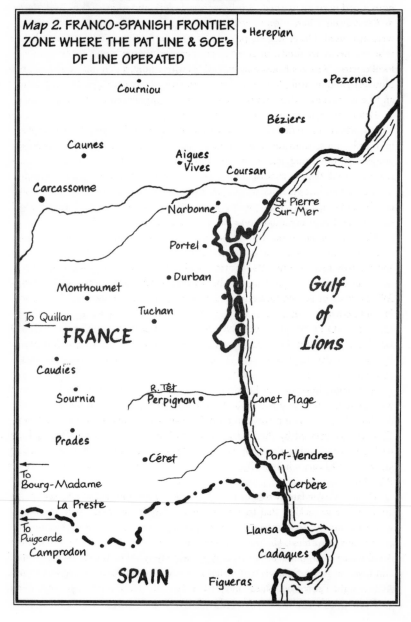

Map 2. FRANCO-SPANISH FRONTIER ZONE WHERE THE PAT LINE & SOE's DF LINE OPERATED

Caskie agreed to help, although he records that he intensely distrusted the guide whom Garrow had hired, and continued to do so until he was arrested in January 1942 and the Mission was closed. But by then a number of other 'safe' houses had been established. Brothels proved ideal, and some of the city's *Maisons de Rendezvous*, where rooms could be rented by the hour and no questions asked, were also used. Other helpers provided more conventional hiding-places, helped raise the necessary funds, or acted as couriers for Garrow's line. They included a local doctor, Georges Rodocanachi, and his wife Fanny; a rich businessman, Louis Nouveau, and his wife, Renée; and two residents of Greek origin, Mario Prassinos and Leoni Savinos, who became the line's most experienced *convoyeurs* (couriers).

Before an evader was accepted he had to report to a Marseilles bar, *Le Petit Poucet*, where his credentials were thoroughly checked. He would then be placed in a 'safe' house until he could be taken by a courier to the border where paid guides – mostly smugglers or Spanish republicans who abhorred Franco's Fascist regime – took them across the Pyrenees on foot, mostly in the area of Perpignan but also sometimes via Andorra. These guides, tough and duplicitous, were organised by a man named Vidal who was eventually betrayed to the Germans in 1944, tortured and then executed, some say by being burned alive.

Garrow's organisation worked well and during the following months as many as 20 or 25 men made their way to freedom every week. But by the time O'Leary and Garrow met in June 1941 Garrow badly needed a fluent French speaker to help him organise the growing number of evaders who were now mostly downed Allied airmen or French Resistance workers escaping the attentions of the Gestapo. He immediately trusted the Belgian, and the idea of working with Garrow appealed to O'Leary, but he pointed out that as a British naval officer he must seek London's permission first. Garrow agreed and sent a message to London, via his Pyrenean guides, requesting that O'Leary be given security clearance and then be allowed to join him.

After some hesitation in London Garrow's request was granted. The approval was broadcast by the BBC with the pre-arranged phrase *Adolphe doit rester* – Adolphe Lecomte being the name on O'Leary's fake identity card – and when Garrow was arrested by the Vichy French authorities in October 1941 O'Leary took command, using the code-name Pat. From that time the line was officially known by O'Leary's initials, P. A. O., but it was more commonly known as the PAT Line.

Donald Caskie later wrote of Pat: 'His sense of humour led him to enjoy situations so nerve-racking that they might have stopped the stoutest heart. But he was strict, kindly, and protective towards those under his command. Fighting the enemy he was ruthless. He knew the methods of the Gestapo, and he hated them. A cultivated man, one felt that he had set everything aside, the things he enjoyed and loved in peace-time, all that makes life worth living, until victory was won ... At first sight Pat seemed slight and frail. I think the clothes he wore contributed to this impression. He was not a tall man. He moved with uncommon grace and agility. As he moved one noticed the powerful shoulders, the brawny thrust of the legs, the steady, almost machine-like grasp of the muscular hands on objects such as coffee cups, pencils, documents. Pat, I suspect, could have strangled a strong man as easily as I might stick a stamp. His efficiency was awe inspiring.'

Pat had many problems. One was the lack of proper communications. MI6's Donald Darling, code-named 'Sunday', was established in Lisbon – he moved to Gibraltar in January 1942 – and for some time he had been supplying the line with funds, and arranging for the reception of evaders and escapers once they reached Spain. But Pat had no wireless to communicate with either Darling or London and messages had to be taken by the Spanish guides across the Pyrenees secreted in toothpaste tubes.

Another of Pat's problems was the behaviour of a British sergeant named Harold Cole who brought evaders south from his 'safe' house in Lille. Cole, who called himself Paul in France, had delivered his first 'parcels'* in November 1940 and had subsequently shown himself to be a brave and resourceful courier. Garrow thought highly of him, as did many of the evaders he had helped.

But there was something about the red-haired, freckle-faced man with the narrow set eyes and toothbrush moustache that engendered immediate distrust in Pat. There was, he felt, something shifty about Cole and he found the sergeant's ingratiating manner, and his habit of calling everyone 'old boy' or 'old man', distasteful.

Shortly before Garrow was arrested, Pat discovered that Cole was partying in Marseilles when he should have been in Lille. When challenged Cole passed the matter off lightly, but both Garrow and Pat now suspected that Cole was spending the Line's money on high living and Garrow suggested that Pat travel to Lille to make inquiries.

In Lille Pat found that an agent, François Dupré, to whom Cole should have handed funds for the Line, had not received any of it. He also soon discovered that those helping the Line in the area were beginning to regard Cole, who was passing himself off as a British intelligence officer named Captain Colson, with distrust because of his extravagance.

His suspicions about Cole confirmed, Pat returned to Marseilles to find that Garrow had been arrested by the Vichy police. A few days later, on 1 November 1941, Pat, the courier Mario Prassinos, and another of Garrow's helpers, an Australian named Bruce Dowding, began questioning Cole in the Rodocanachis' apartment. It soon became obvious that Cole knew nothing about Garrow's arrest and equally obvious that he was lying about what had happened to the money.

After furiously denying any wrong-doing, Cole broke down and confessed when confronted by Dupré. Pat, in a moment of fury, knocked the English

---

*So-called because, before evaders were dispatched to Paris, those receiving them were warned by letter how many were being sent and where. 'I am sending the shirt and trousers in two parcels', a typical message would say, 'which should arrive by goods train at the Gare du Nord on November 8 at 8.45.'

sergeant down, breaking a knuckle in the process and Cole was locked in a bath-room while the others discussed what should be done with him. Dowding wanted to kill him at once, but Prassinos pointed out that you could hardly execute a man for embezzlement and Pat reluctantly agreed. They had just decided to send Cole back to England under escort when they heard a noise from the bathroom, and found that Cole had escaped.

Pat, Dowding and several other agents now moved to the occupied zone to warn the Line's helpers there that Cole was not to be trusted. Those close to Dupré knew Cole for what he was, but other agents were not easily persuaded that the 'British intelligence officer', whose conduct they so much admired, was an embezzler and a possible traitor, and Cole persuaded some of them who had heard about the confrontation that it was just a minor disagreement. Others either could not be contacted or decided that whatever the truth of the matter it was their duty to continue helping the Line and to remain with their families.

For some weeks Cole lay low in the Lille house he shared with Madeleine Deram, one of the line's couriers. On 6 December he was arrested, though this could have been a convenient method of putting him under German protection as by then he could already have been working for the *Abwehr* (German Military Intelligence), or possibly for the *Abwehr*'s principal rival, the Nazi *Sicherheitsdienst*.

It seems more probable that Cole's treachery dated from the time of his arrest, and that the gentlest of hints about what might lie in store for him if he did not co-operate quickly, persuaded him to tell the Germans all he knew, and to agree to become a double agent. The *Abwehr* agent who interrogated him later testified that Cole 'started to tell us everything', and that his deposition amounted to 30 pages of typescript. Professionally the agent, a Dutchman named Cornelius Verloop, was delighted, but privately he found Cole's revelations distasteful. 'One should all the same maintain a bit of self-respect,' he later stated. In fact, though Cole betrayed many of the Line's agents in the north, including François Dupré, he did not at that time reveal anything about Garrow's organisation in Vichy France.

Using Cole as an intermediary, the *Abwehr* began introducing bogus airmen into the escape line to catch those organising it. Just two days after his arrest Cole took a party of five evaders to the Abbé Carpentier, a priest at Abbeville. This saintly man was avowedly anti-Nazi, as indeed were all the French clergy – one of the standard instructions to escapers and evaders was to head for the nearest church spire and seek help from the priest – and although he had already been warned by Dowding of the potential danger Cole posed, he was determined to remain at his task of forging the necessary documents for anyone travelling across the demarcation line into southern France.

What happened next was later confirmed by the Abbé in a letter he wrote in March 1942, and smuggled out of prison. 'I declare that I was ignobly betrayed by Sgt Col(e) in the following circumstances on the 8 December 1941 at about

14.30 Sgt. Col(e) presented himself to me with five other persons who had come to cross the [demarcation] Line secretly with him. He introduced these persons in the following fashion, two Belgian pilots, one English soldier, one RAF Captain, and a Polish pilot. The two Belgians spoke French, and it was easy for me to verify that they were authentic. The English soldier spoke a little French. The Captain of the RAF spoke French correctly, was the "perfect English" type, and appeared to be a *beau soldat*. The so-called Polish pilot spoke neither French nor German.'

The Polish pilot was in fact the head of the Lille branch of the *Geheime Feldpolizei*, the police units used by the *Abwehr*, and once the Abbé had started work on producing the necessary forged documents for the evaders the whole party were arrested. Many others working for the Line, including Dowding, were later also arrested because of Cole's treachery, as were a number of evaders, some of whom were shot as spies because they were in civilian clothes. Cole later even attempted to put his pregnant wife, a member of the PAT Line who was utterly convinced that he was genuine, into the hands of the Gestapo. Little wonder that Brendan Murphy's book, *Turncoat*, which recounts Cole's treachery in detail, was sub-titled 'The Worst Traitor of the War'.

Pat now knew that the Englishman had to be, as he termed it, 'rubbed out', and he told Donald Darling of his intentions. More than 30 years later Garrow wrote to Donald Darling confirming that independently he too had decided to kill Cole. 'I consulted Dr Rodocanachi and told him my difficulty. I had to kill a man in such a manner that it would not invite a police inquiry and investigation which would reveal our organisation, and it would have to appear to be death from natural causes. His solution was a massive injection of insulin, sufficient in a non-diabetic person to produce coma. Thereafter a gentle push into one of the side basins of the Old Port, Marseilles (I had chosen the spot, unfrequented, and in the shadow of Fort Saint Nicholas).'

However, when Darling informed London of Pat's intentions, Claude Dansey of MI6, who oversaw the work of the British escape and evasion organisation MI9 (see Chapter One), demurred, possibly because he thought Cole might make a double agent; more probably because he was already using him as one. Darling was told to tell Pat to desist. 'After much thought I sent a note to Marseilles', Darling wrote later, 'in as ambiguous a way as possible, referring to the need to forgive human frailties, which I hoped Pat would read to mean Colonel Dansey's own soft attitude to Cole ("give him a run for his money"). It was all very well, I thought, to sit in London and issue instructions covering a situation only understood by the man on the spot, who was in danger!'

While the problems of Cole were exercising Pat's mind, J. M. Langley, the MI9 operative in charge of escape and evasion lines in north-west Europe – and who himself had passed down Garrow's escape line after Dunkirk – was grappling with the task of training a wireless operator for him. At that time MI9 was finding that operators and equipment were almost unobtainable because the other secret services had a higher priority for them, but Langley did eventually manage to find a Belgian volunteer, Jean Ferière. Training Ferière was a slow and exasperating business because the man showed no aptitude either for working a wireless or leading a clandestine life. But as Langley later wrote, he was 'my only hope'.

To discuss the problem of Cole and the general organisation of the PAT Line, Langley decided to meet Pat in Gibraltar and to take Ferière with him. Early in 1942 Pat received a message from Donald Darling asking him make his way there as quickly as practicable.

Pat's journey is a good example of the double and, indeed, triple dealing that underlay the highly lucrative business of taking evaders across the Pyrenees during the war. Pat first of all consulted Vidal who declared that he would make sure that Pat had only the best guide. This turned out to be someone named José II whom Vidal described as 'a very distinguished servant of the Generalissimo [Franco] – and oh so clever ...' before adding that perhaps Pat could spare a few moments to invent a little intelligence which Vidal could pass on to José II who, it transpired, worked for Franco, the Germans and Vidal simultaneously, gave all his employers equal satisfaction, and earned astronomical sums of money in the process.

Travelling as a Captain Rogers, Pat crossed the Pyrenees with a party of evaders which was met by José II at the small Spanish station at Villajuiga at three o'clock in the morning. When the train arrived Pat was taken aside by the guide and they travelled separately. Police checks proved no problem as José II had a special police badge which was treated with great deference. At Barcelona José II vanished for a while with Pat's false documents and Pat knew that he had gone to the German Consulate to have them photographed. Then he took Pat to the British Consulate, slipping away before they reached it. From Barcelona Pat was taken to Madrid by car where he was met by one of the British Embassy's attachés, Michael Creswell (code-named 'Monday'), who had already done so much for the COMET Line (see Chapter Eleven) and who now smuggled him into Gibraltar in the boot of his car.

Before Langley had left for Gibraltar he had been contacted by Scotland Yard's Special Branch which had discovered that Cole, who was on their wanted list, might have MI9 connections. It transpired that Cole had a criminal record as a 'con' man; that in April 1940 he had absconded with the funds of his sergeants' mess; and that he had subsequently slipped into France on the pretence that he was returning to his unit.

So when Pat showed Langley the Abbé's letter about Cole's treachery Langley immediately agreed that London must reverse its decision: Cole had to be eliminated. But the opportunity had passed for shortly afterwards Cole – now on the run from his *Abwehr* masters whom he had also double-crossed – was arrested by the French, tried for espionage and imprisoned.

During their conference, which took place in April 1942, Pat, Langley and Darling also discussed the best method of extracting the growing backlog of evaders who were waiting to be taken down the line to Spain. Pat suggested airborne operations to take them out. Langley knew that this was not practicable, but thought Pat's idea of the evacuation by sea from southern France was a possibility, for the Poles were already running such operations from Gibraltar to extricate the large number of Polish servicemen who had been trapped in France or who had managed to escape to North Africa.

Because of lack of suitable personnel and vessels, but also because they lacked the necessary maintenance back-up, these Polish seaborne operations had had mixed success. Then in December 1941 Captain Slocum, who ran the Operations Section of the Secret Intelligence Service (MI6), had visited Gibraltar to regularise these Polish sea operations, and to mount new ones on behalf of MI6 and other intelligence services including MI9. He decided to form a special unit – known for cover purposes as the Coast Watching Flotilla (CWF) – and put it under the operational and administrative control of the Captain commanding the Gibraltar-based Eighth Submarine Flotilla. This arrangement enabled any necessary maintenance to be carried out by the flotilla's depot ship, or by the Gibraltar dockyard.

Until prevented from doing so by the imminence of the Anglo-American landings in North Africa in November 1942, Operation 'Torch', and then by the German occupation of Vichy France which followed the landings, the CWF carried out a number of successful operations to southern France to deliver and exfiltrate MI9 agents, pick up PAT Line evaders, and land such celebrated agents as Odette Sansom.

These operations were mounted only during the moonless period of each month and elaborate precautions were taken – including the overnight painting of ships' hulls – to ensure that when at sea the vessels appeared to enemy air or sea reconnaissance to be neutral Spanish or Portuguese fishing-boats.

So useful did the British secret services find this sea route that the Polish government-in-exile had cause to complain that what had originally been a purely Polish undertaking had been more or less hijacked by the British and used for their own purposes. When one reads about these operations this accusation seems entirely justified.

The CWF mounted seven operations on behalf of the PAT Line. The first was undertaken on 18 April 1942 when Pat, accompanied by Ferière, were put ashore in the neighbourhood of Port-Vendres by the 200-ton trawler *Tarana*. The next was mounted on the night of 14/15 June when the 47ft Polish-manned *Seawolf*, a Spanish Moroccan felucca (coastal trading vessel), picked up a mixed bag of evaders from Port-Miou, a small inlet 2km west of Cassis which is situated 20km south-east of Marseilles.

The third operation, code-named 'Bluebottle', which took place in mid-July 1942, was the CWF's first large-scale evacuation. About 35 evaders from the PAT Line, including the well-known American fighter pilot Whitney Straight, who was serving in the RAF, were picked up by *Tarana* from St-Pierre-sur-Mer on the coast east of Narbonne. The following month *Tarana* picked up seven evaders and a woman, probably an MI9 courier, again from St-Pierre; and, on the night of 21/22 September twenty-five PAT Line evaders (as many as 38 according to another source) were also picked up by *Seawolf* from the mouth of the River Têt at Canet-Plage during an operation code-named 'Titania'.

The sixth operation took place on the night of 11/12 October when *Seawolf* picked up from the same beach 34 British service personnel who, with Pat's help, had made a mass escape from a French fortress, Fort de la Révère, north of Monaco. With them was a French-Canadian sergeant-major named Dumais, who had escaped after the Dieppe raid the previous August and who was to become a future organiser of the SHELBURNE escape line (see Chapter Twelve).

The last operation for the PAT Line was carried out by another of the Flotilla's feluccas, *Seadog*, which, on the night of 3/4 November, as part of a larger SOE operation, landed an MI9 agent at Port-Miou..

Some idea of the difficulties the Polish crews and their cargoes had to face can be given by quoting from reports written by the skippers. The captain of *Seawolf*, Lieutenant-Commander Krajewski, after returning from operation 'Titania', wrote of the evaders' astonishing lack of security. 'At 0030, moving along the coast, which was lit up almost like daytime, we noticed the flashing of a light from a point that bore some resemblance to the agreed meeting point. THEY WERE HOWEVER IRREGULAR SIGNALS [writer's capitals]. After checking the position of a fort about ½ km distant, I realised it was one more case of unfortunate signalling from the land side. Our astonishment was all the greater when, after heaving to, WE HEARD CRIES AND SINGING AND SAW LAMPS BEING LIT [writer's capitals] among the party of people who were to be embarked. One even swam out towards us and in the water called out in our direction; in these conditions, as is well known, the sound carries a long way.'

The swimmer was Vladimir Bouryschkine, alias Val Williams, who had been helping Pat as a courier and was now returning to Britain where he was trained to run a new escape line for MI9.

Despite the behaviour of the evaders, the evacuation went ahead without police interruption and Krajewski's 20-ton vessel, a mere 47 feet long, was packed with evaders. 'Our journey back to base set a new record for our felucca in terms of numbers: in addition to the enlarged crew of ten for that voyage, we had 83 passengers (54 Poles, 23 British, 4 French, 1 Russian, 1 Czech woman). We therefore had eighteen people altogether over the anticipated programme. Our drinking-water being insufficient at the best of times, we had to ration this precious substance more than usual. Of course everybody had to be accommodated on deck, except the woman, a wounded Canadian (from the Dieppe raid), a wounded Pole and a wounded airman (who had been carrying out Special Operations flights and had had an accident on one of his missions). The mood among the passengers was very good, irrespective of nationality, although I must state impartially that our people withstood the unspeakably awful conditions notably better than the others. 21 September was especially hard because of the return of the bad weather.'

The next operation for the PAT Line also ran into problems. Pat, having collected another 34 evaders at his 'safe' house, a villa close to Canet-Plage, was unable to make contact with *Seawolf* which was scheduled to pick them up on the night of 5/6 October. This meant that the party twice had to cross the River Têt, which flowed into the Mediterranean north of Canet-Plage, up to their necks in water, first to get to the meeting point and then to return to the 'safe' house.

Pat then had to arrange another rendezvous which took several days. Eventually, *Seawolf* met up with them on the night of 11/12 October, though by that time, as the official historian of these clandestine sea operations later recorded, 'the evacuees were so overwrought by fear, tension, boredom and frustration that their emotions erupted on a wave of reckless excitement when at last they saw the felucca's dinghy approaching the beach where they were assembled. Maxted [an RNR lieutenant understudying the Polish felucca skippers], who was aboard *Seawolf*, was appalled by the noise and feared that the French police or the dreaded *Milice* (Vichy auxiliary police units) would be alerted.'

Somehow or other the evaders were ferried to the felucca without alerting the police, and were packed aboard. One of the passengers was André Postel-Vinay, a courier of Pat's. After he had been arrested by the Gestapo in Paris, he had tried to commit suicide to avoid giving away information he knew the Gestapo would wring out of him under torture. The suicide attempt had fractured his spine and shattered his pelvis and leg, but when he had partially recovered a sympathetic doctor had allowed him to escape from hospital.

Once aboard *Seawolf* Postel-Vinay was propped against the wheelhouse, but the return voyage must have been a nightmare for him – and indeed for everyone aboard because the weather turned rough, there was a shortage of food and drinking-water, and many were seasick. In fact, it got so bad that the *Seawolf*'s skipper had to break wireless silence to request help, and another vessel from the Flotilla was sent to rendezvous with the felucca off Majorca.

Although Pat agreed to take Ferière back to France with him, he had no confidence in his compatriot's ability. He had already discovered before leaving Gibraltar that Ferière had only volunteered for the job so as to be able to return to his French wife in southern France. Pat's doubts about the wireless operator were soon confirmed, for Ferière lost his nerve the first time he transmitted and on the second occasion missed his scheduled transmission time. In disgust, Pat dispatched Ferière and his wife across the Pyrenees to England, but he still had Ferière's wireless and he soon found a young Frenchman to work it while Langley trained a Belgian fighter pilot, Alex Nitelet, to take Ferière's place. Although he had been blinded in one eye, Nitelet was an ideal recruit because he already knew the Morse Code. He also knew the organisation he was about to join, for in 1941 it had helped him to escape after he had been shot down in Occupied France.

In France Nitelet soon proved himself a brave and resourceful agent. He knew all the tricks for outwitting the Germans who were, even in neutral Vichy, constantly attempting to track down clandestine wireless transmissions. They used such sensitive detectors that their operators could soon identify the 'fist' of those transmitting. To confuse them Nitelet used his left hand and then his right, alternatively using finger and thumb. And he always made deliberate and pre-arranged errors in his coded messages, so that London would know that he was not transmitting with a pistol at his head. He never transmitted more than three messages from the same apartment, and constantly moved from one place to another, disguising his wireless set in various ways in order to transport it safely.

By the time of the conference in Gibraltar Pat had rebuilt the escape line in the north where one of his best agents, Jean de la Olla, had taken over its running. In Normandy Jacques Wattebled had organised an efficient net to help evading airmen, as had the Fillerin family in the Pas de Calais, while close to the demarcation line Madame Arnaud, from her farm at Les Tuyères, helped evaders avoid the more obvious dangers involved in crossing into Vichy France. And shuttling between the two halves of the country was one of Pat's most valued couriers, the chef on the Paris–Marseilles express.

In Vichy-controlled France the Line's helpers were also spread far and wide. Near the prison of St-Hippolyte-du-Fort the young, romantically inclined Morel sisters carried messages sewn in the hems of their dresses and hid evading airmen in their home. In Nîmes the exuberant Gaston Nègre, a black marketeer *par excellence*, found the necessary food for evaders as well as sheltering them in his apartment above his huge, rambling, wholesale grocery store where on one occasion three Allied pilots, two French Resistance workers, and an escaped British POW were hidden at one end of it while local police officials drank champagne at the other. In Toulouse, a vital centre for the PAT Line because all its Spanish guides lived there, Françoise Dissart's apartment, despite being opposite the local Gestapo headquarters, was a constant 'safe' house for evaders, as was the Hôtel de Paris owned by Madame Mongelard. In Monte Carlo the two elderly Trenchard sisters, Grace and Susie, who ran a teashop in the Principality, provided a haven for evaders before they moved on to Marseilles, and other helpers included a member of the Czech Consulate in Marseilles and the American vice-consul in Lyons.

'Led by Pat, the Organisation reached the borders of Belgium, Italy and Spain,' wrote Guérisse's biographer, Vincent Brome. 'Agents were continually shuttling to and fro and something like two hundred and fifty men and women were involved. In Marseilles itself the organisation had at its disposal forged papers, identity cards, clothing and ration cards, money, black-market food, engravers who could copy every fresh French or German pass within three days, and Paul Ulmann, a Jewish tailor, who could produce perfect imitations of any given uniform within forty-eight hours. It had its own post-boxes throughout France – empty flats and the like – where letters to and from agents were delivered without disclosing address. Everywhere eyes and ears reported to Pat. From prison camps, military forts, police stations and even some Gestapo headquarters; from Paris, Lille, Lyons, Madrid, Barcelona and Gibraltar information filtered through continuously ... Extraordinary feats were now achieved by the organisation.'

It was, for example, perfectly possible for an evader who had baled out over northern France to be picked up on the same night, and given shelter, food, civilian clothes and forged papers, before being escorted to Paris where he would be taken quite openly through streets full of Germans. After a few days in hiding in Paris, he would join a convoy of evaders whose couriers knew various ways of crossing the demarcation line. A favourite method was to travel by train to Chalon and then, when night fell, swim across the River Saône.

At Marseilles the evader might have a brief period of lying low in a 'safe' house before being escorted to Perpignan where the Spanish guides would take him over the border and into neutral Spain. Once in Spain Darling's organisation swung into operation and the evader would soon find himself in Gibraltar, and then on a ship or aircraft to England. It took one pilot who crashed 60 miles north of Paris just twelve days to return to his unit.

But it was not always that easy; some escapers took months to return. It was, as Louis Nouveau pointed out, a matter of luck. 'How uncertain and chancy things can be!' he wrote later. 'Some of the fellows spent six months from the day they were shot down, to the day of their arrival back in England. For example, six weeks concealed in some peasant's house, a fortnight staying in Marseilles or Toulouse, a week for the trip across the mountains, then if arrested in Spain, three weeks in Miranda Internment Camp, a week to reach Gibraltar, and another waiting there for a convoy, and finally a last week at sea to reach England.'

And for evaders and helpers alike there was always the fear of discovery and arrest. In April 1942, Leoni Savinos – Nouveau called him 'one of the cleverest and most courageous men I ever met; a cold, calculating realist' – was arrested; in June Nouveau was forced to move to Paris to avoid the attentions of the police; and that August Gaston Nègre and Alex Nitelet were captured by Vichy police while clearing up after a parachute drop of supplies and money from MI9. The loss of Nitelet was a disastrous blow to the Line and it was not until October that Pat received a competent replacement in a young bilingual Australian, Tom Groome.

The sheer size of the Line also made it vulnerable to Gestapo infiltration, and Pat had to be constantly alert. On one occasion the Germans sent a Frenchman to him at *Le Petit Poucet* claiming that he could give Pat information about German counter-intelligence activities in the occupied zone. Pat made inquiries and soon found that the man had previously tried to penetrate Vidal's group of Spanish guides. On a pretext he took the Frenchman to meet Vidal, and the Frenchman under intense questioning soon confessed that he was working for the Gestapo. He begged for his life in vain; his body was thrown into a ravine.

Another constant problem was the acute shortage of money. The financial drain on the resources of those who ran the Line was about 100,000 francs a month. In Garrow's time an arrangement had been made with a British firm that cash in the possession of one of their employees in France could be used by the PAT Line, but by mid-1942 this was beginning to run out and money provided by MI9 was sporadic and insufficient. A number of Pat's helpers had been extremely generous. Louis Nouveau contributed £5,000, another Marseilles businessman, M. Fiocca, contributed £6,000, and his New Zealand-born wife, Nancy (née Nancy Wake) – one of Pat's most resourceful couriers – sold all her jewellery and gave the money to Pat.

Despite all these difficulties, and helped by the sea line to Gibraltar, Pat continued to operate with ever-greater success and by the autumn of 1942 the Line was being used by American evaders of the US Eighth Army Air Force which had begun operations against European targets in August.

American evaders were, apparently, as prone to breaking security measures when under stress as their European allies, as Fanny Rodocanachi later recorded when she had her first encounter with one. 'We had made it an unbreakable rule that no refugee should ever leave the house except accompanied, either to be photographed, or to go to the station ... As a favour and an exception this first American was granted permission to dine with one of the [American] Vice-Consuls. After his long trials – flight, hunger, privations – the shock was too great for him. He was brought back late at night in a state of great exhilaration, and it was not an easy job to bring from the front door of the house two storeys up to the flat, a happy but too merry pilot who would persist in singing patriotic songs.'

Then in November 1942 security of the Line became paramount, for the Germans moved into the Vichy-controlled region of France. Suddenly the Gestapo were everywhere. Patrols along the Spanish frontier were reinforced, the number of detector vans multiplied, and those members of the PAT Line being held in Vichy prisons were constantly in danger of being deported to Germany.

This last threat, which meant almost certain death in a concentration camp, prompted one of Pat's most dramatic operations when news reached him that Garrow was about to be deported. Pat immediately began planning his escape. A warder's uniform, made with meticulous care by the tailor Paul Ulmann, was smuggled into Garrow by a sympathetic gaoler who had been liberally bribed. At the end of the working day Garrow managed to change into it undetected, and was then escorted out of the prison by the warder and into a waiting car. An intensive hunt followed but Garrow was safely spirited across the Pyrenees to safety and once in London he became another useful MI9 recruit.

In February 1943 agents belonging to the line pulled off another *coup* by rescuing Gaston Nègre from prison after he, too, was in danger of being deported. This time a bottle of wine doctored with a sleeping-draught put those warders on the night shift into a deep sleep and a total of eight prisoners were removed to safety in a furniture van.

But gradually the Germans tightened their grip, putting the PAT Line under intolerable pressure. In January 1943 Tom Groome was caught operating his wireless set at Montauban, and the following month Dr Rodocanachi was arrested, for Cole, released to the *Abwehr*, was at work again, betraying his former friends in Marseilles.

However, it was not Cole but a Gestapo agent, a Frenchman working under the name of Roger Le Neveu, who brought about the virtual demise of the PAT Line. Louis Nouveau, who had recruited him in Paris at the end of 1942, was a cautious, clever operator. But Le Neveu had seemed the ideal recruit for he was engaged to a woman who was carrying on the underground resistance work of her brother who had been executed by the Germans. He was also a veteran of the French Foreign Legion – he became known to those whom he betrayed as Roger *Le Légionnaire* – and Nouveau considered this 'a certificate of courage' as well as a guarantee that Le Neveu must be both tough and resourceful. As a standard precaution he asked Jean de la Olla and Norbert Fillerin from the Pas de Calais to meet the new recruit. They had their doubts, but when Nouveau recounted Le Neveu's background and affiliations they reluctantly gave their approval and Le Neveu was hired to escort evaders south.

Le Neveu's first trip was concluded without incident, but he returned from his second to say that the Australian airman he had been escorting had been arrested though he himself had managed, by a trick, to escape. To Nouveau this sounded remarkably like the kind of excuse that Cole used to make, and he began to have his doubts about the blond Frenchman. But when Le Neveu returned from his third trip having successfully delivered another four evaders to Marseilles, Nouveau's confidence was restored. Shortly afterwards Groome was arrested, and Nouveau received a summons from Pat to take over the Line in the south while Pat travelled to Gibraltar. He arranged to travel with two couriers who were escorting five airmen from an American bomber which had been shot down over Brittany.

By now the Germans were tightening their security measures in Paris and, unknown to Nouveau, they had just introduced passes to enter the Gare d'Auster-litz. Without passes the party could not travel, but Le Neveu volunteered to obtain them and in the rush to catch the train Nouveau had no time to reflect on how the new courier had managed this. He only did so when, after changing trains at St-Pierre-des-Corps, a suburb of Tours, he felt the muzzle of a revolver rammed into his ribs as the carriage filled with German plain-clothes police.

Nouveau's arrest led Pat inadvertently into a fatal trap. Le Neveu contacted Paul Ulmann and suggested that he arrange a meeting between himself and Pat so that he could tell the Belgian the exact circumstances under which Nouveau had been arrested. Ulmann did so and Pat agreed to the meeting. By now he knew that there was another traitor at work within the organisation but Ulmann was above suspicion and Pat wanted to hear what Le Neveu, whom he had heard of through Nouveau but had not met, had to say. On 2 March 1943 the two men entered a Toulouse café where Le Neveu and the Gestapo were waiting for them. Both were arrested, and the arrests of most of Pat's other main agents in Paris followed shortly afterwards.

Of those agents who knew how the Line worked, only Françoise Dissart in Toulouse now remained at liberty. The Gestapo knew she existed, they even knew her Christian name, but they could not track her down. Despite vicious torture Pat refused to tell the Gestapo anything, and the astute lady was too canny to take the bait dangled by Le Neveu. As Pat's successor she organised the last party of evaders from Marseilles in April 1943. It then became too dangerous to continue with the old methods, so she escorted evaders herself to the frontier and continued to do so until the Liberation, and for her bravery she was awarded the George Medal after the war.

According to MI9 operative Airey Neave – who was in a position to know as he himself used it after escaping from the notorious Colditz Castle – the PAT Line aided as many as 600 escapers and evaders to freedom. But the price paid by those who helped them was a terrible one. More than thirty were executed, including the Abbé Carpentier and Bruce Dowding who were both beheaded. Others like Mario Prassinos, Georges Rodocanachi, Paul Ulmann, the chef on the Paris-Marseilles express, and the owner of the *Le Petit Poucet* never returned from the concentration camps. Of those who did – they included Pat, Tom Groome and Louis Nouveau who all survived the hideous ordeals of Dachau and Buchenwald – many were permanently mutilated by torture.

At least Pat, who became one of the war's most highly decorated servicemen, had the satisfaction of identifying the corpse of Cole who, in 1945, was shot dead in Paris by French police. Le Neveu suffered a similar fate, executed by the French Resistance after the Liberation.

4

SOE'S DF SECTION

Not all escape lines were formed to bring servicemen to safety. For example, the work of DF Section, part of the British sabotage and subversion organisation, the Special Operations Executive (SOE), was primarily to pass its agents in and out of France, and as a supply line for such essentials as wireless sets. Occasionally, an escaping serviceman did stumble accidentally across a DF escape line. If he did he was certainly helped by it but was also passed on to those run specifically for servicemen as quickly as possible so as to leave DF lines clear for SOE traffic.

DF mainly ran escape lines across France into the Iberian and Breton peninsulas from where, in the first case, passengers were covertly passed on to Gibraltar or Lisbon; or, from Brittany, smuggled by sea to England. As with the escape lines of other organisations such as MI9 (see Chapter One), escapers were always accompanied by a guide across the frontier.

The usual guides were smugglers who, according to the official historian of SOE in France, M. R. D. Foot, were quite secure if they were paid promptly and in full. The largest DF line worked with them through a former general in the Spanish Republican army code-named 'Martin'. Nearly all of them had fought on the Republican side during the Civil War and many were wanted men on both sides of the frontier. They knew every nook and cranny in the mountains, though they did sometimes get lost.

SOE was particularly active in Occupied France where by the end of the war it had established nearly a hundred Resistance circuits (*réseau*). Initially DF Section was part of F Section which controlled these circuits, but in the spring of 1942 it was made independent and came under the command of Leslie Humphreys, a former head of F Section. It was not an operational unit in the sense that F Section was, but it provided escape and evasion facilities just as other administrative elements of SOE provided clothes, weapons and forged documents. But its members in Occupied France lived just as dangerously as did those of F-Section, always in danger of betrayal, arrest and execution.

At its busiest, in the spring of 1944, DF's lines were handling an agent every day. Several hundred were plucked from danger in this way and none was lost. The loss rate among the couriers handling them was 2 per cent against that of F Section where the loss rate was 25 per cent. The basis of DF escape lines was a series of 'safe' houses and a watertight system of passing escapees from one 'safe' house to another until they were spirited out of the country.

To make the system watertight a series of 'cut-outs' was used. The technique is described in SOE files. An agent, who had two escapees in his 'safe' house, telephoned the cut-out, who was a bookseller, and said, 'I have two volumes of Anatole France that need binding; can you arrange it for me?' The bookseller waited until the next link in the line telephoned to ask, 'Have you any Anatole France in stock?' If the bookseller said, 'Yes, two volumes have just come in', the caller knew there were two escapers waiting to be collected from the 'safe' house in Boulevard Anatole France. If he said, 'Sorry, we're right out of stock', the caller knew there were none to be collected on that day.

To increase further the safety of the 'cut-out' system DF introduced the cut-out rendezvous which divided each section of the escape line into sealed compartments. The escapers would not be collected from the 'safe' house but would be taken to a pre-arranged spot such as a park bench where they would be collected shortly afterwards by a guide who would take them to their next 'safe' house. This had the added security that a guide never knew what any of the other guides looked like, and never knew where any of the 'safe' houses were except his own. The most they knew were two telephone numbers and two rendezvous, and both, of course, were constantly changed. Café call-boxes were used as often as possible – but not those in post offices where identity papers had to be shown.

Another cut-out system, using a *poste restante* address, also comes from SOE files. It needed an accomplice in a post office and was slower than other methods, but proved to be secure. An agent wanting to return to England from Switzerland made his way to a 'safe' house in Lyons whose owner would then drop a message to a fictitious individual, a Mademoiselle Marie Labaloue, care of a Lyons sub-post office, making sure that the message indicated how many passengers were to be picked up. The post was sorted at the post office by the sub-postmaster or his wife, both of whom knew all about Marie Labaloue. When they found a letter addressed to her they took it round to the local cobbler. On receipt of the note the cobbler put a particular pair of shoes in his window. The next link in the escape line walked past the cobbler at a certain time every day; if the shoes were in the window the courier went in and collected the letter. A similar cut-out system could be used by telephoning an intermediary.

The behaviour of escapees passing down the lines was strictly regulated, and the operators of the lines had even stricter rules. The Paris sub-organiser of DF's largest escape line, the VIC Line, made a list of the latter and this can be seen in SOE files: 'Members were only known and referred to by their pseudos. Domiciles of the regular staff of the Circuit always remained secret. New members of the Organisation had to drop all previous clandestine activities. All regular members had to sever contact with their families and live at a different address from the one they had lived at before joining the Circuit.'

Couriers were forbidden to carry any incriminating documents when going about their private affairs. When operative they were forbidden to carry any documents that revealed the names or addresses of contacts, and high-risk rendezvous at certain Metro stations, bars, cinemas and black market restaurants were forbidden. Messages passed verbally by couriers were always couched in incomprehensible phrases, but if this were impossible, or the message were too long to be memorised accurately, it was written on tissue paper and inserted into a cigarette, or carried in such a way as to be easily swallowed or simply dropped to the ground. Passwords, the key to establishing any contact, had to be quoted with total accuracy or they were rejected. Escapees hidden in 'safe' houses were never allowed out. Visiting agents or couriers always checked first by telephone and a simple inversion code increased security. If told that it would not be convenient to come, it meant that the coast was clear; 'by all means do come' meant that the Germans were in the house. 'Safe' houses and children were incompatible – children might let slip that there were strangers in their home.

The first DF line was run by E. V. H. Rizzo, a Maltese civil engineer who had taught science in a Paris school until he had escaped to England in June 1940. He was Humphreys' first agent in France when, in April 1941, he was put ashore east of the Pyrenees by HMS *Fidelity*, which was then to embark evaders from the PAT Line (see Chapter Three).

Working out of Perpignan, Rizzo established a highly successful line, known as EDOUARD or TROY, which became the second largest of DF's French circuits. During its four years of operating it was never penetrated or compromised, but tragically its principal courier, Rizzo's wife, was eventually caught by the Germans and gassed at Ravensbrück concentration camp in the spring of 1945.

Other early DF agents included the first woman SOE agent to be used in France, Giliana Balmaceda. An actress by profession, Giliana was a Chilean citizen whose passport contained a visa which permitted her to visit Vichy France. She travelled there in the spring of 1941 and during a useful three-week visit to Vichy and Lyons returned with a wealth of humdrum, but essential, information for escapers, such as railway time-tables, the implementation of curfews, identification documents, and the controls imposed on those travelling on buses and railways.

Two other early DF agents were a French Jew named Daniel Deligant who lived in Lisbon, and a Swiss social democrat, René Bertholet. Both took messages in and out of France. On occasions Deligant even delivered radio transceivers, and was able to do so on either side of the demarcation line which he had made arrangements to cross.

In April 1941 Giliana Balmaceda's husband, Victor Gerson, was put ashore from a submarine off the Côte d'Azur to set up the DF escape line called VIC, which became SOE's largest and best known. Gerson, a Jew, recruited another Jew, George Levin, as his second-in-command in Lyons which was the centre of the circuit's activities. Both ran much higher risks than a Gentile in a job that was, in any event, dangerous enough, but both were highly motivated.

Like Rizzo, Gerson used 'Martin' to smuggle his passengers across the Pyrenees. Most of the crossings were made from Perpignan where the mountains are not high. Before the Germans occupied Vichy France in November 1942 there was one particular route which caused travellers no trouble at all as M. R. D. Foot records in *SOE in France*. 'The escaper took the train, with his guide, on Sunday afternoon to the mountain station of Latour-de-Carol, five miles beyond Bourg-Madame. They left the station and strolled a few hundred yards up to the frontier, where by village custom several score French and Spanish people gossiped for a couple of hours every Sunday afternoon. When people began to drift away, the escaper walked quietly off with the man his guide had been chatting to – a Spaniard who would be his guide for the next stage of his journey, through Puigcerda to Barcelona.'

Even as late as 1943 the Germans, who by now had occupied the whole of France and had spread their *zone interdite* along the length of the Pyrenees, 'seldom exerted themselves unduly at the week-end', according to one F Section agent, John Lodwick, who used the VIC Line. He and a companion slipped across the frontier with their guide after leaving a train at St-Etienne-de-Baïgorry one Saturday evening:

'We had disembarked among a throng of barrel-shaped Basques and, acting upon instructions, plunged into the dark and more inaccessible interior of the covered lorry which served as transport between that town and the village of Urepel, which lies in a bowline loop of the frontier, with Spain on every hand but that of the North Star. At various road blocks, Austrian *Jäger* personnel had flashed torches upon the pile of twisted legs, clawing arms and flattened suitcases beneath which we three struggled like the castaways of the *Medusa*. Effectively deterred by the extreme coldness of the night and the Augean nature of our quarters, the intruders invariably withdrew. We had reached Urepel safely, been escorted to a large and comfortable house, eaten once again more than was good for us, and the next night, with a single guide, made the short but circuitous climb through cork woods required to reach the frontier, and by next morning, on foot and with the omnibus, had got about thirty miles inside Spain before being arrested. That we might have travelled further in the direction of our objective, Bilbao, by moving only at night and on foot, is possible, but unlikely. The security precautions in Spain at that time were not only more rigorous but infinitely more efficient than any imposed by the Germans during their tenure of France.'

Lodwick, who was writing of his experiences some years after the war, does not make the journey sound too onerous. But the diaries of Hugh Dormer, which were compiled soon after he had completed two treks across the Pyrenees in 1943, paint a rather different story. The immediacy of their tone strikes a sombre note quite missing in Lodwick's more flippant narrative.

Dormer, an Irish Guards subaltern, volunteered for SOE in the autumn of 1942, was decorated with the DSO for his work in France, and subsequently rejoined his unit and was killed in Normandy in July 1944. His French was adequate but far from perfect, which indicates – as does the fact that he was asked to return on another mission within days of returning to England – how desperately short of agents SOE were at this time.

Dormer's first operation, in April 1943, was aborted, and after being sheltered in a Paris 'safe' house by the VIC Line he and his one surviving companion were taken to Perpignan. The first night their French guide lost his way in the damp mountain mist. When at last they made their rendezvous with their Spanish guide – and after there had been a terrible row about money – they discovered that the farm where they had been told they could rest and have a meal was non-existent. Instead they would have to walk all the way to Figueras, which 'was not a pleasant discovery'.

The party, three in number, quickly lost confidence in the Spanish guide, a Catalan, though Dormer commented that later on 'we came to realise that he knew from childhood every blade of grass of those hills and knew more about field-craft from years of experience than we should ever have guessed. His contempt for us was one hundred times deeper and better justified than ours for him.'

Such was the bitter recrimination on the dark, cold, wet mountainside that it made Dormer 'weep in silent rage' and he swore to himself that as soon as they reached Barcelona he would kick the guide's teeth out in the street. In fact, once they did reach Barcelona they shook hands warmly, but reading between the lines it is obvious that Dormer and his companions lacked any sense of security. This terrified and infuriated the guide who would have been executed by the Spanish authorities if he had been caught.

It is interesting to note that on this first occasion Dormer was not taken to Gibraltar, as most evaders were, but was escorted by a guide into Portugal and flown back to England from Lisbon. No sooner had he arrived than he was asked to return to attack lock gates on the St. Quentin Canal. This too was aborted, before it was launched, but in August 1943 he returned to France to attack his original target, a shale oil mine and distillery plant near Autun. This time the attack succeeded, though not much damage was done. Only Dormer and a sergeant in the party of six escaped after being hunted by bloodhounds, and the following month Dormer found himself back in Perpignan as a guest of the VIC Line.

This time the party totalled nine, including two married couples. Soon after the start the women became 'exhausted by the remorseless pace, and kept on falling behind at every obstacle – at each stream or ditch. Then they would get nervous of losing contact with the guide, as he disappeared in the distance in front, and kept on crying out in the silence of the night.'

The women had to be dragged along and later in the journey, exhausted and their feet blistered and bleeding, they seemed to succumb to total despair and had to be virtually carried. They begged to be left behind and at some point were administered 'a drug to keep them going', presumably benzedrine. 'It was really terrible to witness their sufferings,' Dormer wrote, 'which were hard enough even for fit men to endure.' The journey soon became a nightmare:

'On and upwards we went towards the summit over the rocks and boulders. I had the sack of bread on my back, and was leading the quieter of the two women by one hand and tapping my way with a stick in the other. We were going along a knife-edge, and on the left was a sheer drop over the rocks below. Every now and again we had to skirt the German observation posts a few hundred feet above us on the peaks, and then again there was no path at all, but just a precipitous scramble over the boulders in the dark. As we approached the final summit of the Pyrenees, there was a great wind roaring in our faces. It was very dark now, and every few minutes there was thunder and forked lightning across the sky. We were right in the middle of a magnetic storm.'

Somehow they all got over the mountains and into Spain without being detected and after resting up in a farmhouse were taken to Barcelona. From there Dormer and his sergeant companion were taken to the British embassy in Madrid, and after a few days on to Gibraltar. At the embassy Dormer had found other evaders, most of them aircrew, waiting to be exfiltrated. One of them, an RAF pilot, had wandered around France for a year trying to get out. At one point he had gone for help to his father who lived in Paris. But his father was a collaborator and had thrown his son out of the house. Another man, an American pilot, had found a guide to take him across the Pyrenees at Andorra, 'the safest but the longest route'. It had taken nine days, some of them above snow level, and of a party of fourteen only eleven had made it.

These personal accounts show the extent of the resourcefulness and physical endurance needed to escape. They also give a flavour of what it was really like, which official documents often fail to do. But official reports also have their place in the story of escape lines for they give the modern reader a more objective perspective against which to measure the personal stories of evaders. For this reason it is worth quoting at some length from a paper Gerson wrote for SOE in January 1944 describing the routine of a typical crossing at that time.

'On the night of the departure the party is grouped in one of our safe houses, where they receive the final briefing on behaviour en route, what they have to say if caught, where and when they will change over couriers or guides, etc., etc. They leave Lyons by the night train. They arrive at Narbonne early in the morning, about 7 o'clock. The courier who accompanies the party is met at Narbonne by one or two of Martin's people. The decision is then made, whether they are to go straight through to Perpignan or round the Carcassonne–Quillan route.'

When they arrived at Perpignan, Gerson continues, the escapers were, depending on the circumstances, either put into a safe house or escorted to a local park where they stayed until evening. They were then collected by one of Martin's agents who led them out of Perpignan to meet the guides who were waiting for them outside the town. When contact was made the escapers were given rope-soled shoes – the most suitable footwear for crossing the mountains – and the party then began their all-night trek. Next morning, having passed through the *zone interdite*, they were passed on to two more guides, who were carrying food and drink for the party, at a pre-arranged rendezvous somewhere south of Céret.

According to Gerson the actual crossing of the frontier was made in daylight. The guides always acted with great caution, one staying with the party while the other scouted ahead. On the evening of the first day they would be handed over to a Spanish guide who would take them across the Frontier Zone on the Spanish side to a farmhouse where they arrived at about midnight. There they were given a meal before resting for the remainder of the night. The following day they began the last leg of the trek in the direction of Figueras where a car met them a few kilometres outside the town and took them into Barcelona.

The trip, from Perpignan to Figueras, took between 30 and 35 hours – which tallies with Dormer's accounts – though actual walking time was between 22 and 24 hours. The longest stretch, from Perpignan to Céret, took about twelve hours, and in his report Gerson commented that during the summer months it would be necessary to have a 'safe' house on this stretch because it was too far to cover by night, and had no doubts that this could be arranged. 'The most dangerous part', he concluded, though Dormer may not have agreed, 'is between Céret and the time when you are handed over to the Spanish side of the frontier; and the most difficult part is the walk through the Spanish Frontier Zone.'

Another highly successful DF escape line, which used the north Breton beaches to exfiltrate escapers and evaders to England by Motor Gun Boat (MGB), was code-named VAR. It operated during the winter of 1943 until the spring of 1944 and though it was formed specifically to land SOE agents and vital stores, and to bring out agents on the run from the Gestapo, evading service personnel inevitably became part of its cargo once the line's existence became known.

By this stage of the war the MGBs used for such operations were under the operational command of the Deputy Director Operations Division (Irregular), or DDOD(I). This was Captain F. A. Slocum RN who, at the beginning of the war, had commanded the Operations Section of the Special Intelligence Service (MI6), which was charged with re-opening physical contact with occupied Europe.

Rather to the annoyance of SOE, which had its own paranaval section on the River Helford in south-west England, the DDOD(I), at the request of the DF Section, undertook the training of DF's GSO III, Captain Peter Harratt, and an agent, Erwin Deman, with a view to their setting up the VAR escape line.

The previous spring Harratt had taken part in a reconnaissance of the beach at Clogourouan to check a cache of supplies which had been buried there, and was obviously struck with the potential efficiency of a sea escape line. Organising such a line by sea was little different from that by land. Those using it were assembled at a 'safe' house before being taken after dusk to a convenient cottage close to the beach. Normally up to six passengers could be carried, though on one occasion when an emergency arose ten were taken aboard for the passage to England.

The MGBs operated on moonless nights and never closed the French coast until two hours after sunset. On the approach, Peter Harratt explained, 'the silencers were turned on to the engines and the speed consequently reduced. At a point fifteen miles from the enemy coast, main engines were cut and we went forward on auxiliaries in complete silence, at a maximum speed of approximately 6 knots. This reduced the wash and consequent phosphorescence.'

When closing the shore the strictest drill was imposed on the beach and on board: no lights, no smoking, no talking. Would-be passengers, commonly known as parcels, were checked to ensure 'he neither rattles nor shines' and were briefed 'to behave as much like luggage as possible. While waiting they should always sit down.'

The MGB usually made contact with the shore by S-Phone, though sometimes an agreed letter in Morse was flashed by torch from the beach party. Occasionally the correct signal was made with a luminous ball held in a closed fist. When contact was made the MGB anchored offshore. A grass rope, not an anchor chain, was always used so that it could be severed instantly by a rating who stood by with an axe. The passengers were rowed to the beach with muffled oars.

Two surf boats were used. An armed look-out took up position in the bows of the first; the passengers followed in the second. Agents going ashore always wore gas capes to avoid having their clothes stained by spray, and these were collected and returned to the MGB. No headgear was worn in case it was blown off and lost, and perhaps found by the Germans. Landings were always made on a rising tide which it was hoped would obliterate footprints, though the beach was always visited early the following morning by someone who made sure there were no traces of the operation. Speed was of the essence, but even so, the MGB was normally at anchor for about an hour and a half. The shortest recorded time was 35 minutes; the longest was $3\frac{1}{2}$ hours when a sudden fog descended.

The French side of the VAR Line had about 150 people working for it and was run by Erwin Deman, a 39-year-old Jew from Vienna who spoke French, German and English fluently. After training with Harratt he began his activities in August 1943 when he was flown into France by a Special Duties aircraft to make contact with a Madame Jestin who lived in Rennes. She had two unmarried daughters in their forties who agreed to organise the line's 'safe' houses and recruit reliable guides and couriers. Aline, the elder, worked in the Rennes prefecture and had no difficulty in supplying blank safe conduct passes for the coastal zone which was a prohibited area for civilians.

Deman surveyed two selected beaches west of Dinard, one of which, the Grève-du-Mousselet, had been recommended by the Irish yachtswoman, Cecily Lefort, who owned a villa above it at Saint-Cast and was at that time undergoing training as an SOE agent (she was later to die in Ravensbrück concentration camp). Deman established his *bona fides* with the housekeeper of Lefort's villa by showing her a ring belonging to her mistress.

The Mousselet beach proved satisfactory and had the added advantage of being close to the home of the parents of Aristide Sicot, Deman's right-hand man, which could be used as a 'safe' house. For cover Deman set himself up as an insurance agent in Rennes and within two months the line was ready to start operating, but before it did so he was asked to return for last-minute consultations in London. He told acquaintances he was taking two weeks off; travelled via the VIC Line to England in the record time of seven days; was returned by MGB to Mousselet beach on 28 October; and was back at his office in Rennes exactly a fortnight after he had left.

The first operation had to be abandoned, but the second, which took place on 1 December 1943, succeeded – though Harratt, in one of the two surf-boats sent ashore by the MGB, nearly shot Sicot as the Frenchman waded out to meet him (it was agreed that in future Sicot would hold his hands in the air to establish his identity).

The next operation, due to be mounted on 23/24 December, did not go so well and is vividly described in Brooks Richards' official history, *Secret Flotillas*: 'At the last minute Félix Jouan, the miller from Bedée, whose van was being used by the VAR organisation to transport passengers through the Prohibited Zone that covered the coast, came to say that a General Allard, whose wife had already been arrested by the Gestapo, was urgently seeking evacuation to England. Deman felt he could not do other than accept this distinguished additional passenger, whom Jouan then delivered in his van. The party, now expanded to considerable size, left the villa that night in Indian file behind Aristide Sicot. They passed through La-Pisotte and made their way down to the Grève-du-Mousselet, using a coastguard path cut into the face of the cliff. Though there was no moon, the night had become calm and clear after earlier rain and the visibility by starlight was good enough to cause Peter Williams, on the bridge of MGB 502, considerable apprehension as he approached the Baie-de-la-Frénaie, its entrance, 2.5km (1½ miles) wide, dominated by high cliffs on either side.'

Sicot and Deman left the party on the beach and hurried to the top of a nearby cliff to contact the MGB by S-phone and warn Williams that he would have to embark more people than he was expecting. The surf boats would have to make two trips to the beach which put pressure on Williams to bring his MGB in as close as possible to cut down the time the operation would now take.

'Williams came close enough to surprise those waiting ashore,' Brooks Richards wrote. 'Sicot recalled that the gunboat seemed to drift over to the Saint-Cast shore. She passed under the noses of the Germans, that is to say, within a hundred metres of their block-houses. Even though she was steaming at slow speed on one silenced engine, the Germans would have been deaf not to hear her. She came on in until she was off the Pointe-du-Châtelet and there anchored. Deman and Sicot watched from the top of their rocky headland, astonished by the audacity of the proceedings. Although there was no moon, the visibility to seaward was such that, even at a distance of over half a mile, the ship's silhouette seemed outlined by a sort of phosphorescent mist.'

At first there was no reaction from the Germans, but as the surf boats were being lowered from the anchored MGB a white flare was fired and illuminated the whole area. This was followed by a red one – the signal to open fire – and as the MGB's grass warp was severed, and she swung round on her main engines to get out of the bay, machine-gun bullets started falling all around her. Luckily she was too far into the bay to be in the field of fire of the heavier calibre guns mounted on each side of the bay's entrance; and when she did come within range of them the German gunners miscalculated her speed and the evasive measures she was taking, and all the shells fell into her wake.

Ashore, Deman and Sicot dashed back to the beach, collected the party and rushed them into a concealed cellar which had been constructed under the safe house. But the Germans concentrated their subsequent searches on the other side of the bay and the following night the party was evacuated in Jouan's van to Bedée and was eventually fed through the VIC Line to freedom.

This setback meant that the Mousselet beach could not be used again, so it was replaced by one near Beg-an-Fry close to Guimaëc, north-east of Morlaix. This was used with great success and none of the 70 passengers, which included a future French president, François Mitterand, conveyed during the line's existence were lost, though in April 1944 a naval rating was killed in a fire-fight with a German patrol boat during one of the sixteen successful cross-Channel passages undertaken. Another sixteen were attempted but failed for one reason or another.

Eventually, the VAR Line became a victim of its own success for it became so widely known that its security was impaired. It was shut down and its personnel – though not Deman who was withdrawn suffering from exhaustion and stress – formed an SOE land escape route via the Pyrenees until the Normandy landings that June made it redundant. Shortly afterwards the circuit's wireless operator was arrested while transmitting. He kept silent under torture and died in Buchenwald concentration camp eight months later.

Two other DF lines, GREYHOUND/WOODCHUCK and PIERRE/ JACQUES, were established in 1943. Both ran between Paris and Belgium. The former was run by a Belgian businessman, George Lovinfosse, from a house near Châteauroux in central France; the latter by a Dutchman, Guido Zembsch-Schreve, and an Anglo–Frenchmen, J. M. C. Planel. They were later supplemented by two more lines, STANISLAUS, organised by Felix Hilton, and LOYOLA, a Polish group run by K. Popiel.

At the end of 1943 the VIC Line was penetrated by the *Abwehr* (German Military Intelligence). During the previous year the *Abwehr* had taken control of SOE circuits in the Netherlands. This gave them the necessary entrée to the VIC Line, and in November 1943 an *Abwehr* agent named Richard Christmann turned up at a VIC Paris address which had been given to the compromised SOE Dutch circuits by SOE in London. He was fed down the line to Lyons where he was told by George Levin that he was urgently needed in London. He managed to extricate himself from this potentially awkward situation and in January 1944 the ten sub-agents who had passed him down to Lyons were arrested, though Levin himself escaped capture because he had left the apartment in which Christmann had met him.

None of the arrested sub-agents could provide their interrogators with any information of substance because of the extremely secure systems on which the line was run by Gerson. He changed his 'safe' houses and contacts every three months, regardless of whether they were blown or not, as he did not wait for trouble before taking measures to prevent it. Such meticulous attention to security meant that the VIC Line survived the arrests and even its most hazardous stretch, between Perpignan and Figueras, remained intact. The compromised 'safe' houses and couriers were replaced by others ready to step into the breach, and the flow of 'bodies' continued with very little interruption.

5

THE ONE THAT GOT AWAY

Allied servicemen were not the only POW who escaped during the course
of the Second World War, but escaping from Britain proved beyond the
resources of the Italians and Germans who found themselves imprisoned
there. So far as is known no Italian even attempted to escape from a UK POW
camp. The Germans were every bit as enterprising as their British and American
counterparts in trying to do so, though only one ever made it back to Germany
and that was from Canada not Britain.

One particularly audacious attempt took place in November 1941. Two
German pilots from KG27, who were imprisoned in Cumbria, bluffed their way
out of their camp and seized a trainer aircraft at Carlisle. They managed to take
off but were recaptured at Horsham St Faith in Norfolk where they had landed
to refuel before crossing the North Sea. The RAF thought so highly of their
attempt that they were feted in the officers' mess before being returned to
captivity.

Nor was that classic means of escape, tunnelling, the prerogative of Allied
POW. In February 1945 69 German officers in a POW camp at Bridgend in South
Wales escaped by tunnelling out of their compound. This created a considerable
panic in the area but all of them were rounded up within a week.

Potentially much more dangerous was a plot hatched in December 1944 by a
number of Nazi POW for a mass breakout from Camp 23 near Devizes, Wiltshire,
which housed 7,000 German prisoners. It was rather similar to the one by
Japanese POW at Cowra camp in Australia (see Chapter Thirteen) in that the ringleaders – battle-hardened NCOs captured during the Normandy landings in June
1944 – planned to kill the guards, arm the escapees, and then liberate POW from
other camps before making a mass attack on London.

This plan was, wrote the British intelligence officer who later interrogated the
ringleaders, 'a startling programme. At zero hour the key men would begin the
mass breakout. A selected handful of truckdrivers would proceed to the vehicle
park, commandeer the vehicles and drive at once to the arms store, where guns
would be picked up. A second squad would make their way to the food stores,
collect as many provisions as possible in a few minutes, then hurry to the trucks,
where they would load the rations.'

Once this had been accomplished the armed prisoners would drive to Sheffield
where another mass breakout from a POW camp had been planned, and the two
groups would join forces and drive due east, fighting their way to the coast if that
proved necessary. On the way a radio station would be captured so that a signal

could be sent to Germany to alert the German Navy which would pick up the POW when they arrived near the Wash.

This fantastic plot came to nothing because two of its ringleaders were over-heard discussing it by a German-speaking American intelligence officer. The 30 main ringleaders were promptly removed from the camp and taken to the interro-gation centre for POW at 8 Kensington Palace Gardens, known as the London Cage. There they were questioned by Lieutenant-Colonel A. P. Scotland, who later wrote of the German plan that 'no escape story of the Second World War was more daring in concept, more fantastic, more ambitious, more hopelessly fanatical than that of the prisoners of Devizes.'

But more bizarre events were to follow. After interrogation the ringleaders were sent to the remote Camp 21 near Comrie in Perthshire. This was a maximum security camp which held a thousand of the most fanatical Nazis. The ringleaders, thinking that their plot had been betrayed – though in fact it was their own lack of security that had revealed it – turned on one of their number they suspected of being responsible and he was beaten to death. The men who committed this murder were put on trial in July 1945 and five of them were hanged at Pentonville prison on 6 October.

During the early years of the war many Axis POW were shipped to Canada and this kept the number of German prisoners in the UK – the only ones who ever even considered escaping – to under 2,000 until March 1944. But after the Normandy landings in June 1944 the numbers rose sharply so that by the end of the war in Europe, in May 1945, there were nearly 200,000 of them and by September 1946 this had risen to a peak of 402,200.

By now German POW were beginning to be repatriated and those due to return awaited their turn patiently – all that is except a young Berliner named Hans Müller and two of his fellows in a POW camp near Colchester on the Essex coast. They got tired of waiting and, having by now a fair measure of freedom, had little difficulty in stowing away aboard a German ship at nearby Ipswich which was bound for Hamburg. When the German skipper found them he was furious and made them swim ashore as soon as the ship reached the River Elbe.

Müller's companions, who were from Bremen, left Müller to make his own way to his home which was in the Russian zone of East Berlin. But he soon found that though it had proved easy to leave Britain and enter Germany, it was impossible to travel, eat or work in Germany without documents. In Hanover he acquired a forged pass which enabled him to get to East Berlin. But the Russians were always carrying out searches for anyone living in the Russian zone illegally and after four months he was forced to move to his grandmother's farm near Dresden.

He stayed with his grandmother for two months but was then picked up by the Russians and imprisoned. He escaped, decided he must have proper documents, and returned to Hanover to try to get some. He did not have enough money to do so but the enterprising forgers, who ran a very successful business providing documents to those attempting to evade Allied justice, suggested that he return to

England for his own documents for which, on his return, he would be handsomely paid. When Müller pointed out that the docks at Hamburg were closely guarded, the forgers offered to give him a pass into the docks provided that he return and sell them his POW documents.

Müller agreed, stowed away aboard another boat, and within a week was reporting back to the POW camp near Colchester from which he had disappeared nearly a year previously. The authorities there simply did not believe his story. He was sent to the London Cage for interrogation where Colonel Scotland soon established that he had been telling nothing less than the truth! When asked by a colleague what he had said to the German, Scotland replied: 'Frankly, I congratulated him. In my opinion the boy deserves a medal.'

There were a number of similar post-war escapes by German POW in the USA (see Chapter Six), but the few who escaped during the war were recaptured. In Britain by March 1945 there had been a total of 420 escapes by German POW. One of the most persistent escapers was Franz von Werra, a Luftwaffe fighter ace, and it was he who eventually became the only German during the war to return to Germany – via Britain, Canada and the United States.

Werra was shot down over the Kent countryside in September 1940 when his squadron of Me 109s was escorting bombers on a raid on Croydon. He was taken prisoner by an unarmed cook from a nearby searchlight battery, spent the night in a police cell, and was taken next day under armed guard to Colonel Scotland's interrogation centre in Kensington Palace Gardens.

Like the British, German servicemen were briefed to give only their name, rank and number if captured, but at this point in the war Luftwaffe personnel were not security conscious, nor had they been briefed as to how to behave under interrogation. But Werra, as well as being an ebullient character, was a canny one. So when he was handed a form which included questions about his unit and his mission he wrote only his name, rank and number; and when he was told to fill in the form correctly he refused. He was questioned briefly by an army captain – who studiously avoided asking questions of a military nature – and was then taken to the MI9 interrogation centre at Trent Park, Cockfosters, in north London.

Werra stayed at Cockfosters for two weeks, undergoing a series of gruelling interrogations, before being returned to Kensington for four days for further questioning. He was then taken to POW Camp No. 1 at Grizedale Hall in the Lake District which at the time was the only camp in Britain for captured officers. A former stately home, it lay in isolated countryside between Windermere and Coniston Water. The prisoners there, mostly U-boat and Luftwaffe officers, ran the camp rather on the same lines as British and American POW ran theirs. The senior officer formed a three-man *Altestenrat* (lit. 'council of the eldest'), which maintained discipline and looked after the welfare of the POW by acting as their representatives with the British military authorities who ran the camp.

At that time the general attitude of the few Germans who had been captured was that the war was nearly over and that Britain would either be invaded and overrun, or would be forced to capitulate. Either way, it seemed more sensible to wait to be released than to undertake the onerous task of trying to escape. But one of the *Altestenrat* had in fact made such a bid. He had acquired some English money, a fake identity card, and civilian clothing, but he had not got beyond the camp's inner ring of barbed wire before being recaptured. Since then security at the camp had been tightened, and when Werra applied to the *Altestenrat* for permission to escape just ten days after he had arrived the three officers were highly sceptical that he would have any chance of succeeding. But the details of his escape plan impressed them and he was given permission to proceed.

On 7 October 1940 Werra joined the route march which was organised daily to give the prisoners some exercise and during a rest he dropped over a stone wall and made his escape. He was spotted almost immediately, not by the guards, who had been distracted, but by two local women. They tried to attract the guards' attention by waving their handkerchiefs. The prisoners responded by shouting and waving back which fooled the guards into thinking that the women were waving at the Germans, and it was not until a count was taken on the return march that Werra was found to be was missing. The police were alerted and the local Home Guard mobilised, and soon hundreds of men had been drawn into the hunt, but the German fighter ace proved an adept escaper. At one point he was found sheltering in a stone hut by two members of the Home Guard, but in the darkness and the rain he soon eluded them.

Werra remained at large for five days, living on what food he had managed to stuff into his pockets and on apples he had found in an orchard. On 12 October, he was seen by a Cumberland shepherd and recaptured. He was returned to Grizedale Hall where he was sentenced to 21 days' solitary confinement in the cells which had been built in the cellars of the hall – the maximum sentence for escaping was 30 days according to the Geneva Convention – but messages and cigarettes were smuggled into him and he was able to send out messages as well. Before he had completed his sentence he was transferred to POW (Officers') Transit Camp No. 13 which was established in a complex of buildings around 'The Hayes', a country house situated near the Derbyshire village of Swanwick on the main road from Alfreton to Ripley.

The relative ease with which he had escaped made Werra determined to try again, and he and another prisoner started what they called the *Swanwick Tiefbau A. G.* (Swanwick Construction Company). This comprised carefully selected prisoners whose job it was to dig a tunnel out of the camp and their ingenuity was the equal of anything displayed by Allied POW. The five men, including Werra, who worked on it from start to finish were to be the first to use it. They decided that their best chance of freedom was to try to get to neutral Eire, or to stow away on a neutral ship at Liverpool. But, Werra, with his good command of English, decided that his best chance would be to steal an aircraft from an RAF air base. He would masquerade as a Dutch pilot attached to a fictitious Coastal Command squadron at Aberdeen who had crash-landed north of Derby. He had been ordered to the air base where he was to be picked up by another Coastal Command aircraft.

Werra was confident that this cover story would be good enough to get him into the base; once inside he would have to rely on luck and bluff to get hold of an aircraft. He chose Coastal Command because he guessed that no one at an inland air base would be familiar with its operations, and that this would lessen the chance of being asked awkward questions. Also, one of his fellow prisoners had frequently attacked Dyce Coastal Command base at Aberdeen and was able to tell Werra quite a lot about it. If he were asked for his identity papers he would point out that these were not allowed to be taken on flying missions. But he knew he that he would have to produce an identity disc, which every serviceman wore. One of the guards innocently provided one that could be copied and a perfect imitation was eventually forged. Suitable clothing could have proved a problem but one of the inmates still had his flying-suit which he gave to Werra, and another donated his flying-boots.

The 16-metre tunnel was completed in a month and all five men escaped without difficulty on the night of 20 December 1940. One was quickly recaptured at South Normanton after stealing a bicycle – unfortunately for him, it belonged to the local policeman – and by the early hours of the following morning a manhunt for the others was under way. A second prisoner was arrested next morning on the outskirts of Handsworth near Sheffield – when he clicked his heels and bowed his thanks to a bus conductor who had handed him his ticket! – and another two on the outskirts of Manchester after a lorry driver, who had given them a lift, became suspicious.

Werra was luckier. His cover story held sufficiently well for him to bluff a local railway booking clerk into calling the nearest RAF station, Hucknall, to say that he had a Dutch pilot who had crash-landed near by. Situated north of Nottingham, Hucknall was an RAF-run training school for Polish pilots as well as an airfield for Rolls-Royce from which ferry pilots took aircraft to other bases. Its duty officer was not very convinced by what the booking clerk told him, but agreed to send a car to pick Werra up from the station, and once Werra was in his office he put through a call to Werra's alleged base at Dyce, near Aberdeen.

While waiting for the call the duty officer asked for identification. Werra reached for his identity disc, which was hanging around his neck, only to find that the heat of his body had turned the forgery into a sticky mess! As Werra fumbled with what remained of the disc, the call came through from Aberdeen. But the line was bad, and while the duty officer was busy trying to make himself understood Werra slipped out and made for the part of the airfield run by Rolls-Royce where he had another break because he encountered a man who mistook him for an expected ferry pilot. But then Werra's luck ran out. He was in fact already seated in the cockpit of a Hurricane, one of the brand new Mk IIs which had not yet been used operationally, and was receiving instructions on its instrument panel from a mechanic, when the duty officer, revolver in hand, caught up with him.

All five prisoners were returned to Swanwick where they were given the comparatively light sentence of 14 days in the punishment cells before the occupants of the camp were all shipped to Canada (where eventually 33,800 German POW were held). Once aboard ship, the Canadian Pacific Line's *Duchess of York*, a special guard was put on Werra. On 10 January 1941 the liner sailed for Halifax. Once at sea Werra soon evaded the ship's security to wander about in forbidden areas of the ship, and he then proposed to the other prisoners that they take over the liner by force and sail it to the nearest German-held French Atlantic port. This had to be abandoned as impracticable, but when the senior German officer ordered all officers planning to escape to report to him, 73 of the 250 officers aboard turned up. Most had hare-brained schemes which were greeted with laughter, but the more determined ones were given lectures by one prisoner who knew Canada well; and, in fact, several of his audience did manage to escape from Canada during the course of the war.

When the liner docked at Halifax the POW were quickly frisked for weapons and their baggage was cursorily examined. Incidentally, this was the first and last occasion German prisoners were treated so casually, for the epidemic of escaping which followed their arrival resulted in much stricter security measures being imposed later on. In fact, when the next contingent of prisoners arrived from Britain, a large number of escape aids were found on them or hidden in their belongings: home-made compasses, maps, sail-cord, cash in several different currencies, hacksaw blades, identity papers stolen from a seaman, and a large amount of the ship's cutlery were discovered.

Once the searches had been completed the prisoners were put aboard a train which was to take them to a newly built camp on the north shore of Lake Superior in Ontario. When Werra learned their destination he decided on a new plan of escape. He decided his best chance would be to try to cross the St. Lawrence River, the border between Canada and the still-neutral United States, which, between Montreal and Ottawa, ran reasonably close to the railway line. It was not the closest point; that was in north-west New Brunswick which the train passed through early in the journey close to the American state of Maine. But the Maine countryside was wild and inhospitable at this time of year and Werra thought he might easily be lost in its endless expanse of forests. He also reckoned that the guards would be at their most alert, and that that would be the place where other POW might make their bid for freedom. (Altogether there were eight escapes from the train during the course of its journey and several other prisoners were caught as they were about to leave.)

Werra and the three prisoners with him in the compartment developed a plan which would enable Werra to escape through the train window after dark while the guards were distracted by other prisoners. Partly through sheer luck, and partly through Werra's courage, the plan succeeded – what's more he was not missed until the following afternoon – and he landed in a snow drift near a place called Smiths Falls, about 40 miles south-west of Ottawa, some 30 miles from the St.

THE ONE THAT GOT AWAY

Lawrence. How he made his way to Johnstown on the St. Lawrence River during the course of the day was never subsequently established – the story he told the American press could not possibly have been true – but he acquired a map from a garage and was almost certainly given a lift by someone.

At Johnstown he tried to walk across the frozen river to Ogdensburg on the American bank, but after stumbling about in the bitter darkness he found that the ice had melted close to the river bank. He returned to the Canadian shore, found a boat, dragged it across the ice and managed to reach dry land. He was quickly arrested after being given a lift into Ogdensburg and was charged with vagrancy, but once he had established that he was an escaped POW the charge was dropped and he was handed over to immigration officials who charged him with illegal entry into the United States.

Next day, 25 January 1941, he was besieged by American pressmen and he made the front pages of the newspapers. He was released from custody on $5,000 bail which was paid by the German Consul who quickly arranged for him to come to New York. There he wrote a report which included details of his interrogation in London, and from then on Luftwaffe personnel were properly briefed on what to do if they became POW.

Werra was the third German to have escaped from Canada into the United States up to that time: the first, a U-boat rating, had escaped from a prison ship in the St. Lawrence during the summer of 1940. He had been allowed to remain in the United States, but the second, a merchant seaman who escaped from a prison camp in Ontario, and crossed the border at International Falls, Minnesota, was imprisoned and then returned to Canada.

Initially, Werra avoided the fate of the merchant seaman because of the publicity that surrounded his escape – many Americans at that time were still sympathetic to the Germans – but when on 22 March 1941 two more German POW escaped to the United States by crossing the frozen St. Lawrence at Ogdensburg they were returned to Canada. Anticipating a protest from Germany, the State Department issued a statement to explain why Werra had been allowed in on a temporary basis while the other two had not: 'The difference was that Werra was not arrested until after he had entered the country, whereas the two officers supposedly applied for admission at the border, and after due consideration, were found to be unacceptable.'

Nevertheless it looked as if Werra might be returned to Canada. and on 24 March 1941 he fled secretly to Mexico; the German Consul forfeited $5,000 in bail money; and Werra eventually returned to Germany via Rio de Janeiro, Barcelona and Rome. He was then attached to the Intelligence Branch of the Luftwaffe Operations staff which subsequently issued a 12-page booklet describing his experiences as a POW.

Apart from alerting the Luftwaffe to the need to train their airmen in resisting interrogation, Werra denied Nazi propaganda that all German POW were maltreated by their British captors. Now German personnel knew that if they were captured and interrogated they would not be tortured or physically harmed, and this gave them confidence to refuse to give any information. As part of his job Werra was also sent to visit several British POW camps in Germany to report on their security compared to those run by the British. What he recommended in the way of anti-escape measures does not seem to have affected the rate of exodus from them, but his reaction to the techniques employed at the German Air Interrogation Centre – at Oberursel, near Frankfurt-on-Main – made a considerable impact. Known as *Dulag Luft*, it was the equivalent of MI9's centre at Cockfosters. Werra sat in on several interrogations and later reported to Göring that he would prefer to be quizzed 'by half a dozen German inquisitors than by one RAF expert'.

At his own request Werra was posted to the Eastern Front after Germany invaded the Soviet Union on 22 June 1941, but by September his *Gruppe* had been moved to Holland. On 25 October his Messerschmitt developed an engine fault and plunged into the sea. Neither the aircraft nor Werra's body were ever found.

6

AMERICA'S ESCAPE FACTORIES

The Americans' principal escape and evasion organisations were MIS-X, P/W&X and AGAS. MIS-X was the equivalent of the British escape and evasion organisation, MI9 (see Chapter One); P/W&X, which catered for aircrew in the European Theatre of Operations, was independent of MIS-X and performed only some of that organisation's functions; and AGAS was the Far East equivalent, and eventual successor, of the British Army Aid Group (see Chapter Nine).

Unfortunately for future historians and writers – and perhaps more importantly for those who had to cope with the problems of escape and evasion during the Korean War – the records of MIS-X were destroyed in August 1945 on the orders of the US Army's Assistant Chief of Staff for G-2 (Intelligence), Major General George V. Strong.

So it is impossible to give a complete picture of how MIS-X functioned or to document in any detail its successes and failures. But when the authors of *MI9: Escape and Evasion 1939-45* undertook further research for the American edition of their book, they did find a number of MIS-X files in the National Archives at Washington. Its publication spurred a surviving ex-member of MIS-X to undertake further research and subsequently to write a book, *The Escape Factory*, published in 1990. This, perforce, relies largely on the author's memory, and those few surviving colleagues of MIS-X that he was able to interview, but he did track down some additional documentary evidence. There is also some mention in British documents of the joint work of MIS-X and MI9 in the Mediterranean Theatre of Operations.

The letters MIS stood for Military Intelligence Service (MIS) which been formed in 1942 as part of the US general staff's Military Intelligence Division (MID). Among other functions MIS was directed to supervise the 'appropriate operational functions concerning matter within the purview of the Military Intelligence Division' which included escape and evasion of US personnel in enemy-occupied territory and the interrogation in the US of enemy POW suspected of having specialised information of use to the Allied war effort.

It is worth pausing here to add that once the Americans entered the war in December 1941 they too had to accommodate an increasing number of Axis POW and by May 1945 a total of 425,871 German, Italian and Japanese POW were being held in the USA in 155 camps. Some of these, particularly the Germans, were as eager to escape as their Allied counterparts and more than 2,000 German POW managed to do so. None remained at large for long and the vast majority were recaptured within 24 hours.

One of the more ingenious, and protracted, escapes was organised in December 1944 by four U-boat captains. They supervised the construction of a 178-foot tunnel under cover of volunteering to build a volleyball field in the compound of their camp in Arizona, and 25 prisoners escaped through it. Armed with false identification papers and disguised as factory workers and merchant seamen, they were free for six weeks before being recaptured while trying to reach the Mexican border.

When, in July 1946, the last of the German POW were being returned to Germany it was found that six had absconded. Five were eventually tracked down and arrested, but the sixth, a sergeant in the Afrika Korps' crack 15th Panzer Division, became a model American citizen and eluded all attempts to trace him until he revealed his origins forty years later and posed the authorities a unique problem. 'He is not an illegal alien, since he was brought to America against his will,' wrote Professor Arnold Krammer in an article in *Soldiers* in December 1985. 'He was urged to escape, as our soldiers are ordered to do. Since he escaped on Sept. 21, 1945, after the war was over, he was technically not a prisoner of war. [He] paid his taxes every year, broke no laws and was married to an American woman for twenty years.'

To cope with this flood of Axis POW – a percentage of whom had information of use to the Allies – an interrogation section, known as MIS-Y, was formed in April 1942 under the command of Colonel Russell Sweet, and in October 1942 MIS-X was formed, the Washington head of which was Lieutenant-Colonel J. Edward Johnson. For administrative purposes both sections became part of MIS's Captured Personnel and Material Branch in Washington when that branch was established on 22 October 1942 under the command of Colonel Catesby ap C. Jones.

Both sections were housed at Fort Hunt, Virginia, a preserved Civil War fortress and First World War command post which lay in 80 acres of ground on the west bank of the River Potomac, twenty miles south of Washington, DC. For security reasons it was always referred to as '1142', its post office box number in Alexandria.

A post-war history of the MID in the US National Archives states that 'Within the [Captured Personnel and Material] Branch there was a section whose activities were secret and whose relation to the activities of the remainder of the branch were superficial. Known as the MIS-X section, it dealt with the escape and evasion activities of our own personnel captured or detained by the enemy. The section was activated 6 October 1942 after the Secretary of War [Henry L. Stimson] had suggested such an agency to the Chief of Staff [General George C. Marshall]. The purpose of the section was to provide escape and evasion information to American personnel overseas. It was to make this information available to key personnel who would pass it on to others. Finally it disseminated intelligence, gleaned from communication with our prisoners. Quite naturally it was expected to develop the means of communication with them.'

MIS-X had five sub-sections: interrogation, correspondence (codes), POW locations, training & briefing, and technical. The interrogation sub-section interviewed returning US POW and internees for information that might be of value to military intelligence and to pinpoint the locations of camps and find out about the conditions in them.

The correspondence sub-section handled coded mail between selected prisoners – called code users (CU) – and their correspondents in the US. This included writing 'phoney letters' (complete with false names, addresses and censorship deletions) which contained special messages for the addressees; and also working with the next-of-kin of prisoners in the composition of letters which could contain coded information.

The POW camp locations sub-section sought the exact location of camps so that the Air Forces could be warned not to bomb them, and an evaluation was placed upon intelligence sent from the camps. The sub-section's sources included the Red Cross, the Protecting Powers, MI9 and other British intelligence sources, and the Office of Strategic Services (OSS) which undertook all American sabotage and subversion operations in enemy-occupied territory. It also kept itself *au fait* with camp conditions and the needs of prisoners, and issued reports on the camps.

The training and briefing sub-section sent 'briefers' to Army Air Force units as well as to certain Marine Corps and other Army units to train selected personnel in escape and evasion techniques, and the use of codes. Much of this work was done with USAAF combat crews and USAAF officers were assigned to the sub-section to help in their indoctrination.

The design, procurement and distribution of escape kits was the responsibility of the technical sub-section which, throughout the war, worked closely with its British counterpart, MI9, which helped in the initial training of the section. The activities of the sub-section 'played a large part in the maintenance of morale in the Prisoner of War camps abroad, and yielded information concerning bomb damage and likely targets in the area visited'. The history concluded: 'As the operations of the [Captured Personnel and Material] Branch developed, its name became misleading. At no time did it concern itself with captured material. The Scientific Branch, the Military Branch and the Intelligence Section of the Technical service assumed responsibility [for this]. The Branch concerned itself with prisoner[s] – both enemy and American. Its operations were carefully guarded secrets, which yielded a fund of intelligence of both tactical and strategical importance.'

Examples of this intelligence, sent by coded messages from US POW, included a warning that the forward emergency hatch on the Flying Fortress B-17 bomber was not working properly; that escapers and evaders should avoid the town of Tours in France because it was exceptionally well policed; that the Germans were using a bogus Red Cross official to extract information from newly captured personnel; and that POW interrogated at some *Dulagen* (special interrogation centres for POW who were thought to be in possession of information useful to the Germans), were revealing too much because they were kept in solitary confinement.

The principal spur to establishing MIS-X was a visit in February 1942 by Major General Carl Spaatz of the USAAF to England where he met Norman Crockatt, the head of MI9. Spaatz was impressed with Crockatt's organisation, so impressed that he requested that one of his staff officers, Captain Robley E. Winfrey, a former professor of civil engineering at Iowa State University, be attached to it to learn every aspect of MI9's operations. This was granted and the following month a British Air-Vice Marshal, Charles Medhurst, flew to Washington to brief the Chairman of the US Joint Chiefs of Staff, General George C. Marshall, and the Secretary of War, Henry L. Stimson, about MI9.

That summer Spaatz also appointed another member of his staff, Lieutenant-Colonel W. Stull Holt, an academic historian from Johns Hopkins University, to form a staff branch, called P/W&X, to liaise with Crockatt and supervise the escape and evasion needs of all three Commands – bomber, fighter and ground attack – of Spaatz's Eighth USAAF which began operating from British soil in the summer of 1942.

Holt's orders from Spaatz were 'to study and perfect the escape and evasion techniques into a program to be used by the American briefers as they indoctrinated US Army air and ground forces troops prior to combat; the proper employment of this indoctrination; how to behave if captured; what to say during interrogation; how to escape from a POW camp; and the selection of certain individuals in combat units who would be taught a secret letter code to be employed if captured by the enemy.'

Holt reported directly to Spaatz and his section was independent of MIS-X, though he liaised as closely with it as he did with MI9.

Initially Stimson was doubtful about the possibilities of forming an American equivalent of MI9, but he was eventually persuaded to give his permission by Marshall, by the head of the MID, Major-General George V. Strong, and by Spaatz. MIS-X was established at Fort Hunt in October 1942 with an initial funding by Stimson of $25,000. MIS-X was given the following directive that indicates that it was to work in very much the same way as MI9:

a. Indoctrinate Air Force intelligence officers who will in turn instruct air crew in the various Theaters of Operation on evasion of capture when forced down or captured in enemy territory.

b. Instructions on escape – including the instilling of escape psychology in combat airmen and communicating plans for escape to American prisoners of war by means of codes.

c. Instruction in proper conduct after capture and to inform intelligence officers of the rights of prisoners of war under international law.

d. To secure military information from American or Allied escaped prisoners on their return to Allied territory.

e. To obtain by means of codes from prisoners of war still in captivity information concerning locations of prisoners, conditions of imprisonment, opportunities for escape, reasons for failure in attempts to escape, and other pertinent intelligence.

f. To assist in the preparation and distribution of escape kits, and emergency kits containing maps, money, and other necessities to be furnished aircrews on missions and to incorporate new ideas and improvements in such equipment.

g. Plan and carry on correspondence with prisoners of war by means of codes which will be taught to key personnel of this organisation.

h. To maintain close liaison with the British MI-9 branch, which is conducting similar operations.

Like MI9, MIS-X used codes to correspond with POW. During air crew training the most reliable individuals were picked to be Code Users – a total of 7,724 US service personnel became CUs – and when requests were received for escape material it was hidden in parcels, though, like MI9, MIS-X never used Red Cross parcels for this purpose.

The first contact made by code, with an American fighter pilot who had been shot down in July 1942, came via MI9. But in May 1943 the first CU letters were intercepted at the New York censor office whose workers had been alerted to look out for any letter or package bearing a return address of a European POW camp, the sign that the contents were encoded.

One of these encoded letters shows how effective the system was. Deciphered, it read 'Give this message to address below. Send part diagram 220 direct and alternating. John C. Bowman 2900 Nichols Street San Diego, Calif. Signed Boxer.'

A check on the signature revealed that Boxer was an American airman, Lieutenant Horace Dale Bowman, and when a security check was run on John C. Bowman he proved to be the airman's brother, an engineer in the aircraft industry. He was considered a good security risk so a member of MIS-X was sent to San Diego to ask Bowman what the message meant. Bowman remembered immediately that it was a diagram for a radio transmitter which he and his brother had constructed before the war. The diagram was hidden in a shoe brush and a coded letter telling him where to find it was sent to Boxer at *Oflag 64*.

As in British POW camps, American prisoners set up an organisation headed by the highest ranking officer (SAO) with an adjutant to deal with administration and liaison, maintain personnel lists and keep a daily log. A messing officer supervised the equal distribution of food and goods from whatever source; a laundry officer organised the laundering of clothes by the wives of camp guards; a mail officer was always present when mail arrived to ensure that none was pilfered by the guards. Finally, an officer was appointed to run the escape and evasion committee and endeavour to implement the directive which called on prisoners to harass, confuse and disrupt their captors, and make every effort to escape.

The identities of the E&E committee were kept secret. In *Oflag 64*, for instance, the E&E chairman was 30-year-old Lieutenant-Colonel John H. Van Vliet, a West Point graduate who had been captured in North Africa while serving with the 34th Division's 168th Infantry Regiment. He was known only as 'Big X' and not even the SAO knew of his activities so that if questioned, during a German alert concerning a possible escape, he could face his German interrogators with equanimity.

'Big X' selected suitable personnel to head every aspect of his escape organisation – Security, Codes, Finance, Nuisances, Maps, Tunnels, Forgery, News, Gadgets, Tailoring, Intelligence, Parcels – but none of these officers, except on a 'need to know' basis, knew what the others were doing. Those responsible made sure that maps of the region were up to date; forgers provided passes and other essential papers, making sure that what they produced had not been superseded; those in charge of finances hid and dispensed German currency sent into the camp by MIS-X; the nuisance groups created diversions during an attempted escape or if tunnelling were under way; the tailoring section made clothes for escapees; the news section was responsible for the clandestine radio which most camps possessed.

The whereabouts of the radio receiver (there were few transmitters and none was ever used) and the identities of the personnel who manned it and recorded news in shorthand were among the most closely guarded secrets in a POW camp. Those responsible shared a room where the radio was hidden. News was passed on by one man from each block who memorised what he had been told and was careful not to give any outward sign that the news was good (bad news was not disseminated) for fear of alerting his captors to the radio's existence.

While working, code users were closely protected from intruders, American or German. It could take a CU up to an hour to decipher a letter, but all evidence of his work could be destroyed within ten seconds of receiving a warning – the length of time it took him to swallow the paper.

To co-ordinate all these activities 'Big X' would appoint an executive officer to head his security branch. Known as 'Big S', his tasks included the monitoring of German personnel's movements in and out of camp, and the provision of sufficient cover for escape activities. One way of minimising the risk of discovery was to confine a particular type of escape activity to one group of huts or 'block' . Each block had its own security officer who ensured that the orders of 'Big S' were carried out.

It was the responsibility of the parcels officer to spot anything that contained escape material before it entered the camp. Nearly all mail sent to American POW in Germany from the US was routed via the neutral countries of Switzerland, Sweden or Portugal, where it was sorted for dispatch by rail to Germany. The Germans took boxcars to the borders of the neutral countries and the mail was loaded into them. When the mail reached the nearest railhead to a POW camp it was off-loaded by POW volunteers organised by the parcels officer and loaded by them on a truck, a chore the German guards were usually only too willing to relinquish.

MIS-X adopted MI9's idea of sending these parcels under the names of fictitious philanthropic organisations and they were easily identified by the coloured labels that MIS-X used. They also stood out from the ordinary mail because they were different in size and packaging. Red Cross parcels were packed in wood and strapped with metal bindings – which were kept by POW for fashioning saws or other escape materials – while MIS-X's Servicemen's Relief parcels were packed in cardboard, wrapped in brown paper, and secured with hemp twine.

The parcels were taken by the truck to a *Vorlager* (receiving area) outside the camp's compound. There they were placed at one end of a long table where their bindings were cut by one of the parcel officer's assistants. The parcel was then pushed along the table for the German censor to inspect it. The parcels officer stood next to the censor, ostensibly to check off addressees' names on his clipboard. But his real role was to spot parcels addressed to code users, which meant that they contained escape material. When the parcels had been identified precautions were taken to ensure that they were only opened by the recipients in secure surroundings in the presence of those authorised to handle escape material.

The escape material that MIS-X dispatched varied, but was as ingenious as anything devised by MI9. One shipment of ten MIS-X escape-aid parcels contained a crystal radio set in a cribbage board; twenty ½-inch compasses in twenty chess pieces; 500 Reichsmarks in 10-Mark denominations and ten counterfeit German work and travel permits in the chessboard itself; ten sets of ration coupons in four checkerboards; and tissue paper maps of the area around Sagan in five pairs of table tennis bats. Parts of maps were also concealed in decks of playing cards.

Gillette razor blades were magnetised so that when dangled on cotton they could be used as compasses, and the Scoville Company in Waterbury, Connecticut, which manufactured buttons for service uniforms, produced five million containing a compass which could be retrieved by turning the face of the button anti-clockwise.

Some escape aids were too bulky or heavy to be sent in ordinary parcels. MI9 called these 'Dynamites' and MIS-X 'Super-Dupers'. The contents were not concealed in any way and were wrapped and marked as if they came from a relative (fictitious) of a particular prisoner. Forewarned, it was up to the recipients to make sure that the parcel was not searched by the Germans, and numerous dodges ensured that this did not happen.

A particularly ingenious method was found for smuggling small radio parts into POW camps. A Cincinnati baseball manufacturer was requested to prepare four dozen balls with an aluminium capsule containing the spares inside. One of the balls, destined for *Stalag Luft III* in August 1944, was delivered to the camp by a prisoner, Captain Jack Oliver, who had been charged with its safe arrival. He stood by as the incoming parcels were opened in front of the German censors. Eventually, the one containing the baseball was opened.

Oliver knew that POW were not allowed to touch the contents of any package until it had been passed by the censors. He began a conversation with a guard, suggesting that he feel the softness of the baseball's covering. The man did so and, as Oliver had guessed he would, picked it up. He then passed it to Oliver who tossed it gently back. The guard obligingly stepped out of the office to continue the ball game, and Oliver followed him. When the guard had been manoeuvred so that he was standing beside the fence of the compound, Oliver threw the ball too high for him to catch and it flew over into the compound; the prisoners carried on the game inside the camp until a member of the escape committee arrived and took the ball away.

In 1943, the Western Allies divided the world's combat areas into spheres of primary interest for escape and evasion. The USA became responsible for China, the South-west Pacific and Pacific Ocean areas; the British were charged with the European, Mediterranean and India–Burma Theatres. In China, as will be seen, this meant that the British organisation was virtually superseded, but in other theatres of operations, such as Europe and the Mediterranean, escape and evasion became an inter-Allied effort. But according to the official history of the British organisation in the Mediterranean, Washington seemed uninterested in the American MIS-X personnel who worked with it and this lack of interest 'reacted unfavourably on the personnel concerned, who, almost without exception – and entirely without justification – blamed their own senior officer (a major) for lack of promotion, lack of rotation for return to the States, etc. Although one or two officers did come direct from MIS-X and one or two officers from this Theatre returned to MIS-X the feeling of both American and British personnel was that Washington took little interest in our affairs.'

The largest MIS-X organisation in the Far East was the Air Ground Aid Service (AGAS). This was formed when Crockatt urged Johnston to form an escape and evasion organisation in China similar to the British Army Aid Group. It was set up on the recommendation of First-Lieutenant Barclay P. Schoyer who was chosen by Johnston to fly to China in September 1943 on a fact-finding mission about the work of the BAAG.

Lieutenant Colonel A. R. Wichtrich was appointed to command AGAS and its headquarters were set up at the US air base at Kunming, the capital of the remote south-west province of Yunnan. From 1943 China fell within the American sphere of influence, and the commander of BAAG, Colonel Ride, soon found that the Americans, with the support of the Chinese themselves, were squeezing him out of the area.

But AGAS had far larger ambitions than Ride had ever contemplated. Working from a forward base at Shanjao, Schoyer soon had 40 forward posts in south China alone, liaising with the local people to spot and rescue downed airmen.

In the summer of 1944 Wichtrich sent Captain Henry C. Whittesley into north China which was largely occupied by the Japanese. He managed to get through to the walled city of Yennan, the headquarters of Mao Tse-tung's Chinese Communists who were fighting both Chiang Kai-shek's Nationalists and the Japanese. Whittesley obtained their co-operation in helping downed flyers, but in February 1945, before he had had time to form a proper organisation with them, he and his interpreter were captured and executed by the Japanese.

By the following June AGAS had spread to French Indo–China and one AGAS agent got as far as Formosa (now Taiwan) to investigate a US POW camp there and to find out if there were any chance of escape from the island (there wasn't; the agent himself only just managed to regain the mainland after the Japanese tightened the rules on who could leave Formosa).

One of the first officers employed by AGAS was an old China hand, Lieutenant Richard V. Hill, who before the war had worked in China for Standard Oil before enlisting in the US Army. After undertaking a two-weeks' course on escape and evasion at Fort Hunt, he was promoted First-Lieutenant on 1 May 1944 and was sent by ship to India; he arrived at Kunming in September.

As one of the members of a three-man team, Hill's first task was to arrange for the location and rescue of downed airmen flying the India–China air supply route across the Himalayas. Known as The Hump, the flying conditions on this route were always hazardous and more aircraft crashed because of the weather than were shot down by the Japanese.

The party was landed in a valley some 9,000 feet up in the Himalayas by a civilian cargo aircraft belonging to the China National Aviation Corporation, the USAAF having refused to undertake such a risky operation. The party arranged for American and British missionaries whom they encountered to start a network of native helpers and to radio Kunming when downed airmen had been brought in from the surrounding countryside (forty years later the American missionary and his two sons were each awarded the Bronze Star for their help in rescuing airmen).

Hill's next operation was into eastern central China. He took with him two Chinese civilians, one of whom, the radio operator, was from Hong Kong, and a British citizen. They were escorted through Japanese-occupied territory by Chinese Nationalist troops and it took them much of the winter of 1944/5 to cover the mammoth journey of 1,550 miles to the province of Anhwei where Hill set up his headquarters in the mountain village of Lihuang. Within a week of his arrival Hill had three evaders brought to him, all of whom had been shot down during raids on Japanese-occupied towns. With the help of the local Chinese Hill improvised a landing strip and radioed for an aircraft to pick them up.

'Early the next morning, 9 March,' Hill recorded later, 'I took the three fliers to the strip. Chinese were marching back and forth to harden the surface. Small white flags were placed around the runway to show the pilot where to land. The first C-47 came in at 1000 hours, creating a cloud of dust, without any mishap.

Captain Birch homed in the plane on a portable radio. The transport was escorted by three P-51 fighter planes, which provided cover while it was on the ground. The P-15s did not land. They continually flew over the field ... The C-47 took off after only twenty minutes on the ground. It was a thrilling sight to see an American plane come to this remote area and get men out who had been shot down. However, being on a slow, unarmed cargo plane in enemy territory was risky for the crew.'

During the short time in which he ran his AGAS post in Anhwei, Hill and his civilian helpers returned 46 escapers and evaders to safety, including a pilot from the American Volunteer Group (the Flying Tigers) and four Marine officers who had escaped from a train moving them from Shanghai prison camp.

At the end of the war Hill was asked for an analysis of the qualifications needed by someone working in escape and evasion. 'AGAS field men came from various backgrounds, education, and training,' he wrote. 'Education is important but a college degree not essential. Being in a ground combat environment, one must have a good army background, preferably infantry, and have thorough training in intelligence and E&E operations. He must be able to cope by himself under severe stress, with physical hardships, poor communications, lack of medical aid and security, and the unexpected. To stay alive he must be careful what he says, where it is said, and to whom. He has to live off the land without benefit of logistical support from Allied bases. Early experiences in Boy Scouting are a great asset. Eagle Scouts especially have the training for path-finding, survival, and living on their own initiative. Of course, a field man must have intimate knowledge of the country and its people, also the enemy he is dealing with. He should also have knowledge of the language of his area. In China, each section of the country had its own dialect. It is important, too, to be acquainted with climate, terrain, and the prevailing government in his assigned territory.'

There were MIS-X units in other parts of the Far East – the one in MacArthur's South West Pacific Area was a section of his Allied Intelligence Bureau based at Brisbane, Australia, and was commanded by Major Paul S. Kraus – but the huge distances involved meant that escape was almost impossible. The section therefore concentrated on evasion, and one of its early operators, Lieutenant Harry Osterweis, was charged by Kraus with the rescuing of downed Allied airmen in the New Guinea Islands. If an aircraft went into the water Osterweis arranged for an Air-Sea Rescue amphibian to pick up the crew, or for the Navy to do so if the water was too rough. If the aircraft had crashed on land Osterweis hired natives to take him to the spot.

It was a task filled with hazards, as Osterweis later recalled: 'We had a couple of planes down on the north coast [of New Guinea] near the village of Aitape. An army recon plane spotted an SOS spelled out on the beach. It looked like a parachute had been cut up to form the signal. It was such a stupid thing to do, as the Japanese could see it as well as we could. I was assigned to investigate and make the rescue in case it was some of our fellows. But I was suspicious, and requested the army to fly me out in a little recon plane for a closer look. We flew over the area at about one thousand feet, but no one could be seen moving around, and an injured airman could not have laid out that signal. We also knew it had not been there the day before, or our daily reconnaissance patrols would have spotted it. So, when I landed, I called the army for a loan of a fast, small, armed boat with a half dozen men. They provided me with six eager soldiers and a forty-foot launch with a twenty-millimeter machine-gun mounted up forward. We knew that, if this was a trap, the Japanese would expect us to come straight in from the sea side, because the beach was in a recessed bay formed by a thousand-foot-high rise on all sides. So we approached from the south in the launch and were shielded by the cliff until we were only a thousand feet away from our target. Then we saw Japanese milling about a camouflaged bunker. The boys were ready on the bow and demolished the bunker with twenty-millimeter shells – leaving a few bodies lying on the beach.'

According to Colonel Russell Sweet, the number of American escapers and evaders totalled approximately 12,000 during the war. Of these 3,069 came from occupied Belgium and from Germany, 47 from occupied Holland and Denmark, 6,335 from Italian POW camps, 18 from North Africa, 100 from occupied Greece, 1,333 from occupied Albania and Yugoslavia, 218 from Japanese-occupied areas, and 853 from China.

7

THE INDRAGIRI RIVER ESCAPE LINE

Another escape line formed by the Special Operations Executive (SOE) was entirely for the benefit of evading servicemen. These belonged to the garrison defending the great British naval base of Singapore which was overrun by the Japanese in March 1942.

When the Japanese invaded Malaya in December 1941, Colonel Alan Warren of the Royal Marines, who worked for the Oriental Mission (the Far East section of SOE), began to organise clandestine 'stay-behind' parties to mount guerrilla operations against the invaders should the colony be overrun. His task was only partially completed by the time the Malayan peninsula was occupied by the Japanese who then began preparing to take Singapore Island to which tens of thousands of British and Commonwealth troops had retreated.

At the end of January three members of Warren's first 'stay-behind' party arrived at Singapore from Malaya where they had been unable to carry out any operations. They had returned to Singapore via Bagan-si-api-api on the north coast of Sumatra, and their report indicated that Bagan might be an ideal place from which to keep in contact with the other 'stay-behind' parties in Malaya. It was also hoped that, via Bagan, it might be possible to extract many of the British soldiers who were still at large behind Japanese lines in Malaya.

The Oriental Mission decided to send an expedition to Bagan, and a small coasting vessel, the *Hin Lee* of about 40 tons, was requisitioned, and two members of the Mission, Lieutenant Brian Passmore, RNVR and Lieutenant A. U. Lind of the Malayan RNVR, were put in charge of it. The party, consisting of five officers and '10 selected Chinese communists', was commanded by Warren. The *Hin Lee* sailed on 3 February 1942 and the party established its HQ at Bagan. Only limited contact had been made with the other 'stay-behind' parties in Malaya before Warren was ordered, during the last week in February, to withdraw his party to Padang on Sumatra's west coast.

Despite Churchill's order that Singapore be held to the last man, the battle for it lasted only a week before General Percival, who commanded the 85,000 British and Commonwealth troops, surrendered on 15 February. The British prime minister's orders to stand and fight had seemed reasonable enough because the troops on Singapore Island far outnumbered the attacking Japanese. But in the long term the position of the British and Commonwealth troops was not viable, a fact obviously recognised by the War Council in Singapore which at the end of January decided that a route should be organised for all those wishing to escape captivity.

The Oriental Mission was given the task of organising the escape route, and on the same day that Warren left for Sumatra, 3 February, a second expedition sailed in the 50-ton *Hongchuan* to reconnoitre the most appropriate route, to arrange food and water dumps on the most strategically placed islands, and to visit native settlements along and near the escape line to alert the local headmen to the arrangements being made.

Among SOE files released to the Public Record Office at Kew in the early 1990s is one which contains the official report on the establishment of what became known as the Indragiri Escape Line. Its author, Basil Goodfellow, a member of the Oriental Mission in Singapore, wrote: 'It was clear that to escape from Singapore to Sumatra would be an easy task for anyone with resource and the ability to handle small craft. The prevailing wind, at least till the end of March, was NE leading straight to Sumatra through the mass of small densely forested tropical islands lying South and South West of Singapore. These would provide cover from aircraft by day for small craft, and shelter from heavy seas. It was expected, however, that troops escaping from Singapore would be short of food and water, which they could not rely upon getting en route, and would be without maps or compasses.'

Two Malayan-speaking officers had been chosen to lead the *Hongchuan* expedition: Major Jock Campbell, general manager of the Labis Rubber Estate in Johore before the war, and a regular army officer, Captain Ivan Lyon, who was to earn posthumous fame as the leader of two canoe raids on Japanese shipping in Singapore harbour in 1943 and 1944.

Their plan was to select the simplest route via easily recognisable islands, the description of which would be circulated in Singapore at the appropriate time. It ran through the islands of the Rhio and Lingga archipelagoes, to the east coast of Sumatra, some 150 miles from Singapore. From there escapers would be able to cross Sumatra, a distance of about 250 miles, in small craft on either the Indragiri or Djambi rivers (see Map 3). When the water became too shallow, lorries, buses, or trains would take them to Padang on Sumatra's west coast where, it was hoped, ships would be waiting to take them to Ceylon or India.

The *Hongchuan* returned to Singapore four days later bringing a report from Campbell and Lyon who had remained in Sumatra to organise the line. They wrote that 'the very greatest help has been given by the Dutch authorities throughout, and by the fishing communities on the islands. A main food dump has been put on a headland at the Eastern tip of Durian Island, conspicuous from afar to anyone taking the obvious route through the Soegi Strait, by a tall dead tree against the skyline, and a rocky islet.'

Three natives had been commissioned to guard the dump and to go out in sampans to bring in passers-by. A second main dump had been established at Prigi Rajah at the mouth of the Indragiri River, and the report requested that a third be made at Pulau (island) Sabu, a small but very conspicuous islet some ten miles south-west of Singapore.

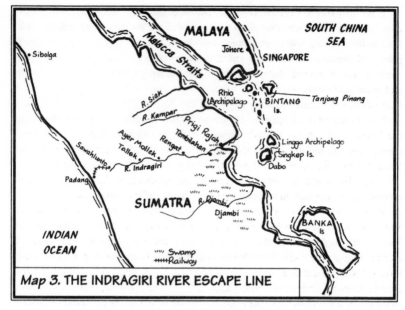

Map 3. THE INDRAGIRI RIVER ESCAPE LINE

The report was used to draft a set of instructions to guide escapees along the routes. 'This raised of course the principal danger of the scheme, that its premature disclosure would be an incentive for desertion.' Although it had not been circulated by 13 February, when the first large exodus from Singapore took place, there is evidence that it was widely known about and that deserters took full advantage of it.

The escape line was formed to handle about 1,000 escapees who would be expected to come through in groups of about 50. This wildly under-estimated the numbers that would try to escape – the first of them, according to the official Oriental Mission report, a full ten days before Singapore fell. The report also remarked that from about 9 February onwards 'a steady stream of small craft was flowing out of Singapore'; that the wealthy Chinese had already left; and that 'virtually every serviceable power-driven craft in the port had been earmarked, largely by civilians who were in touch with the harbour authorities. It is unfortunate that these first-comers who least deserved helping, inevitably availed themselves of the facilities in Sumatra.'

The report prompted a second Oriental Mission expedition in the *Hongchuan* 'with the particular object of visiting the communities on the islands nearer to Singapore'. Under the command of Goodfellow it left on 11 February, established the dump on Sabu island, and then proceeded via various islands to Djambi on the Djambi River which lay to the south of the Indragiri. Here, they were lent a truck by the Dutch in which they travelled to Padang, arriving there eleven days after leaving Singapore.

It fell to Lyon to organise that part of the escape line which ran from Singapore, through the Durian Strait, to the mouth of the Indragiri. He was the ideal man to do it, being a keen yachtsman who knew the area to the south of Singapore well because he had often sailed there in his 3-ton yacht *Vinette*. With a medical orderly named Morris, he now commandeered a 17-foot sailing dinghy and spent some days visiting local headmen on surrounding islands to elicit their help which was readily forthcoming.

In the meantime Campbell, who was to ensure the safe passage of escapees up the Indragiri and thence to Padang, was arranging a first staging-post at Tembilahan, near the mouth of the Indragiri. He also established a small base near Rengat, 100 miles up-river at the highest navigable point for sea-going vessels.

While the escape line was being set up, the exodus from Singapore began in earnest. 'Men who left after the "cease fire" had a difficult time finding any craft at all,' Goodfellow's report stated. 'Some boldly rowed sampans out from the Singapore River and Rochore Canal, well within the city. Others made for the Yacht Club, only to find the remaining craft stove in. One party repaired a damaged dinghy by night and sailed away in it. It has been reported that one party took [a] sliding seat four from the Rowing Club, and got safely to the Dutch Islands. Others, finding no undamaged craft in the harbour, walked for miles along the beaches until they found small native craft of one sort or another hidden away. One man paddled himself on a piece of timber with his hands to Pulau Bukum where he joined others in a sea-worthy boat.'

Many of these escapers reached the food dump on Durian Island or were able to hire junks to take them on to Sumatra. Others went down the Soegi Strait where they were spotted by the Mission's look-out men on Durian Island who went out in their sampans to guide the escapees in. Those who reached the island but were not able to go further because of the frailty of their craft were ferried to the Indragiri.

Not all the evaders knew about the escape line. 'Some of these men,' wrote Goodfellow, 'who arrived tired, often with no food or water and with no certainty of their next move, speak of the discovery of an organisation to help them on as something of a miracle.'

When Campbell arrived at Padang, the terminal point of the escape line, he found that 60 officers and men had already made their own way there from the Malayan mainland. They were put into a rest camp, and by the time Campbell returned to Rengat on 15 February he found 'escapees already arriving up the river *in hundreds*'.

To relieve this unexpected pressure Campbell arranged with the local Dutch commissioner to requisition the abandoned Ayer Mollek Dutch rubber plantation, situated about 30 miles up-river from Rengat, as an assembly point for servicemen who were waiting for transport to take them further along the escape route. An elderly Indian Army officer, Lieutenant-Colonel F. J. Dillon, who had won the MC on the North-West Frontier, took command of this transit camp.

Some of the evaders who reached Rengat were taken further up-river by small river craft to Tallek, where another emergency camp was opened in the market building; but some struck out on their own and walked. Above Tallek the river was too shallow to use boats of any sort. Instead, trucks or buses took evaders by stages to Padang on the west coast, or to Sawahlunto, the railhead for an ancient steam train to Padang which used a chain and ratchet system to help pull it up the steep hills. By all accounts Campbell organised this part of the route supremely well. He was, according to Major L. E. C. (Doc) Davies who escaped with him to Ceylon, 'a born leader of men. His organisation was superb.'

By 16 February 150 men had reached Padang and a signal was sent to the British Naval Commander at Batavia to send a ship to pick them up. Two days later a destroyer arrived and took them off together with 100 new arrivals. Subsequently, the arranging for evacuation vessels became the responsibility of the British Vice Consul at Padang who held the relevant naval codes, and from 18 February to 7 March a total of twelve ships took off 2,586 men.

When it became known that the situation in Singapore was hopeless, the trickle of junks, yachts, ferries, river craft and assorted power boats leaving the great port became a flood. Vessels were commandeered or just hijacked from their rightful owners and crammed with evaders, in scenes of chaos vividly described by the journalist Noel Barber:

'Across the dead calm seas south of the island a flotilla of small ships – Singapore's "Dunkirk" – struggled vainly to reach the sanctuary of Sumatra or any of the hundreds of islands sitting astride the Equator. Every stratum of humanity crouched in the vessels. There were generals, an admiral, an air marshal. There were hundreds of women and children. There were deserters who had slipped away secretly under cover of dark. Some of the larger boats also carried deserters who had forced their way on board at the point of the pistol ...

'Those who escaped were wrecked on the small desert islands that dot the archipelago. Some starved to death, some died of thirst, some of tropical diseases. The tiny launch carrying Admiral Spooner, Air Vice Marshal Pulford and a small party of officers and men was beached on a small malarial island barely twenty miles from Banka. For two months they suffered agonising privations. Eighteen died, including the Admiral and Air Marshal, before the remnant managed to cross to Sumatra in a native boat and surrender.'

A typical user of the escape line was Lieutenant Rolla Edwardes-Ker of the Malay Regiment. He and five others left Singapore in a 15ft sailing dinghy in the early hours of 16 February and made for the island of Pulau Batam, their shallow draft allowing them to sail across the minefield that protected Singapore harbour. They stayed for one day on the island and then sailed to Tanjong Pinang on Bintang Island, the administrative centre of the Rhio archipelago, arriving there in the afternoon. The only official remaining, the Assistant District Officer, who had been left to hand over to the Japanese, was persuaded to give them the government launch on the promise that it would be handed over to a Dutch official when the party reached Sumatra.

They sailed at dusk with some 50 other refugees aboard, reaching Tembilahan, upriver from Prigi Rajah, at midday where they were advised that the Dutch were evacuating the town and that it would be better to press on up the river. This they did, travelling all night before reaching Rengat early the next morning. The launch was handed over and the party was taken in Dutch Army trucks to the rubber plantation at Ayer Mollek where they spent several days. They were then given an old truck and a bus and in these were, in Edwardes-Ker's words, 'driven through the night on primitive mountain roads. We could not use the lights as we had to maintain a strict black-out. This was a most frightening journey as the road surface was very bad and there many hair-pin bends.'

On 22 February they arrived at Sawahlunto and took the narrow gauge mountain railway. This 'meandered through the mountains which were many thousands of feet high' before arriving at Padang 24 hours later. After a few days in Padang the party went to the docks where two ships were waiting to evacuate the servicemen and civilians who had already arrived. The *Rooseboom*, the larger of the two, took most of these aboard and sailed for Ceylon; the smaller one, the *Domayer Van Twist*, took a much smaller number of servicemen, including Edwardes-Ker, to Java.

The *Rooseboom* was torpedoed off Ceylon and only one lifeboat could be launched. This drifted back to Sumatra. By the time it arrived there only five people aboard remained alive. Those in the *Domayer Van Twist* were luckier for their ship reached Java, and Edwardes-Ker and some others then transferred to a larger ship which eventually reached Fremantle in Western Australia.

Gerald Scott, an engineer employed by Shell, also managed to reach safety down the escape line. He left Singapore on 13 February in the 13-ton launch *Mutiara* which was normally used for conveying members of the company's staff between the island of Bukum and Singapore. The launch was crammed with 23 Shell Company staff and two Chartered Bank men. The captain was an installation superintendent who had not been to sea for more than seventeen years and the crew included three marine engineers who were soon to earn their passage.

As the launch passed the Singapore Yacht Club a powerful naval tug passed to starboard. The captain decided to follow it and *Mutiara* was soon joined by an RNVR launch. Scott signalled that they had no navigator and the launch replied that the *Mutiara* should follow it. This proved to be easier said than done because only one engine in the RNVR launch was working and its course was erratic. Nevertheless it led *Mutiara* through the minefields guarding Singapore, but at 2.30 in the morning the leading naval vessel ran aground, as did Scott's launch.

'There was nothing further to do but to try and get some sleep and this we did very successfully,' Scott wrote later. 'When it was light, just after 6 a.m., we found that there were three vessels lying near – but all three got off and went their way without so much as a word or offer of assistance.'

By 8.15 the marine engineers had *Mutiara*'s engine running, but in reverse (apparently a two-stroke engine can run either way) and it was only with some difficulty that they managed to get afloat again. The water was very shallow at first but when they eventually reached deeper water the engine was stopped and reversed. 'Everything was plain sailing now' and *Mutiara* made a steady 8 knots away from Singapore. When Scott looked back he saw the sky above the colony filled with black smoke which trailed far out to sea. It could still be seen when they eventually reached the Sumatran coast.

The launch's engine needed the undivided attention of the marine engineers, but eventually the party arrived at Prigi Rajah where they were met by the headman of the village, magnificently dressed in a uniform of starched white drill, and some Army officers who handed them a sheet of instructions addressed to 'all British imperial forces and personnel'. This stated that they should proceed to Tembilahan, four to five hours sailing up-river. It went on: 'From Tembilahan you must go further up the river to Rengat where there is a camp and food. From there you will be transported to Padang on the west coast from where you will later be evacuated. In navigating the river keep to the outside of the turns. Go slow and keep a sharp lookout for logs and sandbanks.'

At Rengat the party officially became part of what Scott called the Civilian and Army Evacuation Scheme and spent the next five days and nights en route to Padang. 'Arriving in Padang was for me one of the best experiences of my life,' Scott recorded later. 'Here was civilisation! We rode from the station in little two-wheeled gharries to the town hall where we were each presented with a whisky and soda! After registering with the Evacuation authorities we were offered clothing (which we declined as we could buy clothes in the shops) and then billeted on Dutch families in the town who had volunteered to take in evacuees. Two days were spent in this delightful town. I cannot speak too highly of the efficient way in which the Dutch authorities helped us or of the charming manner in which the Dutch residents received us. The problem was to get aboard a vessel – any vessel.'

Eventually the party bought their way on to a Dutch collier. On 1 March this sailed from Emmerhaven – the port for Padang which was situated three miles south of the town – to Tlakjap, the only port still open in Java at the time. After 33 hours of hugging the coast and taking a zig-zag course to discourage a submarine attack, the ship picked up a Dutch broadcast instructing all vessels heading for Java to make for the nearest British port instead. The ship's captain reversed course and then asked whether anybody had any maps or charts. One of the native crew had a map in his diary and with this, and a map printed at the head of a 'Via Imperial' cable, a course was set for Ceylon which was reached on 10 March. In total Scott's escape from Singapore had taken 25 days.

Another evader, a rubber planter named D. C. Robinson, was not so lucky. He also had managed to escape from Singapore in a small boat. He left before Edwardes-Ker but delays en route cost him his freedom. But the notes he later made give some insight into the help given to those moving along the escape route. He left Singapore on the night of 13 February in the 32ft yacht *Candella*. With him was his wife, another married couple and their small son, and the son's '*amah*' (nursemaid). As the engine wouldn't work, they sailed south-eastwards towards Bintang Island and anchored that evening off Batam Island.

Next morning six soldiers appeared and asked to be taken aboard, and that afternoon the crowded yacht set sail for the Rhio Straits. At dawn next day the yacht was overtaken by a junk full of soldiers who told them of the existence of the escape line. After reaching Rempang that afternoon, they sailed for the island of Bakung where Robinson had been told a Chinese *towkay* (merchant) had several motor launches which were conveying parties further along the escape line.

Robinson recorded afterwards that they set off due south but during the course of the day the other man became ill and then delirious, 'and I was in the dark as we were in the midst of dozens of islands. Some mere atolls uninhabited, and dangerous coral reefs, some only a few feet under water so at sunset I made for deeper water, trimmed the ship close reefed, one sail to keep her stationary against the slight current and dozed all night at the tiller.'

After three or four days spent drifting among the islands, during which the other man slowly recovered, a launch appeared and closed the yacht. On board were some of those who had been on the junk.

'Drawing alongside they told us the route was up the Indragiri River but we could not make it with the *Candella* [which had a draft of 7 feet] as the coast around that area averaged from ½ to 1½ fathoms. They drew us a rough map to guide us to Bakung, wished us well and off they went, so we set sail using the rough sketch drawn for us and in about 20 hours sailing we reached Bakung.'

At Bakung the *towkay* made them welcome, gave them a meal and two days later – Robinson reckoned it was 1 or 2 March – they were put aboard one of his launches. 'By dawn we are off the mouth of the north channel of the Indragiri River after a long and tedious journey, constant look-out for patrol boats. All day hot and sticky up river, mangrove swamps, alligators, chattering monkeys, flies, mosquitoes, and God knows what else.'

They were among the last to pass along the escape line and were welcomed by Colonel Warren at Padang with the news that the British Vice Consul 'had panicked and destroyed the code books'. This precipitate action left them stranded because the British destroyer which had been standing by to take the last escapers to safety sailed away when it received no reply to its signals. Instead, Warren told them, he was arranging for two parties, one to go south, the other north, to try to buy seaworthy craft to attempt to reach India.

By now Robinson was wracked with fever. He was taken to the Dutch Military hospital where a few days later he awoke to find three Japanese soldiers standing around his bed examining his helmet, binoculars and his other remaining belongings.

Flight-Lieutenant J. O. Dykes, RAFVR, was another evader who ended up as a prisoner of war, though he managed to get away from Padang. He left Singapore on 13 February aboard a 787-ton Auxiliary Patrol vessel, the *Tien Kwan*. During the night the engines broke down and the ship was anchored off Pom Pong Island where it was sunk by Japanese bombers next day. Dykes was one of those who managed to get ashore and after several days was rescued and taken to Kuala Raja on Singkep Island, part of the Lingga archipelago, where he was fed by the Dutch authorities before being taken by boat to Tembilahan. He and those with him were then put aboard barges which were towed up the river to Rengat by an LCA (Landing Craft, Assault). They spent the night at Rengat and then several more at a transit camp before proceeding up the river to Tallek on 3 March. From Tallek they were taken in buses to Sawahlunto where they spent another night before going on by rail to Padang.

'We were quartered in the Chinese school in Padang,' Dykes later wrote of his experiences, 'and Colonel Warren who was OC British forces in Padang had his HQ in the Eindracht Club. He told us we should wait there for a few days until the Navy sent ships to take us to Ceylon.'

The ships did not come and Dykes and a group of other men eventually decided to make an independent bid to escape. They went down the coast, bought a native 27ft sailing boat (for £81), set sail on 22 March, and made an epic voyage to Burma. They landed seven miles south of Moulmein on 18 May only to find that the country was in Japanese hands, and they were immediately captured.

Two other ships – the *Kuala*, a 954-ton Auxiliary Patrol vessel built in Scotland in 1911, and the 4,636-ton *Kung Wo*, a coal-burning Yangtse River trading vessel belonging to the Indo–China Steam Navigation Shipping Company – left Singapore at the same time as Dykes. They too anchored near Pom Pong, and suffered the same fate as Dykes' vessel; many hundreds of survivors were marooned on Pom Pong and on a nearby island.

The same day the more seriously wounded were taken off by a Dutch hospital launch and next night about 320 women, children and casualties were taken aboard a Dutch steamer. When Campbell heard of the disaster he co-ordinated a rescue mission to take the survivors to the escape route.

The first boat to arrive on the scene from Rengat was the ferry that Lyon had organised. This was an ex-Japanese 70ft diesel-driven fishing vessel skippered by Bill Reynolds, an Australian engineer, with a Chinese crew. He took off 76 escapees on his first visit and 96 on his second.

Reynolds' vessel was originally the *Kofuku Maru*, but after his first trip up the Indragiri River he renamed her *Suey Sin Fan* – Cantonese for the water hyacinth – as 'tons daily float down all Sumatran rivers' and he sometimes had to stop and clear mounds of it from the vessel's bows, because it reduced her speed by half.

Reynolds had begun his rescue work before ever reaching the Indragiri River, having first called at Rhio where he found a broken-down island vessel, the *Silver Gull*, alongside the wharf with some 216 women and children aboard. With 50 escapers in his own ship, Reynolds took *Silver Gull* in tow, made his way across to the Indragiri River, steaming at night and hiding by day, until he was able to berth her alongside a wharf at Chenako. From here the escapers were taken to Rengat some 30 miles away.

When Reynolds reached Rengat later that day, 15 February, he learnt of those stranded on Pom Pong Island. After delivering the second load of refugees from there he 'shuttled back and forth to the islands of the outlying archipelago – the first eight days and nights we did not stop ... we sailed under Chinese colours; this in order to reassure Chinese inhabitants of the islands we visited, and so get information about wounded, and stragglers.'

He also made arrangements with local Malay fishermen for them to take anyone they found to pre-arranged rendezvous on the islands of Moro, Benko, Singkep, Pom Pong and Lingga, where *Suey Sin Fan* could pick them up. In total he rescued 1,519 escapers, a remarkable feat. When there were no more to be found Reynolds undertook what he called an espionage trip for the Dutch Resident and was involved in a fire fight with a Japanese patrol boat which was forced to retreat.

On his return to Rengat Reynolds was ordered to escape while he could and took his ship and crew through the Malacca Straits 'steaming by night and hiding in creeks masked by mangroves and fish traps by day', crossed the Bay of Bengal, reaching India near Negapatam on 31 March, an astonishing voyage by any standards. 'A pretty good fluke,' Reynolds called it, 'considering we had no charts or instruments – a compass and a gigantic ego being their substitutes.'

There is an immediacy about Reynolds' account because it was written only a year later, and there is no doubt that he was one of the unsung heroes of the escape route. He and his boat were later recruited by SOE's India Mission to undertake Lyon's first canoe raid on Singapore, but though *Suey Sin Fan*, after being renamed *Krait*, took part, Reynolds did not.

Another of the rescue boats dispatched from Rengat, the 66-ton coastal launch *Noembing*, was commanded by a gunnery officer, Captain Rowley-Conwy, who had used *Noembing* and a junk to evacuate his complete battery of 120 men from Singapore. After ensuring that they had been safely fed into the escape line he carried out rescue work with *Noembing* and another launch, *Plover*. Over ten days he transported 534 people from Tembilahan to Rengat, including 60 he had evacuated from Pom Pong.

Another British officer prominent in the organisation of rescuing those stranded on the islands was a Royal Naval Commander named Alexander. The Dutch District Commissioner at Singkep estimated that at the height of the exodus from Singapore about 2,000 shipwrecked survivors were scattered among the nearby islands and it fell to Alexander to co-ordinate the rescue of as many of them as possible, to collect them at Dabo, the island's main town, and pass them up the Indragiri or Djambi rivers.

Altogether, Alexander, with the help of the Dutch District Commissioner and local fishermen, evacuated 1,500 survivors, but by 22 February the number of daily arrivals had begun to decline and on 25 February Alexander decided to evacuate the island altogether. He bribed with opium the Chinese owners of the three junks to take the remaining survivors up the Indragiri.

Large numbers of early escapers also arrived at Lyon's base on Moro Island and were supplied with rations before being directed on to Prigi Rajah some 70 miles further on. But when Lyon heard that a Japanese naval squadron was in the area he decided it was too risky to continue using the island. He closed the camp, and he and Morris sailed their dinghy to the mouth of the Indragiri River to join Campbell.

Soon after hearing by radio about the fall of Singapore, those running the escape line received the equally disturbing news that the Commander-in-Chief of ABDA Command, General Wavell, had abandoned Sumatra to the Japanese who had already seized the Palembang oilfields and Banka Strait. This effectively put the escape line some 400 miles behind enemy lines, but as the days passed the numbers of soldiers and civilians the line was handling increased, and their numbers at the first staging-post, Tembilahan, soon swamped the capacity of the local transport allotted to ferrying them further along the line.

The civilians usually arrived with plenty of funds – which, incidentally, drove up the price of food – but the soldiers were often penniless and it was common for roving bands of armed deserters to demand food and shelter at the point of a gun. In an endeavour to bring order to the chaos, Campbell asked Captain Ernest Gordon, who arrived at Rengat on 18 February, to join his organisation and take command at Tembilahan.

Many of those crowding into the town were wounded or sick, and although the shortage of skilled medical help had been partially alleviated by the arrival of an Australian surgeon, Colonel Coates, and the matron and nurses from 12th Australian General Hospital, there were few drugs, surgical instruments or anaesthetics. Apparently Coates, who in one night performed eighteen operations, had to use an axe for amputations. In his report Goodfellow says that Coates 'did heroic work all along the line performing emergency operations' and that he was 'cool and ready to render help in any circumstances'.

Not all senior officers worked with the same selfless devotion as Coates. The behaviour of one brigadier at the transit camp at Ayer Mollek almost caused open mutiny. Like Tembilahan, Ayer Mollek was flooded with escapers and though Dillon dealt with them on a 'first in first out' principle, discipline eventually began to break down. When word spread that a brigadier had arrived at the camp and was demanding transport immediately for himself and his party, those waiting let it be known that if the brigadier did not wait his turn they would start shooting.

The brigadier backed down, but only the strength of Dillon's personality, and his insistence that the Dutch provide additional transport, prevented further serious trouble. Many of the men were eventually moved upstream in two wooden barges towed by an old steam launch, fuelled by wood. The Dutch then provided enough buses to take the rest by road, enabling Dillon to close the camp on 1 March.

Nor was the behaviour of the Australian General, Gordon Bennett, above reproach when he used the escape line. One eye-witness has recorded that when Bennett arrived at Sawahlunto in a bus he ordered that it be ready immediately to take him on to Padang. The duty officer, who had orders to see that the bus returned to Ayer Mollek to pick up more escapers, was wondering what to say when Bennett asked, 'Are you in charge here?'

'I am the duty officer at the moment, sir.'

'Are you a deserter?' the General demanded, and when the duty officer replied that he had been in Singapore at the time of the surrender Bennett said: 'So was I. How is it that you are here before me?'

'I don't know, sir.'

Bennett then demanded to know how the officer had escaped, and asked why he hadn't come via Djambi. When the duty officer told him that he had come up the Indragiri River the General seemed surprised. He then asked if there were any Australians in the town and the duty officer said, very pointedly, that a considerable number had been 'but most of them passed through some time ago', which terminated the conversation abruptly. Bennett then said that he intended using the bus to get to Padang as quickly as possible because 'he had information of vital importance to the Allies'.

But when the duty officer suggested that he apply to the Dutch authorities for a car, Bennett agreed. The Dutch authorities obliged and he duly arrived in Padang where a flying-boat was sent to pick him up. Three days after he had been rescued the BBC reported on his escape, and it gave far too many details of the escape route for the liking of those still using it. Although he was later cleared of deserting his troops, Bennett was reprimanded by the Australian government for leaving his post in Singapore and he never held another operational command.

The behaviour of some of the servicemen in Padang was equally reprehensible. The Dutch Military Commander there seemed to expect Warren, as the senior British officer present, to restore order and discipline because all the other officers responsible for embarking the evaders had left on the first available vessel. The British troops, the Dutchman raged, were 'fucking the native women in the streets and selling their weapons for five rupees', and were no more than a rampaging mob.

When Warren pointed out that his primary mission was to establish clandestine parties behind enemy lines and that he was only in Padang to assess the situation for ABDA Command in Java, the Dutchman replied that 'Sumatra was out of the war', that he had orders to hand over the town to the Japanese, and that he hoped Warren would not do anything to jeopardise this being done peacefully.

To make matters worse for the Dutch, the Nationalist leader, Sukarno, had been released from custody by his guards and was now in the town. A revolt was very much on the cards and already estate labourers in Medan had revolted and killed their European masters. The Dutchman pointed out that Warren and his party were drawing money, food and supplies from the Dutch. Under this pressure Warren reluctantly agreed to take on the role of Senior British Officer until he could get clarification of his position from Java.

On 24 February he wrote asking for this, but as ABDA Command was dissolved the following day, it is doubtful if he received a reply. He remained in Padang and spent the rest of the war in a Japanese POW camp. But he must have been determined that those working with him on the escape line should not share the same fate, for on 8 March he gave an 18-strong evacuation party – which included Campbell, Rowley-Conwy, Lyon, and six other SOE officers – written orders to sail for Ceylon.

The party purchased a 30-ton native prahau, the *Sederhana Djohanis*, which meant 'Lucky John' or 'The Good Ship Johnny', for 3,000 guilders and set sail on 9 March. On 14 April, while fifteen miles south-east of Ceylon, they were picked up by a steamer and taken to Bombay after a voyage which showed again the remarkable attributes of Ivan Lyon (see Map 4).

'Ivan was our expert on sailing,' one of the party later recalled. 'It was magnificently reassuring to see him at the helm puffing contentedly at his pipe or one cent cigar. Every one of us placed implicit faith in his skippering and general advice. Typical of Ivan's calmness was the fact that he sighted Ceylon about three hours before anyone else but refrained from saying anything until he was absolutely certain, though some of the party had a shrewd suspicion he kept silent in order to prolong the sailing trip which he obviously enjoyed.'

Another member of the crew, a naval lieutenant named Geoffrey Brooke, was equally impressed by Lyon's calmness, recalling him as a man of few words who was always cool and deliberate. 'In the very worst moments, when asked his opinion, he would always say, "I keep an open mind", and this is how I shall always remember Ivan Lyon, with the ghost of a smile puckering the edges of very

Map 4. THE VOYAGE OF THE
SEDERHANA DJOHANIS

blue eyes.' There seems no doubt that the loss of Lyon in a second raid on Singapore in 1944 deprived the British Army of an outstanding officer.

It is not known how many perished in the escape from Singapore, but they must have numbered thousands. But thanks to the work of SOE's Oriental Mission and its escape line many escaped who might otherwise have been captured or killed. Although one estimate that about 7,000 civilians and servicemen used the line is probably much too high, an SOE memo of 15 June 1942 calculated that the line rescued 2,586 British troops. But about 900 others were captured when the Japanese arrived in Padang in the early hours of 17 March 1942.

8

THE ESCAPE OF THE
COCKLESHELL HEROES

The story of the Cockleshell Heroes has become one of the legends of the Second World War. The operation – an attack by twelve Royal Marine canoeists on enemy shipping in the River Garonne at Bordeaux in December 1942 – has been made so famous by several books and a film that it need not be repeated here in any detail, but the subsequent evasion by the raid's leader, Major 'Blondie' Hasler, and his No. 2, Corporal Sparks, is not so well known. Yet it is a classic example of how, even quite early in the war, the British escape and evasion organisation MI9 (see Chapter One) was able to arrange for the extraction of British servicemen from enemy-occupied territory and return them to duty.

The operation (code-named 'Frankton') called for Hasler's force of six canoes – *Cachalot*, *Catfish*, *Coalfish*, *Conger*, *Crayfish* and *Cuttlefish* – to be launched from a submarine off the Gironde estuary. As there was no possibility of their being retrieved in a similar manner, MI9 had discussions with Combined Operations, who were responsible for mounting 'Frankton', about the practicalities of the men being put in touch with an escape line which could take them over the Pyrenees into neutral Spain.

Up to that time no potential evader had ever been given a contact name or address for an escape line, it being considered far too dangerous for such information to be given to serviceman who might be captured and interrogated, thereby putting the lives of those running the line in jeopardy. This stringent security measure was introduced after an airman, who had been returned to England by one escape line, gave a friend a list of the names and addresses of those who had hidden him in France. The friend was subsequently shot down and killed, but the list was found on his body, and the families concerned were traced by the Gestapo and executed.

MI9 considered that an exception must be made for these Marines. After all, they were highly trained élite Commandos who were being dispatched to mount a secret operation, and it was thought extremely unlikely that any of them would break under even the most severe interrogation. But the risk existed and a compromise was struck. The Marines were each provided with one of Clayton Hutton's escape kits (see Chapter Two), given a cover story in case of capture, and instructed to make for Ruffec, some 70 miles north of Bordeaux, where they would find an organisation which would help them. They were told the name of a café where contact might be made with its leader, but were not informed that the person they would be seeking was the Comtesse de Milleville, *née* Mary Lindell, alias 'Marie-Claire' – and she could not be warned of their impending arrival because she did not have a wireless operator, and anyway the operation could not be revealed before it had taken place.

The arrangement left a lot to chance. Airey Neave, who at that time was working in Room 900, MI9's operational centre for escape lines in north-west Europe, called it the worst of both worlds, but it was probably the best that could be done under the circumstances. On 1 December 1942 the six canoes and their crews and stores were loaded aboard the T-class submarine *Tuna*.

Once aboard Hasler briefed his men on their mission: to attack with limpet mines at Bordeaux docks shipping being used to run essential raw materials for the

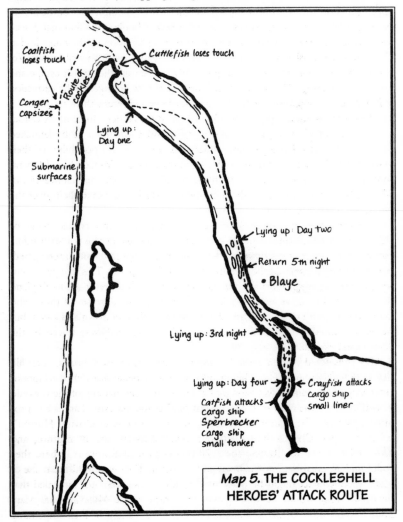

Map 5. THE COCKLESHELL HEROES' ATTACK ROUTE

Germans through the British naval blockade. On completion of the operation the crews were to paddle down river for about five miles, scuttle their canoes and make their way to Ruffec separately.

Tuna arrived off the Gironde estuary in the afternoon of 6 December and the following evening the canoes were launched. *Cachalot* was badly damaged during launching and its crew had to abandon the operation. The other five teams reached the estuary, though only two, *Crayfish* and Hasler's *Catfish*, survived to attack the ships (see Map 5). It took them five days and nights to negotiate the Gironde and then the Garonne, paddling at night, lying up by day. The operation was successful. Six ships were attacked and it was known that one later sank, a second was holed and set afire, and four others were damaged.

Both teams got away downstream, scuttled their canoes and, aided by maps and compasses in their escape kit, began making their way overland to Ruffec. Hasler, who spoke adequate French, begged some civilian clothes from an isolated farmhouse for himself and Sparks, but the other team could not find any and were eventually arrested.

Sheltering where they could at night and sustained by food they begged from farmers, or by raw potatoes and turnips they found in a field, they eventually reached Ruffec (see Map 6), but could not find the café they had been told to make for. Instead, and by sheer luck, because 'Marie-Claire' was known to the proprietors, the two men entered a small bistro, the Hôtel des Toques Blanches. Here they were able to order potato soup, the only food that was not rationed. When they had eaten the *patronne* seemed anxious for them to leave (she thought they were German Army deserters). In desperation Hasler wrote a note which said: 'We are escaping English soldiers. Do you know anyone who can help us?' and handed it to the woman with money for the meal.

The woman's expression did not alter as she took the scrap of paper, but with his change was a note saying, 'Stay at your table until I have closed the restaurant.' This they did and after being questioned by the *patronne*'s husband they were allowed to stay the night.

The next day the Marines were closely questioned by two Frenchmen who wanted to know who they were and what they wanted. When Hasler explained that they did not know the name of the person they were trying to get in touch with, one of the questioners said that it must be 'Marie-Claire', but as she was elsewhere the two evaders would be put in touch with one of her lieutenants next day.

The Marines stayed a second night and the next afternoon were whisked off in a baker's closed van to the demarcation line which ran south-east of Ruffec. Originally this had divided Vichy France in the south from occupied France in the north and though, by the time 'Frankton' was mounted, the Nazis had taken over the whole of the country, the line was retained to prevent those who had fled into Vichy France from returning to their homes.

Right: Brigadier Norman Crockatt, head of MI9.

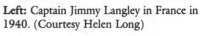

Left: Captain Jimmy Langley in France in 1940. (Courtesy Helen Long)

Below, left and right: The traitor Harold Cole. (Courtesy Helen Long)

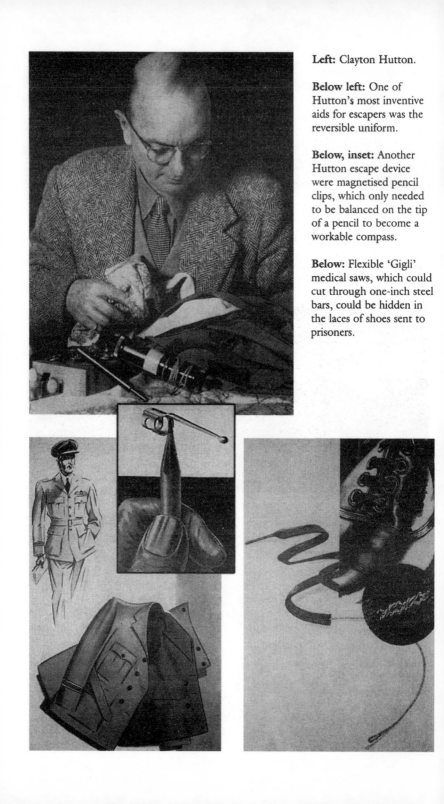

Left: Clayton Hutton.

Below left: One of Hutton's most inventive aids for escapers was the reversible uniform.

Below, inset: Another Hutton escape device were magnetised pencil clips, which only needed to be balanced on the tip of a pencil to become a workable compass.

Below: Flexible 'Gigli' medical saws, which could cut through one-inch steel bars, could be hidden in the laces of shoes sent to prisoners.

Above: HMS *Fidelity*, which was used to land MI9 agents in the western Mediterranean in 1941. (IWM AD 5229)

Below: Pat O'Leary outside Buckingham Palace with his wife and companions after being decorated with the George Cross. (Courtesy Helen Long)

Above: The tattered remains of the Sumatran prahau *Sederhana Djohanis*, in which those SOE members who organised the Indragiri River escape line sailed to Ceylon in the spring of 1942. (PRO, Kew)

Below: The party included five SOE members: number 7 is Jock Campbell, and number 8 is Ivan Lyon. (PRO, Kew)

Above: Major 'Blondie' Hasler, the leader of the Cockleshell Heroes. (RM Museum, Eastney)

Above right: Mary Lindell, whose escape line helped the Cockleshell Heroes.

Right: Franz von Werra, the only German to make a 'home run' during the war.

Right: Donald Caskie.

Above: Caskie's mission building in Marseilles, which was used as a 'safe house' by the PAT Line. (Both illustrations courtesy Helen Long)

OMNIUM ISOLATION

BRITISH ARMY AID GROUP

英軍服務團

Left: A British Army Aid Group truck at Kweilin in Kwangsi province. (IWM)

Above: A wartime photograph of Dédée de Jongh.

Right: The Basque guide Florentino Goicoechea, whose work with the Comet Line earned him a George Medal.

Below: 'Bonaparte' beach, near Plouha, Brittany, where MI9 agents were landed and escapers and evaders embarked during Operation 'SHELBURNE'.

Above: Japanese prisoners playing baseball outside their living quarters at Cowra Camp before the mass escape in August 1944. (AWM 067187)

Below: Improvised weapons recovered from the Japanese sector of Cowra after the escape. (AWM 073486)

Some twelve miles from Ruffec they were told to leave the van and wait for their guide who arrived some two hours later. He led them across the line to a farmhouse where they were handed over to its owner. The farmer, a close colleague of 'Marie-Claire', told them that they would have to remain hidden for a few days in the farmhouse until 'Marie-Claire' could be contacted and someone sent to collect them.

The days turned to weeks, but no one seemed to know where 'Marie-Claire' was. Bored stiff, the Marines turned to carving wood to while away the time. Christmas came and went, and still nothing happened. Sparks, when Hasler told him who they were waiting for to rescue them, wrote later that he 'did not feel too happy about leaving my fate in the hands of a woman. But in time I would come to realise that Marie-Claire was one of the most extraordinary and courageous people I could ever hope to meet.'

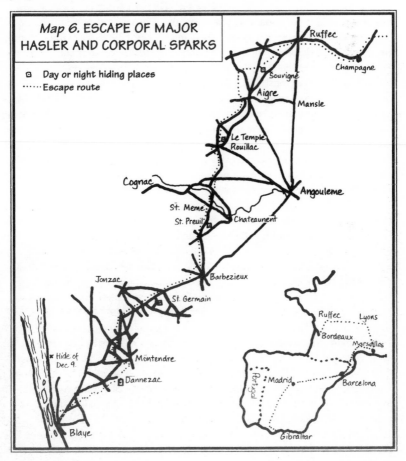

Map 6. ESCAPE OF MAJOR HASLER AND CORPORAL SPARKS

- ⊡ Day or night hiding places
- ····· Escape route

Sparks was perfectly correct in his assessment of Mary Lindell. But it must also be added that, from the accounts of some of those who encountered her, she had more than a touch of *hauteur* that was not always particularly endearing, but which, no doubt, helped her survive the war. Born into an upper class English family in 1895, Mary had served as a nurse with the French Red Cross during the First World War and had been awarded, among other decorations, the Croix de Guerre for her bravery under fire. After the war she married a Frenchman, the Comte de Milleville, by whom she had two boys, Maurice and Oky, who were 17 and 16 years old when the war began, and a girl named Barbé. The marriage did not prosper and by the time Mary had become active in the Resistance in 1940, she and her husband were leading separate lives.

Like most of those who became involved in escape lines, Mary fell into the business by accident. The French Red Cross had refused to return her to active service but she was determined to 'do her bit'. Helping British servicemen at large in France seemed as good a way as any, and when the opportunity came to smuggle an evading British Army officer into Vichy France from the occupied north she took it. One thing led to another, including interrogation by the Gestapo which resulted in a 9-month prison sentence for helping escapers.

In July 1942 the British Consul in Barcelona cabled MI9 that a woman dressed in French Red Cross uniform, with a British passport in the name of Ghita Mary Lindell, had arrived in Barcelona from France having crossed the frontier by train as 'a stranded governess'. She told the Consul that in Lyons the American Vice Consul had obtained the necessary visas for her, and an exit permit. She described her escape and evasion activities up to that date and volunteered to return to France to start a new organisation with a radio operator. At that moment, the Consul's cable said, she was on her way to London from Lisbon.

Neave and Captain J. M. Langley, Neave's colleague in Room 900, received this news with no little amazement, but also with some caution, for anyone who had been in Gestapo hands had to be treated with the greatest reserve.

Writing of his first meeting with this remarkable woman, Neave recalled: 'She was standing in the sunshine, dressed in the royal blue uniform of the French Red Cross, with a row of French and British decorations. She was at this time about 45, but looked considerably younger. She had dark brown eyes and chestnut hair, and her face was finely proportioned. Her figure was slight, and her uniform was well cut. She seemed very feminine, but in her expression there was an intensity, a stubbornness which somehow did not fit her smart appearance. As soon as she spoke, I understood why. She was very definitely English and used to getting her own way ... I noticed that she wore two English decorations in front of her French Croix de Guerre, loudly proclaiming her nationality. She gave an immediate impression of fearlessness, independence and not a little arrogance ... Her contempt and disdain for the Germans was enormous.'

It did not take Langley and Neave long to decide that Mary was genuine, but remained doubtful as to the wisdom of employing someone who had already been in the clutches of the Gestapo and allowing her to return to France. But they badly needed an alternative escape line to the endangered COMET and PAT organisations (see Chapters Eleven and Three) so she was recruited; the first female agent to be specially trained by Room 900.

Although Langley and Neave overcame their reservations about risking Mary's life by returning her to France, Claude Dansey of MI6, the overseer of MI9's work, was opposed to her doing so. But, Langley wrote, when he summoned her to tell her that he would not sanction her mission, 'Mary took control of the interview and informed him of all his shortcomings as far as helping evaders were concerned. When he pointed out that he was only trying to save her life she replied that it was not her life she was interested in but his reputation.' For once the wily Dansey had met his match and after she had left he told Langley he was to spare no effort to get her to France as soon as 'humanly possible'. According to Langley, Dansey was not the only member of the 'Establishment' to feel the same way about Mary with the result that she returned to France without a radio operator.

Mary's intuition regarding Dansey was undoubtedly correct – he was, according to some sources, a shit of the first order – but, typically, she had not got on with the radio operator allotted to her and as there was no time to train the Belgian with whom she wanted to work, it was decided that he must follow later, by parachute. But he was never sent either, so strongly were some in London opposed to her methods and personality.

They were not entirely in the wrong because Mary undoubtedly did act foolishly on occasions. For example, after her return to France, Donald Darling, MI6's man in Gibraltar, 'received a report that a Red Cross nurse, looking very English, had aroused considerable interest when seen walking along the *Promenade des Anglais* in Nice', and he was certain that this must have been Mary. This information caused dismay at MI9 because she had been briefed to confine her activities to the central provinces of France which were not so closely watched by the Gestapo.

On 21 October 1942 Mary was landed in France by Lysander light aircraft with instructions to form an escape line to Spain. Re-establishing herself in Paris was out of the question so Room 900 agreed that she should set up her headquarters at Ruffec. This made sense because she had many contacts in the town and earlier in the war had organised an efficient method of crossing the demarcation line and providing 'safe' houses for those travelling south. (It was in one of these safe houses, known as 'Farm B', owned by Mary's agent and guide, Armand Debreuil, that Hasler and Sparks were sheltered after crossing the demarcation line.)

Mary arrived safely and was soon re-united with her elder son, Maurice, who was in Monte Carlo (which ties in with Darling's account of her being seen in Nice). They then travelled to Lyons where Mary contacted the American Consul, who was to provide her with funds, and with a staunch supporter, Inspector Jo Deronne. Maurice and Deronne agreed to take on the task of setting up alternative escape routes across the Pyrenees and Mary then left for Ruffec, where she established her headquarters in the Hôtel de France, owned by an old and trusted friend, François Roullion.

Plans for the line were developing well when shortly before Christmas Mary was knocked off her bicycle by a car and severely injured. On Christmas Eve 1942 Maurice de Milleville returned to Lyons from visiting his mother in hospital in Loches and found waiting for him a note from Debreuil which said that 'two important parcels of food' were waiting for him. Maurice returned to the hospital for instructions and Mary told him to arrange for the 'two parcels' to be taken to Lyons and kept in safe houses there. Debreuil was to be told that the evaders would be picked up on 6 January.

Two days later Mary, though still very ill, discharged herself and returned to Lyons to make sure everything was in order. Maurice followed his mother's instructions and took Hasler and Sparks on bicycles to Roumazières-Loubert where the stationmaster would ensure that they were able to get on the night train for Lyons even though they did not have identity cards. 'There's one very important point which I'd better tell you now,' Maurice said before they started. 'You must avoid speaking on the train. Should anyone speak to you, the best way of getting out of it is to use a very guttural voice and just say "Breton". Fortunately there are still people in Brittany who do not speak ordinary French.'

Before they left, Debreuil asked Hasler to arrange for a message to be sent by the BBC once he reached England. 'Certainly,' Hasler said. 'We shall be sending one for the people who first gave us shelter. Our message will be: "*Le poulet est bon!*". Would that do for you as well?' But Debreuil looked disappointed and asked if it was not possible to have one broadcast specially for himself, and Hasler immediately agreed to Debreuil's suggestion of '*Les deux poulets sont arrivés!*', and in due course both messages were broadcast.

The evaders arrived in Lyons early next morning and Maurice took them to meet his mother. Mary still had one leg in plaster and her collar bone was heavily strapped, and she was probably not in a good mood. She certainly nearly lost her temper with her son when she saw the two men, for Hasler was sporting a very large English-looking moustache. Even more dangerous, both were still carrying their frogmen outfits in their rucksacks!

Mary's first instructions to Hasler were for him to remove his moustache, which he reluctantly did. She then gave both men a forceful lecture on security. 'We've got only one rule for Englishmen in our care,' she stated. 'NO GIRLS. From past experience we know that once they meet a pretty girl everything goes to hell. So we shall take care to keep them away from you.' (In fact she had other rules: she insisted on interviewing personally every evader before she allowed him to be sent down the line, and no man was allowed to drink more than two glasses of wine a day.)

She told Hasler that the proposed escape line across the Pyrenees had 'folded up' because she had not been able to find a suitable guide to take anyone across the mountains; they would have to lie low until she could arrange for them to be smuggled into Switzerland. But first she would have to enter Switzerland herself to obtain funds because the whole of France was now occupied by the Germans and the American Consul had left. This she managed to do, taking with her a coded message for Combined Operations from Hasler. The message read:

'Tuna launched five cockles seven Dec. Cachelot torn in hatch. Pad hatches. In bad tide-race SW Pte de Grave Coalfish lost formation fate unknown. Conger capsized crew may have swum ashore. Cuttlefish lost formation nr Le Verdon fate unknown. Catfish Crayfish lay up in bushes Pte Aux Oiseaux. Found by French but not betrayed. Ninth in hedges five miles north of Blaye. Tenth in field south end Cazeau. Eleventh in reeds thirty yards south of pontoons opp Bassens South. Attack eleventh. Catfish Bordeaux West three on cargo ship two on engines of sperrbrecher two on stern of cargo ship one on stern of small tanker. Crayfish Bassens South five on large cargo ship three on smaller line. Back together same night. Separate and scuttle cockles one mile north of Blaye. Sparks with me. Fate of Crayfish crew unknown.'

The message was received in London on 23 February 1943, but as Hasler had forgotten how to encipher properly it took some time to break it. Mary made contact, as she had been told to do by MI9, with the British military attaché in Berne. He cabled London that Mary was still seriously ill as a consequence of her accident. She had told him that the two Marines were in hiding in Lyons and that she was trying to arrange for them to be smuggled into Switzerland because she had not been able to send them into Spain.

London wanted Hasler and Sparks back in England as quickly as possible. At first MI9 considered arranging for them to be taken out of Mary's hands and passed to Pat O'Leary, now running his PAT Line north of Toulouse, but on reflection this was thought too risky because Pat's wireless operator had just been arrested. Instead, MI9 instructed the military attaché to make sure that Mary received the necessary medical treatment and when she was fully recovered to return her to Lyons with extra funds to arrange the exfiltration of the Marines into Spain.

This plan did not suit the impatient, imperious Mary. With the help of a Swiss intelligence officer, she recrossed the border, returned to Lyons where Hasler and Sparks, driven to distraction by boredom, had again taken up woodcarving to pass the time.

It was now February and Mary, still desperately ill and knowing she must return to Switzerland for treatment, eventually put her two charges in the hands of a courier named Martineau. She eventually recovered and, according to Donald Darling, between October and December 1943 her line managed to get a further ten servicemen to safety in Spain, and an eleventh, a left-over from Dunkirk, reached Gibraltar in January 1944.

From this point the facts about the Marines' escape are not entirely clear. When Hasler was debriefed in London it was thought that Mary had handed them over to another escape organisation – probably one run by Communists – but Neave wrote in his book *Saturday at MI9* that this was not the case. Yet it is certain that Martineau took the two Marines to an apartment in Marseilles which must have belonged to the PAT Line.

In Marseilles another long wait ensued during which the Marines were joined by other evaders. These included Werner de Merode, a Belgian prince serving in the RAF, and his flight sergeant. After nearly a month a man appeared at the apartment and told the party that they would be moving next day. In his memoirs Sparks described the man as a French-Canadian. 'He was heavily built with ginger hair and spoke only French. His name was Pat – we were not to learn his surname, nor even if Pat was his real name.'

O'Leary's cover was as a French-Canadian, but Sparks' description bears no resemblance to the Belgian. Besides, O'Leary was in Toulouse and was arrested there on 2 March. But whoever went to the apartment to brief the Marines was almost certainly a member of the PAT Line, because Donald Darling later confirmed in his book *Secret Sunday* that the guide (or guides) who took the party into Spain belonged to O'Leary's organisation.

The next day, 1 March 1943, the party boarded a train for Perpignan accompanied by a young French courier. At Perpignan the courier left and at some point each of the party was given a small canvas haversack and two pairs of Basque *espadrilles*. They were joined by another young Frenchman and were taken by van beyond Céret (see Map 2) where their Basque guides were waiting for them. It was now dusk and after walking along a path for two miles they came to a hut where they slept the night. Up before dawn, the party began its ascent of the Pyrenees. Although the route across the mountains did not take them much above the snowline, it was rugged enough to deter regular patrols by the Germans and Spaniards. It certainly stretched the two Marines to the limit, though the two airmen seemed able to cope and the young Frenchman had no trouble at all. When the guides seemed not to know where they were the young Frenchman took command and after another two nights – one spent in a cave and another in a farmhouse – they arrived at the small country town of Bañolas some 60 miles from Barcelona.

The young Frenchman now disappeared – he was later suspected of being a Gestapo agent – and the others were hidden from the local police for several days before a lorry arrived and took them to Barcelona. Here the two Marines were debriefed and sent to Madrid whence Hasler was flown home while Sparks was sent to Gibraltar to board a troopship.

Operation 'Frankton' took a very heavy toll of the raiders and of Mary Lindell and her organisation. Two of the Marines were drowned and six were captured, interrogated, and shot in accordance with Hitler's Commando Order. Mary recovered and managed to start an escape line with the help of guides who took evaders across the frontier at Andorra before she was eventually tracked down by the Gestapo and arrested at Pau railway station on 24 November 1943. She was sent by train to Paris for interrogation and on the way tried to escape but was shot in the back of the head and through the cheek. A German surgeon saved her life, but she was imprisoned in Dijon for eight months and was then transferred to Ravensbrück concentration camp.

Miraculously, Mary survived all her ordeals and was again awarded the Croix de Guerre, but the 'Establishment' in London got their petty revenge on her, for the only award she was given by the British was a Mention in Dispatches.

9

THE BRITISH ARMY AID GROUP

On Christmas Day 1941 Hong Kong surrendered to the Japanese, and for several days the occupiers made no attempt to restore order to the chaos that followed their invasion of the British colony. While Japanese troops looted and raped, the defeated British troops were left at liberty to roam the streets. Eventually, they were ordered to assemble at Murray Parade Ground on Hong Kong Island, and were then ferried across to Kowloon to the looted and wrecked British Army barracks at Sham Shui Po (see Map 7).

More than 7,000 POW were gathered at the barracks, and other camps were formed, one at the Quarry Bay end of King's Road on Hong Kong Island (North Point Camp) and two at Argyle Street, Kowloon (The Argyle Street Camp and Ma Tau Chung).

Among those taken to Sham Shui Po at the end of December 1941 were men of the Hong Kong Field Ambulance, commanded by Lieutenant-Colonel Lindsay Ride. A professor of physiology at Hong Kong University, Ride was an Australian medical officer attached to the Hong Kong Volunteer Defence Force. Frustrated by the Japanese refusal to allow him to help wounded British personnel, his thoughts, influenced by the classic escape book, *The Road to En-dor*, which he had read as a medical student, had already turned to escaping before he was incarcerated in Sham Shui Po. Before moving to the barracks he had hidden in his belongings a 1/80,000 map which covered the New Territories and the shores of Mirs Bay, a likely route to escape into Chiang Kai-shek's Nationalist China. He also took with him as much tinned food and medical supplies as he could carry though these were nearly all consumed during the first days in the camp.

The conditions in Sham Shui Po were horrendous and the Japanese did nothing to alleviate the suffering of the sick and wounded. Ride quickly concluded that he could do more for them if he escaped and organised the smuggling of medical supplies into the camp. When he discussed the possibility of escape with a number of officers he was surprised at how little interest was shown. Eventually he found three eager recruits, two naval reserve officers and a Cantonese-speaking Chinese, Lance-Corporal Francis Lee Yiu Piu, a member of Ride's Field Ambulance Unit who had been his clerk at the university. They began to study the sentries' routines and, with the aid of the map, memorised their escape route through the Kowloon hills which they could see from the camp.

Time was short because security, almost non-existent at first, daily became more efficient. Ride soon pinpointed a corner of the camp where they could leave unobserved. Lee left first, on 8 January, and returned next night with a sampan.

They embarked from a jetty close to the camp, crossed the bay to a beach and made their way into the hills beyond Kowloon.

After ten days of narrow escapes and extreme hardships, during which they were helped by anti-Nationalist Chinese guerrillas who were fighting the Japanese as well as the Nationalists, the party arrived at the Nationalist Government town of Waichow. Ride cabled the British Ambassador in Chungking, the National Government's capital, and was eventually ordered to report to Chungking where he arrived on 17 February. For his part in leading the escape Ride was awarded the OBE; Francis Lee, who had proved an invaluable member of the team, received the Military Medal.

Ride's idea of setting up an escape line for the POW and civilians they had left behind in Hong Kong, and of smuggling in medical supplies to those who were unable to escape, was received enthusiastically by the military attaché at the British embassy, Brigadier G. E. Grimsdale, who approached his superiors and the Nationalist Chinese with the scheme. General Wavell, the Commander-in-Chief at the time, immediately agreed and when Grimsdale and the British Ambassador had a personal interview with Chiang and Madam Kai-shek, who also endorsed the

Map 7.
WARTIME HONGKONG
PRISONER OF WAR CAMPS

plan. They did so despite the fact that they knew that Ride's unit would have to work with the anti-Nationalist Communist guerrillas who controlled the land approaches to Hong Kong.

At the end of February 1942 Ride was instructed by Grimsdale to return to South China and 'do what he could' to assist POW in Hong Kong and to encourage as many of them as possible to escape from the colony. Grimsdale also informed Ride that because his organisation was more a clandestine unit than a military one it was, through Grimsdale, to be controlled and administered by the Indian section of the British escape and evasion organisation, MI9 (see Chapter One), which was attached to the Directorate of Military Intelligence at GHQ Delhi.

Because he was only a volunteer, Ride's military status caused difficulties. Initially it was thought preferable to appoint a regular officer to command the new unit, but this never happened. The difficulty was only partially solved when he was commissioned into the Indian Army as a second-lieutenant on 1 August 1942, and promoted acting lieutenant-colonel the same day! A dispute with the military bureaucrats about his substantive rank continued until the end of the war.

It was of course the duty of every serviceman to escape if humanly possible and Ride was quite uncompromising in ensuring that all prisoners understood this. And he was equally adamant that it was the duty of civilians to escape if they were particularly required to help the Allied war effort. Some found his attitude controversial. A number of doctors, for example, strongly held that their duty was to their patients; if their patients were in Hong Kong that was where doctors must be. Ride's view was that some of these doctors, by co-operating with the Japanese in order to ease the plight of the sick and wounded, were collaborating, but many thought that this was too harsh a line to take.

To help prisoners and would-be escapers, Ride decided to form a base head-quarters close to the Chinese VIIth War Zone HQ at Kukong in northern Kwang-tung Province. He arrived there on 6 March and found not only a handful of service personnel who had escaped from Hong Kong but a much larger number of Chinese refugees who had served with one or other of the essential services, or with the armed forces, during the fighting there. Many had their families with them. They had no money, food or clothing and Ride realised that his new organisation would not only have to cope with escaped military personnel but also with civilian refugees. Eventually the British embassy sent a branch of the Refugee Relief Department to Kukong, but it remained Ride's responsibility to carry out security checks on every individual.

It was from these refugees, as well as from escaped service personnel, that Ride picked his first recruits for what was soon to be called the British Army Aid Group (BAAG). The numbers serving in it varied, but at times total maximum strength exceeded 500. About a hundred including thirty officers wore uniform, the remainder were civilians or servicemen from a variety of nations, including Portuguese and Chinese, who worked in civilian clothes as agents. By 1945

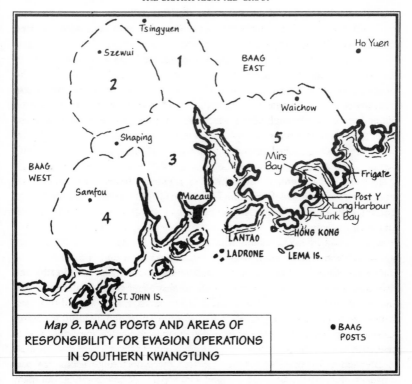

Map 8. BAAG POSTS AND AREAS OF
RESPONSIBILITY FOR EVASION OPERATIONS
IN SOUTHERN KWANGTUNG

Southern Kwangtung was divided into five BAAG zones for evasion operations
(see Map 8).

BAAG's first office was set up in Ride's bedroom in the compound of the
Methodist Medical Mission's Ho Sai Hospital in Kukong, the wartime capital of
Kwangtung Province as well as being the HQ of the Chinese VIIth War Zone.
After a few weeks a temporary headquarters was established in two river boats
which had previously been used as brothels: one served as an office, the other as
living accommodation and the mess.

Ride's first task was to establish medical aid posts as close as practicable to
Hong Kong. Two of them were at Ho Yuen, at Waichow on the East River, and
at Takhing on the West River, from which agents in Macao were contacted. The
task of these posts was to collect escapers, treat them if necessary, and pass them
back to safety. To man them Ride obtained personnel from the Canton Red Cross,
but they did not include any doctors and an immediate task was to make arrangements for the escape of a number of doctors from Hong Kong.

BAAG's principal agent in the Portuguese colony, code-named 'Phoenix', was
a Chinese businessman of considerable initiative. His shop became BAAG's HQ in
Macao and his primary responsibility was to run an escape route to China for all

who managed to reach Macao. He had his own agents among the guerrillas who controlled the area through which any escapee must pass, and he maintained contact with BAAG by buying time on Macao radio to transmit coded messages. He also operated a transmitter from a junk which kept on the move to avoid detection. When he needed replacement items for it – the Japanese had enforced the withdrawal of spares from the shops – he flooded the basement of the Portuguese bank where they had been stored and in the resulting confusion took what he required. Two American airmen escaped via his line in 1943 and three more did so in 1945.

A BAAG intelligence officer was appointed to collect, collate and disseminate relevant intelligence to aid would-be escapers and to determine conditions in Hong Kong and monitor the movement of Japanese shipping. To perform this important task Grimsdale recruited Lieutenant J. D. Clague who, with three others, had made a remarkable escape from Sham Pui Po on 11 April 1942.* In fact, intelligence became an important subsidiary task of the BAAG.

First contact by BAAG agents with POW in Hong Kong was made between agents posing as Chinese coolies and prisoners working on the extension of Hong Kong's airfield at Kai Tak, but ceased in December 1942 when the POW were withdrawn from the airfield. Contact was resumed in January 1943 through a Chinese truck driver who delivered the daily rations of rice and vegetables to the camps. Messages were passed concerning news about the war, requests for information about conditions in the camps, details of escape procedures, and appeals for certain medicines and drugs.

To maintain some sort of control over escapes, an escape committee was formed in the Argyle Street camp under Colonel L. A. Newnham. A would-be escapee had to submit his plan to his commanding officer. After discussion the plan was put to the escape committee. If sanctioned, the applicant had to wait his turn in the queue. When his time came he was given such help as was possible – such as having someone answer for him at the daily roll call.

The majority of escapees were local men. They were encouraged to try to escape to China, but were always enjoined to make the safety of their families their first priority; some of them simply returned home and merged with the local community. Europeans were instructed to head for China. POW in Sham Shui Po were provided with a tracing from the map Ride had smuggled into the camp, and

---

*The party had crawled through a storm drain which passed under the sea wall and led to the harbour. The sea wall was patrolled by a Japanese sentry. Elaborate measures were taken to avoid detection as the escapers' report revealed. 'One assistant above centre manhole with cover half replaced held rope to which a brick was attached. One knock on floor of manhole denoted "danger", three knocks "go ahead", according to position of sentries. Also accomplice played accordion at vantage point on verandah of Jubilee Building. Code of tunes indicated position of sentries e.g. "Happy Days Are Here Again" etc., for "go ahead" signal and "Stormy Weather" for "danger".' From the harbour the party had to swim 800 yards to reach a suitable landing area and then spent three days in the Kowloon hills before making contact with the Communist guerrillas who had helped Ride.

were advised to escape via the Hakka villages on the eastern side of the New Territories where Ride had found the local people sympathetic to the Allies. Escapees were taught a few phrases in the Hakka dialect and were given a letter in Chinese which certified that the carrier was an Allied serviceman and promised a reward after the war to anyone who helped him. These promises were honoured after the war when money to certain villages, and cash rewards or certificates of merit to individuals, were handed out at a ceremony at Government House, Hong Kong, on 15 February 1947.

The Japanese responded to the escapes from Sham Shui Po by electrifying the camp's fences, erecting arc lamps around the perimeter, and increasing the number of guards. A number of POW were shot while trying to escape and others were executed when their plans were discovered. In May 1942 the Japanese demanded a written undertaking from POW that they would not escape. Many decided that a promise extracted under duress was not valid, but when those in Sham Shui Po heard that the officers in the Argyle Street camp had signed most did so, too. Those who did not were put under armed guard and were later 'persuaded' by the *Kempetai*, the Japanese military police, to sign.

The Japanese also increased the reprisals on those left behind by putting them on a starvation diet and making them stand for excessive lengths of time on parade, and special treatment was meted out to an escapee's friends and hut-mates to force them to reveal what they knew. So brutal were these reprisals that the dilemma for any potential escaper was acute.

'From the point of view of the escaper the problem was clear-cut and simple,' wrote Ralph Goodwin, who escaped from Sham Shui Po in July 1944. 'Success meant freedom and a return to battle; failure meant torture and execution. For those left behind the problem was confused, unpredictable and therefore the more terrifying. Anything could happen, from a spate of tortures and execution of individuals, to a mass starvation of the whole camp.' In fact, so debilitated did the remaining prisoners become from malnutrition and disease that by October 1942 escapes had practically ceased, though the BAAG continued to encourage them.

One of the rare escapes from the camp after October 1942 is worth noting for its sheer audacity – and simplicity. In Hong Kong at the time of the invasion was a Portuguese Red Cross unit which subsequently tended the wounds of both Allied and Japanese personnel, and whose members subsequently visited Sham Shui Po to give what aid they could. In February 1943 a red-haired private in the Royal Scots, Charles Salter, stripped his uniform of any insignia, made himself a Red-Cross armband, strolled up to the guard at the camp gate, pointed to the arm band, said 'Portuguese Red Cross', and, to the utter amazement of his friends who were watching, was waved through by the guard who must have been more than half-asleep. Even more astonishingly, Salter managed to get to his girl friend's apartment in Kowloon. She provided him with Chinese clothes and dyed his hair with ink. With BAAG's aid he made his way to Kunming and just three months later was at Buckingham Palace being invested with the Military Medal by the

King. That he had successfully escaped was communicated to the camp's escape officer, Captain Douglas Ford, in a letter from Clague dated 30 April 1943.

At one point a simultaneous mass break-out by the inmates of all three camps, aided by hidden caches of arms and a diversionary attack from the New Territories by local guerrillas, was being planned. It was calculated that about a third of the POW might get away to China, but the plan was never activated.

In mid-April 1942 Francis Lee was dispatched to Hong Kong to make contact with a number of doctors there and to deliver messages to individuals in Sham Shui Po camp. Much depended on the success of this mission. Initially it went well, but on 26 April Lee, and the smugglers he had accompanied to Hong Kong, were arrested by the Japanese and it soon transpired that one of the smugglers had betrayed the rest of the party. Although the Japanese had no idea why Lee had entered Hong Kong, he was accused of being a Chinese Nationalist agent and was severely beaten and tortured. A combination of his own courage, and that of his friends in Hong Kong who spoke up on his behalf, saved him from execution and he was eventually released. He returned to Waichow in early June and made a complete recovery from his ordeal.

In March Ride decided that if the lines of communication in and out of Hong Kong were to be developed safely and efficiently there had to be an advanced HQ closer to Hong Kong than his base at Kukong. He therefore sent Paul Tsui Ka Cheung, a former student at Hong Kong University, to Waichow to act as the BAAG representative there and to prepare the way for an Advanced Headquarters. This was opened in mid-July under the command of Clague.

To help smuggle out escapers the BAAG also acquired its own small junk in September 1942. Manned by agents Nos. 19, 46 and 48, and by two relatives of No. 19, it was permanently based at Ngam Tau Sha. It ran fortnightly trips from Hong Kong and played an important part in the escape of the two Hong Kong bankers, Fenwick and Morrison, described below.

In November 1942 Francis Lee returned to the New Territories to report on Communist guerrilla operations as they affected the BAAG, and to determine whether it was feasible to open a forward aid post in the New Territories. The purpose of this post, known as Post Y, was to gather reports from agents working in Hong Kong, supervise BAAG communications between Waichow and the New Territories, and act as a supply depot for drugs being smuggled into the Hong Kong camps. Additionally, it acted as a liaison post with the guerrillas who would also be given medical aid as necessary.

Initially the guerrilla leader, Tsoi Kwok Leung, suspected that BAAG was colluding with the Nationalists and that Post Y was being established so that BAAG could spy on his activities, but eventually he was persuaded to allow it to be set up with the guerrillas' mobile HQ at Chik Kang on the east arm of Long Harbour. To minimise the risk of detection it was manned only by Chinese and Eurasian staff. It was the only forward aid post in what was technically enemy-occupied territory (though it was effectively controlled by the guerrillas) and it performed much useful work until it had to be closed in July 1943 when relations between the Nationalists and the Communist guerrillas deteriorated.

Lee's work was so outstanding during this period that Ride recommended him for the DCM, and although the recommendation was not accepted Lee was commissioned (he ended the war as a captain) and was awarded the military MBE for his work. In his citation Ride wrote that 'Lee has spent almost the entire period in occupied areas acting as liaison officer for AHQ [Waichow] with the guerrillas, concurrently with the position of Officer i/c Post Y. Lee's work has been beyond reproach and he has displayed extreme loyalty, honesty, efficiency and reliability throughout the entire period. He has been responsible for the smooth working of one of our most important lines of communication with Hong Kong and has carried out his liaison work with skill and unremitting zeal.'

Ride's brief to Paul Tsui Ka Cheung stressed the importance of working with the local Chinese military at Waichow. As the Nationalist Chinese Army was Kafkaesque in its structure and organisation this could not have been easy to achieve – it was said at the time that to work successfully in China during the war one needed a very strong constitution and a copy of *Alice in Wonderland* for guidance. A particularly sensitive issue was BAAG's relationship with the Communist guerrillas, which was excellent, and the Nationalist Chinese were forever accusing the BAAG of giving overt help to them. There was also a deep, abiding suspicion that BAAG were only in South China to keep a foot in the door, as it were, for the British return to Hong Kong. After the war Ride, in his final report, stressed how complicated it had been to liaise with the Chinese Nationalist Army.

'The complex military set-up', he wrote, 'complicated by local politics, personalities, and intrigue, made the work of any foreign military organisation most difficult. In the first place, it took years to get to understand how the system worked; in the second place, a policy which might work in one area would fail in another because of the local values of the various military organisations which were totally different; and thirdly, the BAAG never had at any time formed an integral part of this military set-up.'

The Advanced HQ's first task was to create a proper organisation for BAAG agents and runners moving in and out of Hong Kong. Recruiting these was not a problem because many of Ride's former students from the university had escaped from Hong Kong and they made ideal agent material. Many of them belonged to well-known Hong Kong families. They proved to be trustworthy and courageous, and could travel without difficulty provided that they disguised themselves as peasants.

Administration was complicated. All agents and runners were known only by a number. New recruits were entrusted with only minor missions for which payment was small, and were told that payment would depend on results. Only after they had been in and out of Hong Kong several times and their information had been checked and double-checked, were they given more important missions.

A report Ride sent to Grimsdale on 15 June 1942 gives a good insight into the way BAAG worked. Three of Paul Tsui's agents, Ride wrote, 'have direct family contacts through a shop in Shaukiwan with Chinese employed by the Japanese guards at North Point (POW camp). Through them it is hoped to institute and maintain a postal service into North Point. For this it is expected we shall have to pay fairly highly ... Two agents have already been dispatched to attempt to contact North Point, BMH (the British Military Hospital in Hong Kong), and the French Hospital. It would seem likely that British doctors who are free are on parole and it may not be possible to get any of them out. We are concentrating on the BMH for two reasons: (i) there we are most likely to be able to get most of the information from all the camps and (ii) they have a surplus of RAMC doctors there now and quite a number could come out. No. 34 (Yip Foo) has already gone south. We have engaged him for three months. His twelve men are to report on shipping in Hong Kong and Canton, movements and distribution of troops in the Hong Kong area, enemy defences both fixed and mobile, AA (anti-aircraft gun) dispositions and activities at Kai Tak, and prison camp information. He has been given letters of contact to North Point, Argyle Street and Ma Tau Chung camps. No. 100 (S. B. Tan) is setting up a shop in his family village near the Hong Kong border. He intends to trade with clients in the New Territories and in Kowloon. In order to try out his methods he has been given the specific but innocuous task of contacting the Hong Kong and Shanghai Banking Corporation officials. If this proves successful it is proposed to use him to make contact with a shop in Hong Kong owned by No. 42 (Ah Mui) and this shop-to-shop trade route will be used for letters and medicines.'

At the end of May Ride made his first attempt to contact Hong Kong POW personally. He wrote to his former second-in-command, a Canadian officer, still held captive in Sham Shui Po, and asked for a plan of the camp showing its buildings, disposition of sentries, and anything else that might assist BAAG in helping the prisoners in the near future. 'Also let me know if you have a group of men willing to have a shot at coming out ... No money or food will be needed, just guts and determination. China is not full of robbers and bandits but of brave friends.'

Ride's letter was entrusted to agent No. 63 (Joseph Tsang Yuk Cheung) who travelled with another agent, No. 36 (Lau Teng Ke). By sheer bad luck they were both picked up by the Japanese for interrogation and the letters had to be destroyed. But these two agents were successful in contacting the Vice-Chancellor of Hong Kong University, Duncan J. Sloss, at Stanley camp, the civilian internment camp on the south-east side of Hong Kong island, when Ride wrote to him early in July about the possibility of escaping. The plan, for various reasons, could not be carried out, but Ride's instructions to Sloss do reveal his thinking on how he could help those imprisoned in Hong Kong and how an escape could be planned.

This was an attempt, he wrote to Sloss, to establish a regular information service between BAAG and the prisoners in Stanley camp because prisoners' relatives were naturally very anxious to receive news of them 'and I trust this will be the quickest and safest method of getting news in and out ... I understand you need money badly. Here is $100 from me as a trial; if it gets through you will know that the route is trustworthy ...'

When Sloss replied that he had received the money, Ride wrote back saying that he had worked out a way for about 50 civilians interned in the camp to escape. As the plan involved the escapees swimming about 500 yards, those who could not swim would have to be excluded. All those who were 'psychologically unfit at present for the task or for war-work when they are out' would also have to be excluded as would any who talked too much or were not amenable to discipline ... 'If there are any spare passages, when you have applied the pruning knife to this list, fill it with any whom you know to be of value to the war effort, and that means that women are not debarred as long as they can be relied upon to last the course.'

Ride warned that the escapees would have a crowded, uncomfortable sea journey, but that it would be short. They would be accompanied on board by an armed escort which would be replaced by a BAAG escort immediately they reached shore. They were not to bring any luggage. Sloss was not to give lengthy advance notice to those he had chosen, but he could take two or three people into his confidence if they were absolutely trustworthy. The remainder would have to be the type who would obey orders at a moment's notice and without question. 'That is why the final choice must be left to you for you know by now all those who would be willing to come out at a moment's notice,' Ride concluded. 'There must be no good-byes ... Doctors, engineers, wireless operators, master mariners and young fellows fit for the Army should come out.'

This letter was also delivered by No. 63 who was accompanied by No. 85, an ex-Hong Kong policeman named Chow Ying Kwan who knew the police at Stanley well enough to pick those who would collude in the kind of escape Ride was planning. Another agent became the principal BAAG representative for contacting the Sham Shui Po and Argyle Street camps.

Although the plan to extract civilians from the Stanley camp never came to fruition, the rescue of two senior banking officials in June 1942 did work, and was one of the most daring and efficient operations undertaken by BAAG. These officials, and others, had not been interned. Instead they had been kept under close guard in a Chinese hotel and compelled to co-operate with the Japanese in the liquidation of the Hong Kong and Shanghai Banking Corporation for which they had formerly worked. Because London wanted to know what financial plans the Japanese had for the Colony, it was decided that BAAG should try to smuggle out one or two senior bankers, and during June and July Ride was in correspondence with several of them. It was eventually decided that T. J. J. Fenwick and J. A. D. Morrison, two members of the Hong Kong Bank, should be got out of Hong Kong if the opportunity arose, and in October 1942 the two men were contacted by Agent No. 64 (Lo Hung Sui) who was accompanied by No. 48 (Tsang Tak).

'64 and 48 told Fenwick and Morrison to stand at a nearby tram stop and wait for their signal,' Ride later wrote. 'This they did, and at approximately 1945 hours all four boarded a tram and proceeded toward Shaukiwan. En route two Chinese policemen, a Japanese naval warrant officer, and over a dozen Japanese ratings and salvage corps men joined the vehicle. Although it was unusual for foreigners to be seen in that locality, no notice was taken of them; and all the Japanese had alighted by the time the tram reached North Point.'

At Shaukiwan the party descended from the tram, walked down the main road about fifty yards and turned into an alley-way leading to the beach. No. 48 went to the water's edge and hailed a sampan lying offshore. When it reached the shore, No. 64 with Fenwick and Morrison jumped aboard and lay down out of sight. They crossed the harbour unchallenged and landed at Sai Tso Wan where they were met by another BAAG agent, No. 19 (Joseph Tsang Yiu Sang), who took the two bankers overland to Junk Bay.

During this walk they were joined by an armed guerrilla guard. At Junk Bay they boarded two fishing sampans which took them to Hanghau. There they walked to Silverstrand Bay where the BAAG junk was waiting for them. This took them to Kau Sai where they boarded a larger junk and were taken to a Communist guerrilla base at Shek Hang where No. 19 left them. They reached there at 0530 and after resting for the day they walked over the hills to Cheung Sheung, a two-hour journey.

The party stayed at Cheung Sheung for a couple of days and then, still accompanied by armed guards and No. 64, walked to To Ka Ping on the west arm of Long Harbour where they boarded junks that sailed across Mirs Bay to Sha Yu Chung. After a night's rest they were carried by chair to Tamshui. They stayed the night there and next day were taken to BAAG's HQ at Waichow by taxi-bicycle, arriving in mid-afternoon with their sole piece of luggage, a Hong Kong basket containing half a bottle of gin. Within a few weeks they were in London.

This was the first escape that BAAG had planned and executed from start to finish, and it naturally had a remarkably good effect on the unit's morale. But BAAG's largest and most successful undertaking, known as the 'Mateys Scheme', was its plan to deplete the Hong Kong dockyards' skilled workforce. During the course of 1942 the Japanese had repaired the various dockyards in the Colony and in September that year Ride sent in an agent to make contact with some of the specialist workers employed in them. He was delighted by the positive response he received, and by the end of that month 153 dockyard workers and their families had reached BAAG's new HQ at Kweilin (see below) for onward transportation to India where their skills could be put to good use.

On one occasion three Danes living in Hong Kong added, involuntarily, to the numbers rescued by BAAG. The three men were pounced on by a Communist guerrilla band while picnicking in the Kowloon hills one Sunday afternoon in December 1942, and, despite their protests, were processed smartly along the escape line to BAAG's HQ at Waichow. In his report of the incident Clague remarked that 'Although it is regrettable that these neutrals should have been inconvenienced, it is considered that in war time the Sai Kung Peninsula is not the most suitable place for a gin tiffin. One's only regret is that they finished their gin before arriving in Waichow.'

By early 1943 a new degree of sophistication in BAAG communications had been achieved: secret inks (mainly starch developed by a weak iodine solution) began to be used, and escape aids, such as cloth maps and miniature compasses built into collar studs, were smuggled into the camps. To encourage those fit enough to escape, Clague had two special maps smuggled into Sham Shui Po. These gave details of the possible escape routes, what aid escapers could expect en route to safety, and the positions of Japanese and guerrilla outposts between Kowloon and Waichow.

Concentrated foods, energy tablets, medicines, drugs and vitamins were also smuggled into the prisoners, which alleviated conditions for the lucky few. In his book *Passport to Eternity*, Ralph Goodwin explains how the Ma Ta Chaung camp was contacted and supplied with drugs and other necessities. 'British officers from the Indian regiments had made contact with their men in Ma Ta Chaung while working in the adjoining vegetable garden, and soon they established regular communications. Messages and packages concealed in the garden were collected at night by Indians who were being used by the Japanese as guards, and they in turn left messages to be collected by the gardeners the next day.'

Despite all BAAG's efforts, conditions in Sham Shui Po continued to be deplorable and by the end of November 1942 196 men had died there. The diet was vitamin and protein deficient and there was an acute shortage of drugs. Beri-beri, dysentery, diphtheria, malaria, pellagra and quinsy all took their toll.

In August 1942 a new HQ was set up in Kweilin after it was found that refugees and escapers were using new routes via Macau and Canton through to Kwangsi Province. Before the end of the year, another Advanced Headquarters was established at Samfou, south-west of Canton, to cover the main Macau route to Hong Kong. This still left one or two escape routes which were not covered, the sea route from Hong Kong via Kwang Chow Wan being one of them, but by 1943 BAAG had effectively covered the Kwangtung coastline from Mirs Bay to Kwang Chow Wan.

The same month as the Kweilin HQ was established, British members of BAAG were deployed for the first time in Hong Kong when an attempt was made to reconnoitre a possible escape route for prisoners held in Argyle Street, but this also had to be aborted. BAAG agents had better luck with Ma Tau Chung camp which housed members of the Indian Army of all ranks; the escape of a number of them was successfully arranged. But in May 1943 a BAAG agent was tricked by some Indian collaborators into revealing his connections in the Ma Tau Chung camp and this resulted in the arrest of 170 people including many who worked directly or indirectly for the organisation. More than thirty British, Indian and Chinese were executed including the senior Indian officer at Ma Tau Chung, Captain A. M. Ansari, who was subsequently awarded a posthumous George Cross for his bravery under torture.

In June 1943 the two agents in contact with Sham Shui Po and Argyle Street camps were also arrested, as were some Formosan guards and even a Japanese officer on the staff that controlled the camps. For the next six weeks all communication between the camps and Waichow ceased, and in early July there was a wave of arrests of British POW in Sham Shui Po and Argyle Street, and the truck drivers were also arrested. In this purge more than 40 people were executed, including Newnham and Ford, both of whom were subsequently awarded a posthumous George Cross. These deaths, plus a further wave of arrests and torture, meant that the operators in China lost all contact with the camps for a time.

After the base HQ moved to Kweilin a close association began with General Claire L. Chennault's 14th USAAF. American aircraft would take important mail from Kweilin to Chungking or New Delhi; the BAAG reciprocated by supplying the Americans with weather data. The excellent relationship between them was finally sealed when, at the end of 1942, BAAG rescued two American airmen who had been shot down south of Waichow. And even when BAAG's escape capabilities were brought to a halt by the wave of arrests in 1943, it was still able to help airmen evade capture, and for a time in 1944 this became one of its main tasks.

By the end of the war the BAAG network had managed to bring a number of American airmen to safety, including one who, on 11 February 1944, had baled out within sight of Kai Tak airport, had been hidden in a cave by a Chinese boy, concealed in a house on Tolo Harbour until the hunt for him had died down, and then successfully smuggled across Mirs Bay into China.

In April 1944 the Japanese launched their ICHIGO offensive in China. By October they were closing in on Kweilin and BAAG HQ was forced to evacuate the town. The Advanced HQ at Waichow and the BAAG forward posts in Kwangtung Province also had to withdraw, and it was not until January 1945 that Ride was able to establish a new permanent base, at Kunming. The forward zone around Hong Kong was now divided into the East and West areas, the North River being the boundary between the two.

It was during this reorganisation that the British Secret Intelligence Service (MI6), working under its cover name of Inter-Services Liaison Department (ISLD), took over BAAG's secret intelligence role. This had serious consequences for Ride's organisation because it brought to an end BAAG's close relationship with the Americans who had come to rely on BAAG's ability to assist US air operations with intelligence reports which ISLD refused to continue. This had a knock-on effect with BAAG's relationship with the Nationalist Chinese who quickly realised that the British were being supplanted by the Americans.

These changes adversely affected BAAG's work around Hong Kong because the enemy-occupied area from which American evaders could be recovered had been increased by 70,000 square miles by the ICHIGO offensive. BAAG did not have the personnel to cope with this extra burden and its area was limited to the zone south of the 26th Parallel and bounded by lines north from Swatow in the east and the Luichow Peninsula in the west.

The rest of the area was covered by MIS-X (see Chapter Six), the American equivalent of MI9, which later became known in China as the Air Ground Air Service (AGAS). But AGAS soon encroached upon the BAAG area of responsibility, reasoning that as BAAG could not operate without its help it might as well take over completely. By mid-1945 AGAS had almost totally excluded BAAG from escape and evasion operations in South China, and Ride found himself in no position to act independently of AGAS.

The Japanese surrendered on 16 August and signed the surrender terms on 2 September. That day Ride and senior officers of BAAG flew into Hong Kong. For a short time he was seconded, as Senior Military Officer, to the staff of Rear-Admiral Harcourt, whose force of warships had officially liberated the Colony four days previously. BAAG was officially disbanded in Hong Kong on 31 December 1945. During its three and a half years' existence it had given invaluable aid and comfort to those imprisoned in Hong Kong, provided valuable intelligence about the Japanese, and had assisted the escape or evasion of more than 1,800 civilians and servicemen, including 33 American airmen. A total of 93 BAAG members, agents, runners and contacts lost their lives.

10

THE SCARLET PIMPERNEL
AND THE ROME ORGANISATION

On 3 September 1943 Allied troops began landing in the toe of Italy and five days later, a few hours before they stormed ashore at Salerno, 30 miles south-west of Naples, Italy surrendered unconditionally.

Under the terms of the surrender the Italians had to release all Allied prisoners of war. It is estimated that these numbered just under 80,000, scattered across the country in about 72 camps and twelve hospitals. The largest number, about 42,000, were British, but there were also more than 26,000 Commonwealth troops, mostly South African, and some 1,300 Americans, the remainder being Free French, Greeks and Yugoslavs.

Before the secret armistice came into effect, the senior officer in each camp had been ordered – presumably via coded letters coupled with BBC radio announcements – to ensure that all POW remained within the camps until Allied troops arrived. This 'stand fast' order proved disastrous, because the Italians did not 'release' the POW at all; the guards simply deserted their posts and left the camps to the mercy of the Germans who reacted to the armistice with speed and determination by occupying all those parts of Italy not in Allied hands.

It is not known who issued the 'stand fast' order. The authors of *MI9: Escape and Evasion 1939–45* presumed that it was 'a catastrophic staff muddle, at a level so senior that no has quite cared to clear it up', but the most recent authoritative text on the subject, Roy Absalom's *Strange Alliance*, states that 'there is informed speculation that Montgomery, during a "working leave" in London when the Tunisian campaign was coming to a close [in May 1943], instructed Brigadier Richard Crockatt, the head of MI9, to use his secret channels to order all prisoners of war in Italy to stay put in the event of a surrender. No doubt he was banking on a rapid withdrawal by the Germans and did not want hungry, undisciplined and disoriented prisoners of war wandering around and distracting his advance units. Somehow Crockatt's steps to carry out this order were never brought to the attention of the War Cabinet, nor of Churchill in particular' who, a few days before the invasion of mainland Italy ordered the ground force commander, General Alexander, 'to rescue all prisoners of war at any cost'.

The result of this 'staff muddle' was that for a few vital days most POW stayed put and by the time it was realised that the swift German reaction had made the order redundant it was too late to act, or nearly so. In places the Germans were opposed by the Italian Army, but by the end of September they controlled most of Italy north of Salerno. Nevertheless, in what has been called the largest mass escape in history, some 50,000 POW took to the hills in a last-minute bid for freedom, and those who remained were sent to camps in Germany.

Those POW who were at large tried to reach Switzerland to the north or Allied lines to the south, or simply hid with or near Italian families who valiantly helped them at great danger to themselves (the Germans soon announced that anyone sheltering Allied POW would be shot, and a number were).

To help those on the run, 'A' Force, the cover name under which MI9 (see Chapter One) operated in the Mediterranean theatre – and whose units were by now being run jointly by MI9 and its American equivalent, MIS-X (see Chapter Six) – created field sections to operate with the two Allied Armies (Fifth and Eighth) that were fighting their way up the toe of Italy, and on 23 September formed an operational HQ (SIMCOL) at Bari to augment the efforts being made to rescue POW from behind enemy lines (see Map 9).

Generally speaking, rescue work by the field sections at the front was limited to no more than 50 miles behind German lines, while SIMCOL specialised in 'deep penetration' using parachute teams and small boat units to find and exfiltrate POW from four designated areas (see Map 9). Both groups sent agents into occupied territory, known, because of their function, as 'forks'.

Finding POW hiding in the countryside was a difficult enough task, as was arranging for them to be evacuated by sea or back through the Allied lines, but often it was not easy to persuade them to move at all. Many quickly found girl friends; others settled into the rural life and had no wish to return to war. The history of MI9 operations in the Mediterranean records that when one field section, headed by a Captain McKee, tried to persuade the POW it had managed to track down in the vicinity of Sulmona to return to British lines there were few takers. Initially, the POW affected to believe McKee was a German agent and even when he distributed maps, compasses and money to help them return they refused to budge.

Infuriated by the stubbornness of one group, McKee climbed on a rock 'and in a rather broad Scots, said something on the following lines: "You blank blank bastards. I've walked 500 blank miles to fetch you, and you blank well come back. You're all under arrest – follow me." Despite this and similar harangues only 23 of the 1,300 prisoners agreed to return!

More successful – probably because they only bothered with those who felt duty-bound to escape – were the escape organisations formed by the Italian anti-Fascist National Liberation Committee (CLN) which 'considered it its duty to take care of it [the problem of POW], both from a humanitarian point of view and for the good name of this country'. The most prominent of these was the Milan-based *Ufficio Assistenza Prigionieri di Guerra Alleati* (Allied Prisoners-of-War Assistance Service) whose main operative was Giuseppe Bacciagaluppi. He was married to an Englishwoman who attempted 'single-handed to free a camp of 50 Allied prisoners of war', and between them, and their helpers, this intrepid pair exfiltrated more than 1,800 Allied POW across the Swiss border.

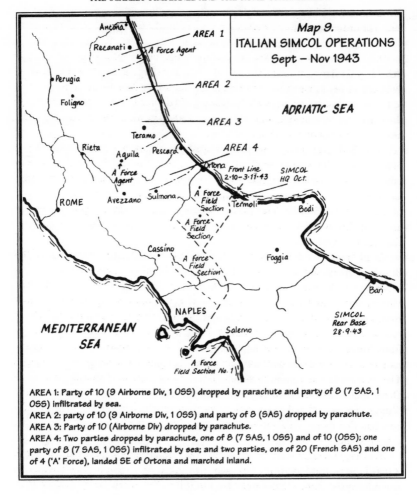

Map 9.
ITALIAN SIMCOL OPERATIONS
Sept – Nov 1943

AREA 1: Party of 10 (9 Airborne Div, 1 OSS) dropped by parachute and party of 8 (7 SAS, 1 OSS) infiltrated by sea.
AREA 2: party of 10 (9 Airborne Div, 1 OSS) and party of 8 (SAS) dropped by parachute.
AREA 3: Party of 10 (Airborne Div) dropped by parachute.
AREA 4: Two parties dropped by parachute, one of 8 (7 SAS, 1 OSS) and of 10 (OSS); one party of 8 (7 SAS, 1 OSS) infiltrated by sea; and two parties, one of 20 (French SAS) and one of 4 ('A' Force), landed SE of Ortona and marched inland.

But the price paid was a heavy one: of the 359 sub-agents employed by Baccia-galuppi six were executed; five were killed while protecting POW; three were permanently disabled; 26 were deported to concentration camps, nine of whom died; 48, including Bacciagaluppi, were arrested and imprisoned. After the war Bacciagaluppi was among 447 Italian resistance workers recommended to receive a British decoration by the Allied Screening Mission. Seventeen were awarded the Medal of Freedom by the Americans, but the British refused to sanction any awards at all.

It must be pointed out that, according to one MI9 document, the 'lavish friendliness' of the Italians towards escaped POW after the Italian surrender, 'is an interesting contrast to the hostility shown by all Italians to escaped POW prior to the armistice. Although nearly 1,500 escapes are recorded from Italian POW camps prior to the armistice, only three are on our MI9 records as having got clear out of Italy.'

Despite the efforts of SIMCOL and the CLN, about 50 per cent of escaped POW had been recaptured by the end of 1943, and only some 10 per cent reached Switzerland or managed to get through the lines into Allied-held territory. The rest remained scattered across Italy, being looked after by the local populace, by partisans, and by a unique unit which came to be known as the Rome Organisation, run by a Major Sam Derry.

Derry had had no opportunity to escape from his prison camp and was one of those put on a train for Germany, but he managed to escape from it some fifteen miles east of Rome and was hidden in a haystack by some peasants. His intention had been to make his way south to cross into Allied-held territory, but the sight of the great dome of St Peter's on the horizon, and a chance encounter with a group of British POW who were in hiding nearby, and who badly needed help, changed his mind.

As an officer it was his undoubted responsibility to care for the welfare of the British escapers, and as he puzzled over his predicament in his haystack he was suddenly struck with the thought that Rome contained the Vatican City, that the Vatican was neutral territory, and that he remembered reading somewhere that British embassy staff had taken refuge there when Italy had entered the war. Derry reasoned that if he could get into the Vatican, he would be able to borrow money from British representatives there, for money was the prime requisite for any escaper to survive. He sought the help of the local priest who spoke some English. The man looked at Derry quizzically, but did not appear overly surprised when Derry requested that a message be smuggled to a British representative in the Vatican. He agreed and Derry simply wrote under the heading 'to whom it may concern' that money and clothing were needed for escaped British POW in hiding east of Rome.

To Derry's delight – and amazement – the priest returned three days later with 3,000 lire (a little less than £10), which in those days went a long way, and a second request from Derry produced 4,000 lire. But when Derry made a third request the priest replied that his superior wanted to meet Derry – in Rome. More than that he would not say. Derry agreed and on 20 November 1943 he was smuggled beneath a cart load of vegetable produce into the city and handed over to a rather shifty-looking individual dressed as a priest (it turned out that he was not one). This individual handed him over to an English-speaking Italian, Aldo Zambardi, who gave him a change of clothing and took him to the Vatican.

It gave Derry something of a shock to cross a St Peter's Square full of German soldiers. 'I continued to follow the silent Zambardi,' Derry wrote later, 'keeping my gaze firmly at ground level, careful to avoid catching the eye of the German soldiers who passed too close for my liking. Ahead of us, almost in the shadow of the noble colonnade that curved round both sides of the *piazza*, I could see a very tall, lone figure, wearing the long black robe of a priest. He was standing with his hands folded in front of him, and his head slightly bowed, as though in prayer, yet I had the feeling that he was watching our approach.'

The priest was a remarkable 44-year-old Irishman, the Right Reverend Monsignor Hugh O'Flaherty, who became known as the 'Scarlet Pimpernel of the Vatican'. A towering, burly, athletic man – he was a scratch golfer – O'Flaherty had worked before the war in the Vatican's Sacred Congregation of the Holy Office, the lineal successor to the Inquisition, and, under the Pope, the ultimate arbiter of the Church's faith and morals. When, because of the war, the Holy Office had not been able to carry out its normal functions, O'Flaherty had been appointed secretary and English interpreter to the Pope's Nuncio (messenger) to Allied POW camps in Italy.

O'Flaherty had trained as a priest during the Irish troubles that followed the First World War, when he had been an IRA supporter and implacably anti-British. Despite this he became such a persistent champion of Allied POW that by the end of 1942, as a result of Fascist pressure, he was asked for his resignation. Back in Rome he became, as Derry described him, 'a sort of rallying point for the underdog; Jews and anti-Fascists who were in danger turned to him for help, and he found places for them to hide', and he also gave what succour he could to escaped POW.

The British Minister to the Vatican, Sir D'Arcy Osborne, had known O'Flaherty for some years before the war. He too was very much involved in helping escapers, and from his sanctuary in the Vatican's Hospice Santa Marta (see Map 10) had managed to harbour a handful – all but one or two were, in due course, exchanged for Italian POW – but after Italy surrendered the trickle threatened to become a flood which not only jeopardised Osborne's diplomatic status but the security of the Vatican itself.

Technically the Vatican was a neutral state and under international law was obliged to intern all escaped prisoners. But as one author has pointed out, like having the right to illuminate the Vatican at night, internment was not a practical possibility because hundreds if not thousands of POW might have tried to seek sanctuary there. It was known that the Germans would not hesitate to raid the Vatican if so many were given shelter, and there were even threats that they might occupy it.

The Swiss Guards who protected the Vatican were therefore given the strictest instructions to keep out all unauthorised intruders, and a special identity card was issued to any one who had the right to enter its territory. But when Osborne began to receive desperate pleas for help from escaped POW scattered across German-occupied Italy – Derry's message was just one of many carried by O'Flaherty's network of country priests – he knew he faced a terrible dilemma.

On the one hand if he did nothing, he would not only be ignoring his own inclinations as well as his duty to help his own countrymen, but would be creating the very situation he wished to avert – namely, encouraging escapers to seek sanc-

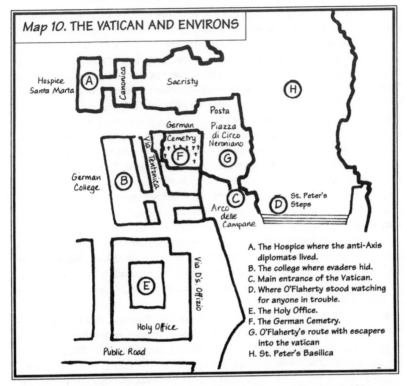

Map 10. THE VATICAN AND ENVIRONS

A. The Hospice where the anti-Axis diplomats lived.
B. The college where evaders hid.
C. Main entrance of the Vatican.
D. Where O'Flaherty stood watching for anyone in trouble.
E. The Holy Office.
F. The German Cemetery.
G. O'Flaherty's route with escapers into the vatican
H. St. Peter's Basilica

tuary in the Vatican for lack of any other refuge. On the other hand, if he were caught helping POW to survive where they were hiding, the logical thing to do, the Germans would demand the expulsion of all members of the British Legation.

It was a difficult choice, but without hesitation Osborne chose the latter option. The Foreign Office backed him, but decided it was too risky to fund him direct. Instead, it initially guaranteed a loan to him from the Vatican bank. The first loan was for three million lire, a second was for two million. It cost 120 lire (4 shillings) a day to keep an escapee in Rome, a lot less in the country. Even so the expenditure mounted alarmingly. In the first six weeks up to 9 December 1943 some 69,000 lire was distributed, but in the next four weeks this spiralled past the million mark. By April 1944 Osborne had borrowed £27,500.

The American Minister in Rome, Harold Tittman, who also resided at the Hospice Santa Marta, paid the costs of evading American airmen helped by the organisation. These tended to be rather higher than for other servicemen because, knowing how important they were to the Allied war effort, evading airmen demanded only the best accommodation! What's more they tended to stay longer, because the Americans had a rule that if an evader or escaper were reunited with his unit within 28 days he was returned to combat duty, otherwise he was entitled to six months' home leave. So quite a few USAAF personnel made sure that they were not available to be smuggled through the lines until 28 days had passed!

Osborne was careful to stay in the background, delegating the ground work to his major-domo, John May. O'Flaherty was the ideal go-between with the British inside the Vatican and the escapers outside because he was widely known and respected throughout Rome and had many contacts among Rome's aristocracy and anti-Fascist elements who, together with Osborne, helped fund the organisation.

When Italy surrendered, and the influx of POW into Rome increased, O'Flaherty formed a Council of Three: himself, Count Sarsfield Salazar, a British subject who was the Swiss Legation's representative in dealing with POW, and John May. Together they arranged for escapers who had reached Rome to be given new clothing, a safe hiding-place, and money on which to subsist, while those in the country were sent money and supplies via the network of local priests that O'Flaherty built up.

May proved especially valuable because he had contacts everywhere and knew immediately if any food or spare clothing became available on the black market. Apartments that could be used as 'safe' houses were rented by O'Flaherty, but POW were also sheltered by individuals who ran great risks to help the Allied cause. One of the most active of these was a Maltese woman whose apartment was in the same street as the Rome headquarters of the SS. Many of these '*padrones*' were caught in the following months and lost their lives as a consequence, for while the POW were simply sent to camps, those sheltering them were often shot or sent to concentration camps in Germany.

Such was the situation when on that November day in 1943 Derry first met O'Flaherty in St Peter's Square. By then Osborne had already decided that the escape organisation needed a full-time military leader who would be able to instil discipline among the POW and run the organisation along military lines. Which was why Derry, the most senior officer yet to contact the British Legation, had been asked to Rome.

O'Flaherty told Derry to follow him and, to the British officer's dismay, led him into the Collegium Teutonicum (German College). At first Derry thought it was a trap, but soon discovered it was where O'Flaherty now had his office and his bed sitting-room. It was to prove a useful and secure refuge for Derry, who slept on the Monsignor's sofa, because although the building was not within the Vatican walls, it was extra-territorial property and therefore treated as neutral ground. For a while Derry was to find that so long as he was discreet he could come and go as he pleased.

That night Derry was smuggled into the Hospice Santa Marta dressed in a cassock, and was given dinner by Osborne. The British Minister explained that the *ad hoc* organisation needed a full-time head to co-ordinate it, not only to keep Allied POW out of German hands but to arrange their evacuation by sea. Derry seemed the ideal man for the job. Would Derry accept?

Derry agreed, provided that he could return to his own group of POW first to ensure that the best NCO was appointed to command them and to arrange the distribution of the money they needed to survive. This was arranged and while Derry was away Osborne sent a signal to London to check Derry's credentials. When he returned he was courteously but closely questioned by the British Minister before being allowed to proceed with his enormous task of feeding, clothing and hiding the ever-growing numbers of POW making contact with the Vatican.

Derry was passed off by his host as Patrick Derry, an Irish writer in the Vatican's employ. He was given a Vatican identity card under this name and thenceforth used the code-name 'Patrick'. His helpers included three British officers interned in the Vatican who kept a 'registry' of all POW passing through the organisation's hands; a New Zealander, Father Owen Sneddon (code-named 'Horace'); the English-speaking announcer on Vatican Radio, who sent messages of reassurance to the relations of escaped POW who would have been simply reported as missing; numerous brave Italian families who sheltered POW in their homes; and the Swiss military attaché in Rome, Captain Leonardo Trippi who, until the Germans put a stop to it, issued Red Cross parcels to those POW who turned up at the Swiss Legation, and who, via his diplomatic bag, sent information about them to their families.

In December Derry was joined by two gunner subalterns, John Furman and William Simpson, and a multi-lingual Palestinian of Cypriot extraction, Private Joe Pollak of the Pioneer Corps, all of whom Derry had known in his POW camp. He called them his 'billeting officers' and it became their task to find safe hide-outs for escapers, and to make sure they, and those looking after them, were regularly supplied with money. They were an invaluable addition to the organisation's staff because, unlike Derry, they all had knowledge of the Italian language. Pollak spoke it like an Italian, and his physical appearance enabled him to pass himself off as one; Simpson's grasp of the language was good enough to take in most Germans; Furman, who knew German as well, employed a system which seemed fool-proof. When he was speaking to a German he pretended to be Italian, and when conversing with Italian Fascist collaborators, of whom there were plenty in Rome, he pretended to be German.

These three new assistants were lodged at the home of an Italian film director, Renzo Lucidi, code-named 'Rinso', and his wife Adrienne. Both were keen opera-goers. Sometimes they took their lodgers with them and in the course of time Pollak introduced some of his escapers to its pleasures. On one occasion, with two of them in tow, at the box office Pollak kept turning to them to tell them in English what seats were available. The two escapers kept changing their minds, a queue formed, and to his horror Pollak found a German officer standing next to him. 'Are you going to be much longer,' the officer demanded irritably in perfect English. 'No,' Pollak replied, also in English, 'we're leaving now,' which they did, very quickly.

At the height of its complexity a nucleus of about forty people ran the Rome Organisation, including two RAMC officers who provided dental and health care, and ten priests including, of course, the indefatigable O'Flaherty. The organisation did not exist in complete isolation because it did have some contact with the 'forks' who had been dispatched by SIMCOL.

SIMCOL's 'forks' were nearly all Italian. One, a bilingual journalist from Milan named Peter Tumiati, had been imprisoned before the war by the Fascists. Because of this he knew O'Flaherty. He went straight to the Irish priest who put him in touch with Derry. Derry asked Tumiati to take back to British lines a list of POW who were in touch with the Rome Organisation so that their families could be contacted. The list numbered almost 2,000 names, with ranks and numbers, which had been compiled by the 'registry'.

Tumiati agreed to do it, but Derry couldn't think how the list could be concealed. When he discussed this with May the English major-domo said that he knew exactly how it could be done. He microfilmed the list and had it baked in one of the small loaves commonly carried by all Italians for sustenance while travelling, and Tumiati got the list safely into British hands.

Another agent who helped Derry was an Italian paratroop major named Umberto Losena. He had been sent north with a suitcase radio by the British – probably by the Secret Intelligence Service, or ISLD as it was called in the Middle East – to report what he could find out about the Germans. Derry helped him by obtaining intelligence gleaned from his POW contacts which, as he said, 'comprised two thousand potential agents behind enemy lines'. But Derry thought he got the better of the deal because, through this valuable radio link, he was able to arrange supply drops from the air for two of the largest groups of escaped POW who were in hiding at Montorio Romano and Nerola some miles north of Rome. Four separate drops were made which relieved the strain of smuggling out of Rome large quantities of stores for those in hiding.

Losena's radio also facilitated three successful evacuations of POW concentrated near the Adriatic beaches, but unfortunately he broke the elementary rule of never transmitting from the same place more than once, and he was eventually caught. 'The lesson of the gallant Italian was taken to heart,' Derry commented afterwards, 'and thereafter secret radio operators working in Rome – in time there were four – sent each message from a different place, often working from park benches while apparently making love to a girl.'

It says much for Germany's deteriorating situation in the war that Derry also gained much help from the First and Second secretaries of the collaborationist Vichy French Ambassador, who were ardent supporters of de Gaulle; and from Blon Kiernan, the young daughter of the ambassador of what was meant to be the strictly neutral country of Eire. Other helpers came from underground organisations operated by Yugoslavs, both Royalist and Communist, Italian Communists, and Greek exiles. Eventually all these groups were looking to Derry, as the senior Allied representative, for guidance and leadership so that he came to be what he called 'the mandatory leader of a unique underground army – or, as I preferred to think of it, the honorary president of a sort of United Nations conglomeration of "kindred societies".'

By Christmas 1943, some three weeks after its three new 'billeting officers' had joined it, the number of POW that the Rome Organisation was helping to shelter had exceeded 2,000. Despite Derry's best efforts to keep them out of the capital, about 80 of them were hidden in forty different 'safe' houses in Rome itself – though a percentage were in transit until hiding-places outside Rome could be found.

There was also at least one ex-POW in Rome, an English army officer named John Miller, who knew nothing at all of the organisation at that time. He was being sheltered by an Italian family who had found temporary refuge in a village close to where Miller had jumped from the train that was taking him to Germany. The family had sheltered him and taken him with them when they moved back to their Rome apartment in November. But it wasn't until the following May that Miller first heard about Derry and received the funds from him that saved the family from complete starvation. The contact came about when the grandmother of the family mentioned Miller while making her confession to a Polish priest in St Peter's. The priest told her that Miller must write a letter to the British Minister to the Vatican and that she must deliver it to him the next day. This was done, and a reply from Derry told Miller to stay where he was, and concluded: 'I am sending you 6,000 lire. Let me have a photograph and I will try to send you some documents.'

Through their efficient network of informers the Germans had been aware for some time that an organisation existed to hide escaped POW, and after Christmas they began to clamp down. In the Arde Valley, where as many as 600 had been hiding at one time, the police arrested eighteen Italians who had helped shelter them, and rewards were offered for information about the origins of the money that was being supplied to them. In Rome the nightly curfew was imposed from 7 p.m. instead of 11 p.m., and for the first time it became impossible to reach the sanctuary of the German College without passing through a check-point.

Then, on 8 January 1944 a series of betrayals led to raids on several of the 'safe' houses and Pollak, Furman, one of the RAMC doctors, eleven other escapers and several '*padrones*' were arrested. From now on Derry made sure that his helpers only knew the location of the few 'cells' they looked after, the whole network being known only to Derry, O'Flaherty and Simpson.

Now the Germans struck another blow. The German Ambassador warned O'Flaherty that he knew of his activities and that they must cease. O'Flaherty laughed this off, but then the Vatican Secretariat, which the Irish priest had to take seriously, also warned him not to continue. Continue he did, but from then on he delegated all his visits outside Vatican territory to priests who were not being so closely watched.

The Germans knew that Derry, under his *nom de guerre*, was also involved, and demanded his removal from the College. Osborne's solution was to hide Derry in the British Legation without the knowledge of the Vatican authorities. It was no use having him officially interned, the British Minister explained to Derry, because the Germans knew all about the activities of 'Patrick Derry', and probably suspected that he was really a senior British officer. If an extra British internee took up residence in the Vatican after 'Patrick Derry' vanished the Germans would soon put two and two together, and that could well cause the British Legation serious trouble.

Derry, reluctant as he was to curtail his freedom, saw the sense of what the British Minister had said. He would be able to direct the organisation from inside the Vatican, which he could not do if he was in hiding in the capital, so on 13 January 1944 he moved out of O'Flaherty's bed sitting-room into the British Legation.

By mid-January Italy was in the grip of the worst winter for many years. This made it all but impossible for POW to make their way south through to the Allied lines – which were now static – and encouraged them to leave their exposed hiding-places and try their luck in Rome. The added influx and unremitting pressure by the Gestapo, not only on the Rome Organisation but on various groups of dissidents with which it was associated, brought about more raids on billets, including the Lucidis' apartment where Simpson was staying. Simpson narrowly escaped arrest by pretending to be a half-witted nephew, but he continued to take the most outrageous risks which were sometimes but not always justified.

On one occasion he was alone in a bar when a group of Germans, including the famous heavyweight boxer, Max Schmeling, entered. Knowing that if he walked out the Germans would regard it as the act of an unfriendly Italian – and knowing that their suspicions would be equally aroused if he continued to sit alone in silence – Simpson called them over and offered them a drink. This was gladly accepted, the alcohol flowed, and before long they were all gathered round the piano singing popular songs, Simpson being the life and soul of the party. The Germans invited Simpson to eat with them, but deciding enough was enough, he made his excuses and left.

On that occasion such calculated bravado probably kept Simpson at liberty, but on another, when he could not resist greeting in the street the Fascist adjutant of a prison camp in which he had been held, it could have been the end of him. The man was walking along with a pretty girl on his arm and Simpson went up to him, offered him his hand, and asked 'Remember me? I was one of your guests at Chieti.' The startled Fascist refused to shake hands and demanded to know why Simpson didn't think he would have him arrested immediately. 'You are an officer and a gentleman,' Simpson replied blithely. 'You could never bring yourself to take advantage of a social meeting like this.' Simpson had judged the conceit of his man well. Aware that the eyes of his girl friend were on him, the Fascist merely warned him to be more careful in future – which no doubt is what Derry did, in rather more forceful terms, when he eventually heard about the encounter.

The incorrigible O'Flaherty was another who was not always bound by caution. On one occasion, to relieve the boredom of Major-General Gambier-Parry, Derry's most senior escapee, the Irish priest took the General to a reception in honour of the Pope's birthday, which was packed with German officers, and introduced him as an Irish doctor.

When Derry heard of this he was horrified. 'At the first opportunity I took the Monsignor to task, telling him quite frankly that I considered that he had taken an unwarrantable risk. "Ah, the poor fellow needed a breath of fresh air," he replied simply. "He's been cooped up for weeks. Not good for him, you know."

'"Now look, Monsignor," I said earnestly, "you know damn well I can't give him orders. He's a General, and if he chooses to go out and get himself recaptured there isn't much I can do about it. But I have every reason for wanting you to stay in circulation, and, Heaven knows, you've attracted quite enough attention already. I do beg you to be as cautious as you possibly can, at least until the German interest in you has died down a bit."

'"Never fear, me boy," said the Monsignor, treating me to one of his vast, room-filling grins.'

But Derry did fear, and in the end O'Flaherty agreed to be more discreet. In March the General was moved to a new 'billet' which gave him more freedom. He became a 'patient' at a hospital run by nuns at San Stefano Rotondo where he was able to exercise in the grounds, and remained there until Rome was liberated.

The Allied landings at Anzio on 22 January which had Rome as their objective brought temporary hope to Derry and his organisation, but these too, like the main advance, were soon bogged down by determined German resistance.

On 25 January Furman smuggled out a note from his Rome gaol to tell Derry that all British prisoners were being moved to camps in Germany. Derry feared that he had seen the last of one of his most valuable aides. But within three weeks Furman was back in Rome. He had escaped from the train taking him north and was soon back to his duties as a 'billeting officer'.

Pollak also returned in due course having had a very close brush with death. After his arrest he was unable to establish his identity as a POW. The Gestapo, knowing that he was not British, accused him of being a Jew and he was then charged with being a spy. A firing-squad seemed unavoidable, but one morning, on his way to the court where he was being tried, the Palestinian encountered a group of British POW whose officer knew him and was able to establish that he had been in Chieti prison camp. So instead of being sentenced to death Pollak was just bundled into a train bound for Germany, but just then the RAF bombed the station and he managed to escape.

The months that followed were exceptionally difficult for those in hiding and for those who were looking after them. The pressure of raids and check-ups by the Gestapo and their Italian Fascist helpers was constant; and once the Anzio landings had taken place Rome was filled with German infantry. This made it even more hazardous for those in hiding to leave their billets, and led to frustration and impatience, and not infrequently to drunkenness and other misdemeanours. Derry, incarcerated in the Vatican, attempted to maintain discipline by sending messages to those who had been reported to him as misbehaving. Mostly his rebukes were mild, pointing out to those who misbehaved that they were endangering the families they were staying with as well as themselves, but occasionally he had to be severe. To one offender he wrote: 'I have received a full report on your atrocious behaviour during the last week. I have made out a full report which will be sent to the proper authorities. You are to get out of Rome at once. Immediately after the liberation of Rome by the Allies, you will have to answer charges.'

By March Derry had 3,423 escapers and evaders on his files – including 400 Russians to whom help was given by a Russian priest appointed by O'Flaherty – and those in the capital had increased to 180. This put an enormous strain on the black market operations for food and clothing, and expenditure escalated alarmingly (Derry was always fearful that the money would dry up).

Footwear was in especially short supply until May discovered that a building which backed on to the garden of the Irish Legation had been acquired by the Germans for repairing boots. At night the building was unguarded and after a means of entering had been found, quantities of boots were regularly taken – never too many so that they would not be missed – and hurled over the wall into a secluded part of the Legation's garden from where they were later collected.

Despite the pressures, the organisation recovered from its earlier setbacks and by the early spring was functioning well. The better weather allowed some POW to escape into Switzerland, and others joined Partisan bands who were adequately supplied with food and clothing. But on 22 March 1944 another disaster occurred. This time it was precipitated by the Communists who had various factions in the city and whose primary objective in life was sabotage. Mostly they attacked industrial targets but on that day they had planted a large bomb in a rubbish cart which exploded as a large squad of German soldiers was marching past it. Thirty-two soldiers were killed and many more were wounded.

Derry knew the Germans would wreak terrible vengeance for this act, and though their search would not be directed against escapers the Rome Organisation was now so closely linked with all the various groups of dissidents in Rome that some of the 'billets' were bound to be compromised. He sent out warning messages for all 'billets' to be cleared. Escapers might have to spend an uncomfortable night or two in public parks or gardens, but at least those looking after them would be in the clear and would escape German vengeance.

The Germans did indeed react strongly and swiftly. They brought forward the curfew to 5.30 p.m. and shot anyone who disobeyed it. But instead of an intensification of the raids and round-ups Derry had been expecting – they came later – the Germans took at random ten prisoners from the city's gaols for each soldier who had been killed. The victims were a motley collection, ranging from prostitutes to political prisoners. They included the radio operator, Umberto Losena, and five of Derry's Italian helpers who were awaiting trial. They were all taken to the Ardeatine caves on the outskirts of Rome where the Germans machine-gunned them to death before blowing the entrance to the caves.

After this massacre the security screw in Rome was further tightened. All males aged between 15 and 70 were rounded up to undertake forced labour outside Rome, large numbers of extra German security troops were drafted into the city, and – in what Derry called the worst development of all – the most vicious elements of the Italian Fascist movement were given free rein. They were, wrote Derry, 'formed into a special security gang, with full German support, and powers overriding those of the police and Republican Guard ... This Fascist neo-Gestapo, answerable to no judicial authority, and consisting largely of brutal, sadistic morons, rapidly established itself as the most terrifying body in Rome. It set up its headquarters in a block of flats, and within a week all the other tenants, unable to stand the screams of the victims of its "interrogations", quit the building.'

Derry's helpers were now in constant danger, but the Ardeatine caves massacre, as it came to be called, did have one positive effect: the Italians, never fond of their one-time allies, turned totally against the Germans which led to many more volunteers for the Rome Organisation. For instance, it almost certainly prompted two Italians to start providing invaluable intelligence, a stroke of luck that Derry badly needed. John May was approached by a man who said that he knew someone who worked in the Questura, the headquarters of the SS and the Fascist Carabinieri, and that for an appropriate sum would pass on the HQ's Routine Orders. Derry was frankly disbelieving, but he and May agreed that it was worth risking some of the organisation's precious lire.

To Derry's astonishment copies of the Orders – which included the proposed locations of the nightly routine raids – came through regularly and helped him to second-guess all efforts by the Gestapo and the Fascists to round up hidden escapers. While it did not give those in hiding complete protection – the Gestapo could turn up anywhere at any time if someone had been denounced to them – it certainly prevented many being recaptured.

However, those in the areas to be raided had to be moved to other billets immediately. 'These evacuations called for some fast thinking,' Derry wrote, 'since the routine orders and detailed raids scheduled for the same evening were not published until midday. Then it took time to cover the devious route from the Questura to the British Legation, and the vital information did not reach me until quite late in the afternoon. Orders for raids usually related to a fairly broad area, and I had to rush through our card-indexes and maps to find out if any of our "cells" were in danger, for with the increasing number of new billets, and the sheer number in occupation in the city, there was too much detail to be committed to memory. If billets were found to be in danger areas there still remained the physical task of warning the occupants and arranging evacuations. This was complicated by the security precaution that any one messenger should know of no more than a handful of "cells". Consequently, we sometimes found that to get warnings to four or five billets quite close to each other, we had to trace and dispatch as many messengers.'

Besides providing the Routine Orders, the informer in the Questura began supplying intelligence which showed that many of the raids on 'cells' and random arrests which had been put down to sheer bad luck had in fact been the result of denunciations. The same source confirmed Derry's suspicions that the Germans were now sending out some of their agents dressed as priests who would make contact with escapees with promises to take them to safe hiding-places. The principal informer was soon found to be a man who had been part of O'Flaherty's original organisation.

But worse was to come. This informer knew enough about O'Flaherty and his circle of helpers for the Germans to complain to the Vatican authorities with the result that two of the Monsignor's most useful assistants were confined to their religious houses. Worse still, on 18 April Simpson was arrested by the Gestapo and all enquiries about him failed to discover his whereabouts. He simply disappeared.

Then in May the Gestapo arrested one of O'Flaherty's helpers, Father Anselmo Musters (code-named 'Dutchpa' because he came from the Netherlands). He was dragged off to Gestapo headquarters in the Via Tasso, interrogated, stripped, and beaten up, the Gestapo being convinced that they had captured a British officer in disguise. For three weeks the priest stolidly maintained his innocence under intense questioning. At the end of that time he was thrown into a dark cell in isolation for two weeks before being put on a train for Germany from which he managed to escape and return to Rome.

Simpson's place was taken by Renzo Lucidi who dropped all his business commitments to take on the task of looking after Simpson's 'cells'. His wife, Adrienne, stood in for Furman when it was too dangerous for the British 'billeting officer' to go out on the streets, even though Furman had altered his appearance by dyeing his hair and shaving off his moustache.

By now the streets had become highly dangerous because the Italians, knowing that liberation was near, could not help but vent their hatred on the occupiers. Sabotage and assassination multiplied and this brought reprisals from the security forces, making it so hazardous to hide escapers that quite a number of '*padrones*' begged that their guests be removed. Derry, of course, complied with their requests, but it created an extra strain on the organisation which was already stretched to its limits.

There were, during this time, several close shaves with the German security services. Perhaps the closest was experienced by Flight-Lieutenant E. Garrard-Cole who had been in hiding in Rome for some months. One day two uniformed Germans challenged him after he had left a tram and though he produced his false documents they ordered him to accompany him to the Via Tasso. With one each side of him the RAF officer had little choice but to obey, but he knew about the Via Tasso and had no intention of ever entering the Gestapo building if he could possibly help it.

As the trio marched towards the Via Tasso, Garrard-Cole noted that his captors did not look particularly bright and that they were armed only with pistols which were well secured in their holsters. As they were passing close by the building in which the Lucidis lived, he tripped one of them up, helped him on his way with a rabbit punch, and ran. A bullet whistled past him but he dodged into the apartment block and hid behind the door as the Germans rushed in and up the stairs. In minutes the whole area was swarming with Fascist police and Gestapo but by then Renzo had immobilised the lift and had hidden Garrard-Cole in the small compartment on the roof which housed the lift's mechanism.

'Given a change of raincoat and hat,' Derry wrote, 'Garrard-Cole eventually emerged from the building and made his way past two or three groups of Germans searching for him. He was hand-in-hand with the Lucidis' small son, Maurice, who chattered continuously in Italian to his "father" all the way to safety. It was an example of something we had always believed: that if the Germans were told to look for a tall man in a light raincoat and dark hat, they would never think of stopping a tall man in a dark raincoat with a light hat.'

Such was the strain on the organisation that towards the end of April Derry had to ban any more escapers from entering Rome and advised any who arrived to leave immediately. O'Flaherty's room, so long the outside headquarters of the organisation, was suddenly cut off when German complaints closed all outside approaches to the College.

For a while there was no communication at all until John May was able to persuade the Swiss Guards to allow one or two of those working outside, including Furman, to visit their guardroom next to the gate. The guards agreed that when any of these selected individuals turned up they would contact the British Legation on the internal telephone system. May would then go down to the guardroom – the limit of movement allowed him – and could talk to the visitor in relative privacy. This meant that money could continue to be sent out and that Derry and Furman could exchange information and instructions.

Simpson was at last traced to the Regina Coeli gaol where he had been incarcerated under the name of William O'Flynn which he used in his false documents. O'Flynn was meant to have been employed in the Vatican, but when inquiries were made by the Germans the Vatican naturally denied any knowledge of him. This put Simpson and those who wanted to extract him in an extremely difficult position. The only hope was to prove that he was an escaper, but the fact that he was using an assumed name and was in civilian clothes was sufficient excuse for the Germans to shoot him as a spy, something that had already happened to a number of POW who had been caught in civilian clothes without proper identification.

A deal was struck with the head of the Fascist security forces in Rome who wanted his family moved out of harm's way, and Simpson and a number of other prisoners were left behind as the Germans began to withdraw from the city. They were all able to gain their freedom when their Italian guards deserted their posts, leaving the cell doors open.

On 4 June the first American units entered the city, at which time the organi-sation had on its books a total of 3,925 escapers and evaders. A total of 1,695 of these were British, 896 South African, 429 Russian, 425 Greek, 185 American, and the remainder coming from as many as twenty other countries.

It is worth recording that O'Flaherty, who died in 1963, was a priest who would endeavour to help anyone who was in trouble. The head of Rome SS, a Colonel Herbert Kappler, who had so often tried to ensnare O'Flaherty during those months when the Germans were in occupation, was in due course sentenced to life imprisonment by the Allies for the Ardeatine caves massacre. Apparently the only person who ever visited him in gaol was – O'Flaherty. And it was the Irish priest who pleaded first with the Allies, and then with the Italian authorities, that Kappler should be released. After six years he was freed, and in March 1959 O'Flaherty baptised him into the Roman Catholic church.

11

THE LITTLE CYCLONE

One of the war's first, and most successful, escape and evasion organisations in north-west Europe was never controlled by MI9 at all, but by a 25-year-old Belgian girl, Andrée de Jongh.

Initially the line, which saved more than 800 Allied servicemen from possible capture, took in hand some of the numerous soldiers who had escaped captivity after the Fall of France, and during the course of the war it also helped a number of escapers from POW camps and agents on the run from the Gestapo. But it specialised in returning aircrew shot down over western occupied Europe and tried, as the authors of *MI9* succinctly wrote, 'to create a basket of sub-agents into which airmen could safely fall, and out of which they could be safely tipped on to a reliable route home'.

The COMET Line, so called by its founder to indicate the speed with which evaders could be returned to their homeland, achieved some remarkable results. On one notable occasion, in late 1942, the Line's members picked up, hid, and escorted over the Pyrenees, the entire crew of a bomber who found themselves safely in Gibraltar exactly seven days after they had baled out near the Dutch–Belgian border.

By the end of 1943, when the number of raids began to increase substantially as the hugely powerful US Eighth Army Air Force got into top gear, many of those living in the Low Countries and France became experts in the art of what was known as 'parachute-watching', which meant scanning the skies for any aircrew who had baled out and then beating the Germans in the race to retrieve them.

'Whenever a giant thrumming in the sky by day revealed that a large American bomber force was passing near,' wrote the authors of *MI9*, 'thousands of people would go out of doors to watch. The hardiest among them took bicycles, and perhaps a spare garment or two (if they had them: there was a fearful shortage of clothing and shoes), in the bicycle basket or over the shoulder or simply worn. If parachutes were seen, bicyclists would hurry towards their presumed point of impact, in the hope that the parachutists were Americans and could be spirited out of sight or at least out of flying-gear before any Germans arrived.'

This resourcefulness in sheltering downed airmen is confirmed by George Watt whose B-17 Flying Fortress was shot down over Belgium in November 1943. Eight of the crew of ten baled out. Five of them were captured immediately, but the remaining three were hidden by civilians and eventually passed to members of the COMET Line.

Watt, when he hit the ground, was immediately surrounded by villagers and had some trouble in shaking them off as he ran for a suitable hiding-place to which he was guided by one of them. Later, while still crouching in a ditch, he was visited by two Belgians, one of whom spoke passable English. 'He told me that I had escaped not a minute too soon. Immediately after I had left the spot, the "Black Brigades" (Belgian pro-Nazis) had arrived and asked everyone where I had gone. No one knew. Someone volunteered that I had run off in the direction opposite [to] the one in which I had fled.'

Within days Watt was spirited away to Brussels and thence to Paris, and on 20 December 1943 he and another member of the crew were back in London reporting to 8 USAAF Command HQ. He is listed in Cecile Joan's book, *Comète: Une histoire d'une ligne d'évasion*, as the 60th Allied airman to be rescued by the line.

It was not possible to give RAF crews, who bombed their targets at night, the express service some American flyers experienced – darkness and strict curfews saw to that – but if they were sensible and hid themselves quickly they had as much chance as the Americans of being whisked to safety when daylight came.

The feats of rescue that the COMET Line achieved were not only invaluable to the war effort – trained aircrew were a scarce commodity – but increased the morale of those flying bomber raids over enemy-occupied territory, for it was encouraging to know that if one was shot down there was at least a 50–50 chance of escaping capture and returning to England.

Nearly all those Andrée de Jongh recruited were in her age group. Nicknamed the 'Little Cyclone' by her father, the headmaster of a Brussels school, because of her prodigious energy as a child, she was known to everyone as Dédée. She was one of the most extraordinary characters that the Second World War produced and her bravery and resourcefulness – she made the perilous double crossing of the Pyrenees no less than sixteen times – was a source of inspiration to all who met her. Her biographer Airey Neave wrote of her as 'a woman of true greatness', and for many years after the war she continued to work for others.

In 1940 Dédée was living at her home in Brussels, and when Belgium was invaded on 10 May she was working as a nurse in a hospital which contained many wounded Allied personnel. Inspired by the courage of Nurse Edith Cavell, who had been shot by the Germans during the First World War for harbouring British servicemen, in early 1941 she and some young friends began hiding British soldiers and airmen, and young Belgians too, who wished to get to England and continue the fight. At first she did not tell her family, but soon they were all involved, her father Frédéric becoming a linchpin of the organisation.

That spring Dédée made her first journey along the Line. Helped by a young Belgian named Arnold de Pé, she took an Englishwoman who wanted to avoid internment, and ten Belgians being hunted by the Gestapo, to the Spanish border. To avoid German frontier controls they left their train at the Franco–Belgian border town of Quiévran and walked through fields to Blanc-

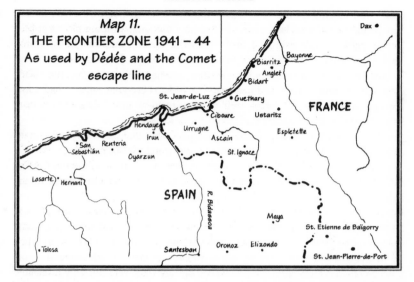

Map 11.
THE FRONTIER ZONE 1941 – 44
As used by Dédée and the Comet
escape line

Misseron in France where they caught a train to Lille, and then another to Corbie on the Somme. The normal river crossings were strictly controlled so, to continue southwards, a boat had been hidden for them by one of their helpers who lived nearby. But they were unable to retrieve it and had to swim across before resuming their journey by train.

Eventually, the party arrived at the house of Dédée's aunt, Elvire de Greef, in the village of Anglet between St-Jean-de-Luz and Bayonne near the Spanish border. Elvire, who was known to all as Tante Go, had been forewarned of Dédée's plans and had willingly agreed to help her. She found a professional Basque smuggler named Thomas to take the party across the Pyrenees and into Spain. This, for an exorbitant price, he did, but the party was subsequently arrested and interned. This made Dédée determined that in the future she would help her evaders to freedom and not into an internment camp. So when she returned to Tante Go in August 1941 with a British soldier and two Belgian officers she decided to accompany Thomas across the Pyrenees to deliver her charges personally to the British Consulate at Bilbao.

The Consul was away so Dédée was seen by the Vice-Consul, Arthur Dean. He listened to her story with some astonishment, finding it hard to believe that this slightly built, if determined-looking, girl had managed such a difficult crossing of the mountains. She told him that she and her father were in the process of establishing a series of 'safe' houses in Brussels, Paris and the Spanish frontier zone to form an escape line for British service personnel. What she needed was money to fund the line.

At a subsequent meeting the Consul asked how much it would cost to bring a man from Brussels and Dédée replied: '6,000 Belgian francs to St-Jean-de-Luz, plus 1,400 pesetas for the mountain guides'. The Consul said he thought this rather expensive but he would refer her request to the relevant authorities at the British embassy in Madrid, and Dédée said she would return in three or four weeks.

But Dédée and her helpers were playing a dangerous game. Before she had crossed the Pyrenees that first time, Arnold de Pé had been arrested and her father, Frédéric, had had his first brush with the Gestapo. For the Germans knew that British servicemen were being hidden and smuggled out of Nazi-occupied France, and that someone answering Dédée's description was involved (though they may have been searching for one of Dédée's couriers who looked like her).

The Gestapo had questioned Frédéric closely. He denied knowledge of his daughter's whereabouts, but was forced to reveal where he taught, remembering as he did so that he had left a pile of false identity and ration cards in his desk. The Gestapo got nothing more out of him and fortunately failed to search his school, but it was now much too dangerous for Dédée to work from Brussels. She moved to the house of a helper who lived at Valenciennes and later to Paris.

In October Dédée returned to Bilbao, taking with her this time two soldiers of the 51st Highland Division who had evaded capture when the division had surrendered at St Valéry the previous June. In the meantime the Consul at Bilbao had sent a report of his meeting with Dédée to Michael Creswell, one of the embassy attachés in Madrid who worked for MI9 under the code-name 'Monday'. He had concluded his report by saying that she could be a German stooge but that he himself did not believe this.

Creswell reported back to London where Claude Dansey of MI6, who had overall control of MI9's activities, was at first convinced that Dédée *was* a stooge, though it may be that he did not like the idea of a woman running an escape line. It was only after rigorous checks had confirmed that Dédée was genuine that he was persuaded to change his mind. His change of heart was probably prompted by the interrogation of the three men she had brought with her from Belgium for they spoke of her 'incomparable courage and firmness'. So when she re-appeared in Bilbao on 17 October Creswell said he was prepared to fund her Line (as did the Belgian government-in-exile later). Aircrew were, he explained to her, priceless assets and they should have the highest priority. Dédée agreed, but insisted that control of the Line remain in her hands; other than providing the necessary funds, the British were not to interfere. Creswell readily concurred and the two of them had soon set up a routine. Dédée would warn Tante Go when she was bringing a party of evaders south and Tante Go would pass this to Creswell by coded message. Creswell would drive his Bentley to Bilbao or San Sebastián from Madrid, bringing money for Dédée and anything else he thought she might need.

From the start the de Greef family was an essential link in the COMET Line. Tante Go's husband, Fernand, worked as a trusted interpreter at the local German headquarters which enabled him to steal or counterfeit official stamps for identity cards and passes; her daughter Janine escorted evaders when they arrived at St-Jean-de-Luz to 'safe' houses in the town; and her son Freddy acted as her courier. The family also had living with them an Englishman named Albert Edward Johnson who had stayed behind in France when the country surrendered. Known simply as 'B', his bravery and resourcefulness in escorting evaders across the Pyrenees made him a valued member of the line.

Dédée's methods initially caused some doubt and misunderstanding among the more senior members of MI9, but they soon came to admit grudgingly that they were effective. For one thing her choice of couriers was impeccable. She always recruited from her acquaintances young men and women who were discreet and inconspicuous, and who were quick-witted enough to have plausible explanations for the evaders they were escorting. Then too, the Basque guide she now used, Florentino Goicoechea, charged a reasonable price for his services. He spoke only Basque – *doucement, doucement, espère un poco*, and *tais-toi* were the only foreign phrases he knew – and despite a fondness for alcohol he proved totally reliable.

'Florentino's knowledge of the mountains was fabulous,' wrote Dédée's biographer. 'He was able to find his way even when under the influence of copious quantities of cognac. He knew every path, every defile. He scented danger like a wild animal. His tremendous physical strength enabled him to withstand the rigours of constant journeys, summer and winter, from 1941 until the liberation of France in 1944. If there was fog, damp and choking, blotting out every landmark, Florentino found the path. He would stop for a moment in his tracks, tapping the hard ground with his *espadrilles*. When he had found his way, he moved off at a great pace, with his party stumbling and slipping behind him. Often they called after him to go more slowly. He mumbled with impatience and came back and collected them. Sometimes he stopped on the blackest night and marched to a tree-trunk or a rock. He alone saw it in the gloom. He searched rapidly and brought forth a pair of *espadrilles* or a bottle of cognac left there months before.'

Any doubts the British may have had about Dédée soon vanished when in the following months she began to arrive in Spain with evading airmen, and a routine was soon established for escorting them to safety. The evaders would either go by train to St-Jean-de-Luz or would leave the train at Bayonne and ride there by bicycle. After being collected from their 'safe' houses they went on foot to a farmhouse at Urrugne where Florentino would be waiting for them. There they were prepared for the 20-hour journey. Each was given a stout stick; instructions that they must march in single file and in absolute silence until they were in the foothills; and the principal landmarks along the way were pointed out to them on a map in case any of them fell behind and got lost.

Once over the foothills of the Pyrenees the party would go down into the valley of the River Bidassoa across which they would wade at the point that marked the Franco–Spanish border. There was a bridge, but this was dangerous because it was guarded, and it was only used as a last resort if the river was in full flood. Florentino and Dédée would lead the party over one by one, gripping their hands in the waist-high water. Sometimes they formed a human chain, gripping hands to avoid being swept away.

The greatest moment of danger came when crossing the road which ran along-side the Spanish side of the river and ascending the steep slope on the other side where one could easily be spotted by a Spanish border patrol. At the top of the slope the party would rest, and food and drink would be dispensed from Florentino's rucksack before the final leg of the trek began.

By now all but the very fittest of the evaders would be close to exhaustion, but Dédée's example and strength kept them going. As dawn began to break they would reach a farmhouse where the evaders were fed and had their clothes dried while they slept. But there was no sleep for Dédée. She changed into a skirt and blouse and walked five kilometres across the fields to the town of Renteria to take the tram to San Sebastián. There she would spend the day resting in the flat of a friend before returning that evening to the farmhouse in the friend's car. The evaders were picked up and the party would motor back along the main road to San Sebastián until they saw Creswell's Bentley with its CD plates parked by the roadside. The evaders would be bundled into it and whisked away to the British Consulate. Dédée would then rejoin Florentino so that they could recross the frontier under cover of darkness.

In the early days of the Line, Dédée did not find it so easy to follow Creswell's instructions to give top priority to aircrew. They were hard to find because not many raids were being mounted by British bombers, and people hiding crews that had been shot down would not relinquish them to anyone they did not know. To overcome this problem it was arranged that the BBC would insert a message among those broadcast to all Resistance fighters after the nine o'clock news every evening. 'Wait until you hear *la plume de ma tante est noire*', those secreting aircrew were told. 'That will show you that we are genuine.' This established the trust that was needed and the trickle of airmen steadily increased as the months passed.

So successful did the COMET Line become at spiriting aircrew from under the noses of the Germans that Göring, head of the Luftwaffe, personally ordered the Line's destruction. In February 1942 – the same month that the German commanders-in-chief in France and Belgium announced that anyone hiding or assisting Allied escapers and evaders would be executed – the Luftwaffe's secret police began an intensive search for the Line's leader. Dédée's elder sister and three of Frédéric's principal helpers were arrested, and Frédéric was forced to flee to Paris.

This setback seemed to spell the finish of the Brussels end of the Line, but in April Jean Greindl, a 36-year-old Belgian aristocrat, assumed command of it. Code-named 'Nemo', Greindl ran a Swedish Red Cross canteen in Brussels which fed and clothed destitute children, work which provided ideal cover for running the line. He set up its headquarters there – evaders became known as *les enfants* – and established centres at Ghent, Namur, Liège and Hasselt to which airmen who had been shot down in the surrounding areas could be brought by local sub-agents.

In July Greindl met Dédée for the first time when she visited the Belgian capital briefly. By this time Airey Neave, who had escaped from the German high security Colditz Castle early in 1942, had been in charge of MI9's Room 900 – the operational centre for keeping contact with those running escape lines – for only two months. He had followed the events in Brussels with great anxiety, and was much relieved when Greindl took control there. Greindl evidently had a strong character and a cool head and there was every reason to believe that the Brussels end of the Line would survive.

Neave was less certain about the Paris organisation where Frédéric had set up his headquarters in the rue Oudinot and where a villa at St-Maur had been rented to hide airmen waiting to be escorted south. The dangers that Frédéric and his helpers were running were intense – the number of German agents trying to infiltrate the escape lines was increasing as fast as the genuine evaders who were using them – and after the near collapse of the Line in Brussels Neave tried, unsuccessfully, to persuade both Frédéric and Dédée to escape to England while they could. Both refused and during the remainder of 1942 Dédée and Johnson took it in turns to take *les enfants* into Spain. Dédée made nine such journeys and Johnson eight, and a new recruit, a 23-year-old Belgian aristocrat named Baron Jean-François Nothomb, alias 'Franco', made one.

These journeys were always hazardous. On one occasion two German soldiers fired on Dédée and her party as they approached the border; on another she cut her legs badly when she and Florentino were ambushed by Spanish guards; and on a third she was stopped by French gendarmes after returning from crossing into Spain. On all three occasions she escaped, but arrests and deaths did occur. The most tragic of these was, as will be seen, the loss of Count Antoine d'Ursel.

Neave was right in his assessment of Greindl's character and for a while the Brussels end of the Line worked well. But then the inevitable happened and it was penetrated by German agents pretending to be evaders. The courage of those arrested in resisting the Gestapo's torture and beatings saved Greindl for the time being but there were mass arrests and one of Greindl's new helpers, Victor, was gunned down in the street.

Dédée now realised that the Gestapo's net was closing on her father, for the Germans had long suspected him of running the entire Line. She insisted that he escape to England and reluctantly he agreed. Just before they travelled south in mid-January 1943, Greindl and two of his associates arrived in Paris. He had come to tell Dédée that after the recent wave of arrests in Brussels it was too dangerous for him to continue and that a successor must be found.

'The British do not understand how difficult it is to persuade our helpers and guides to go on,' he told Dédée. 'People have heard of poor Victor's death. They know many hostages have been taken. Over one hundred people arrested in two days!' Dédée replied that London was delighted with their work. 'Perhaps, but they do not understand the risks that we run.' 'That is not the point,' Dédée said forcefully. 'We have got to go on, and the reason is this. The numbers of airmen coming back are now so large that they are helping the morale of the aircrew. When a man returns alive and safe he is a living proof to his friends that over here there are people to help them if they, too, are shot down. It gives them heart on their raids.'

This was Dédée at her inspirational best. It was just what Greindl wanted to hear and Dédée spoke with such fierce conviction that the three Belgians were convinced. They knew now how essential their work was and Greindl agreed to continue. He would take extra precautions but he would continue. Dédée left him with no illusions. 'You realise', she said at the close of their conversation, 'that there are nine chances out of ten that you will not come out of this alive?' Greindl shrugged his shoulders, not dismissing her statement but accepting it. They shook hands and he left.

A few days later Dédée and her father left for the south with three airmen, but when they arrived the weather was too bad to permit Frédéric to accompany his daughter across the Pyrenees, though the rest of the party left for the farmhouse near Urrugne. But the storm was too bad even for Dédée and Florentino, and Dédée and the pilots remained in the farmhouse overnight while Florentino returned to his home in nearby Ciboure. It was well for him that he did so for the following day the farmhouse was raided by French gendarmes. It is not known who had tipped them off, but the chief suspect is a local mountain guide Dédée had occasionally used before dismissing him for suspected dishonesty.

Dédée, the three pilots, and the owner of the farmhouse, Francia Uzandizaga, were all arrested and more arrests followed when one of the pilots broke down under interrogation. Dédée was imprisoned at Bayonne and then Biarritz and finally at the notorious Fresnes prison outside Paris. Tante Go organised several attempts to rescue her but they all failed. At first Dédée told her interrogators that the headquarters of the Line was at Bordeaux and that she was just a local courier, but when she realised that the Gestapo were edging ever closer to her father she decided to tell the truth. Initially, her captors were as sceptical of her story as the British had been. How could such a young, slight girl have the strength and organisational powers to run so large a secret network as the COMET Line had become?

Altogether Dédée was interrogated nineteen times by the Luftwaffe's secret police, and twice by the Gestapo. Ironically, what possibly saved her life was the bitter enmity between these two organisations. To spite the Gestapo, the Luftwaffe sent her to Germany where she became 'lost' in the concentration camp system.

Shortly after Dédée's arrest Airey Neave managed, after many delays, to have the Line's first wireless operator, Sergeant Henri Decat, parachuted into Belgium.

He arrived safely but his first message spelt out yet another disaster for the Line. 'Nemo (Jean Greindl) arrested sixth of February,' it said. Then Decat went off the air and London never heard from him again. In April 1943 his body was found. He had been murdered, though by whom nobody knows.

For a while the Brussels end of the Line was broken, but then 'Nemo' was replaced by the Belgian aristocrat, Count Antoine d'Ursel, alias Jacques Cartier. He resumed the work of sending airmen down the line to Paris where Dédée's father had again taken command, determined now never to leave the continent while there was any chance of seeing his beloved daughter alive.

The week after Greindl's arrest, the southern end of the Line narrowly escaped two disasters. The first occurred when Nothomb and Johnson took into Spain Greindl's younger brother, now on the run from the Gestapo, and three airmen. The car in which they were being driven by a well-paid Spaniard was stopped by a patrol. Johnson and Greindl managed to escape, but Nothomb and the pilots were arrested. Nothomb told his captors that he, too, was an evading pilot. They accepted his story but some French pilots who shared his cell were not so easily convinced, and Nothomb spent an uncomfortable week in their company being treated as a German stooge. During that time Johnson managed to contact the British Consul at San Sebastián, and Nothomb and the pilots were eventually released.

Then, the following month, it was the turn of Tante Go and Johnson to be arrested when Tante Go decided they should both travel inland to find a new route across the Pyrenees because the coastal zone had become too dangerous. Together with a friend of Tante Go, who helped with the Line, they boarded a local train at Bayonne which would take them to Ustaritz some ten miles to the south. After about a quarter of an hour a German patrol entered their carriage and demanded their papers. The patrol became suspicious of Johnson's English appearance and accent and all three were arrested and taken to the frontier town of St-Jean-Pied-de-Port.

Tante Go was a formidable character who had always treated the Germans with total disdain, and she negotiated the release of herself and her two colleagues with a mixture of blackmail and bribes. When she explained to Johnson that he had been exchanged for a hamper of black-market food, he exclaimed indignantly: 'I thought I was worth more than that!' He was indeed, for he had personally taken 122 servicemen across the Pyrenees, but on 13 March he crossed into Spain for the fifteenth and final time, and was soon back in England.

In Paris Frédéric found a reliable new recruit, Madeleine Bouteloupt, and together they continued to escort the ever-increasing number of air force evaders across Paris to the Gare d'Austerlitz where Nothomb took over to escort them south. In April 1943 Frédéric recruited a new courier, a Belgian who called himself Jean Masson, to take evaders from Brussels to Paris. Masson appeared to be everything that was required of a man undertaking such dangerous work: he was efficient, discreet and bold. But he was a traitor whose cunning had enabled him to penetrate the security checks set up by the Line and, at the beginning of June,

Frédéric, Madeleine and three other helpers were arrested in Paris. Shortly afterwards many members of the Line in Brussels were also duped and then betrayed by him, though Antoine d'Ursel escaped arrest.

All through that summer d'Ursel was forced to lie low, but with more and more airmen being shot down over occupied territory he knew that the Line must at all costs be carried on. From his refuge he recruited two more Belgians who kept the flow of evaders moving south. D'Ursel remained in hiding until the end of the year. Then, determined to discuss the formation of a new line with the British, he travelled south and Nothomb took him into Spain.

Unfortunately for the party the indefatigable Florentino was ill, and the journey was a disaster. D'Ursel was nearly fifty years old and the Bidassoa, flowing high and fast and bitterly cold, was too much for him. He and one of the evaders were drowned, and the others were arrested by Spanish guards, though Nothomb and the guides he had hired escaped.

After Frédéric's arrest in Paris it had become too dangerous for Nothomb to pick up evaders from the Gare d'Austerlitz. Instead, they were taken to Bordeaux before changing to a local train to Dax, close to Bayonne. At Dax bicycles were waiting for evaders in the luggage office and, escorted by Nothomb, Janine, or by Tante Go herself, they were taken to Anglet to await their turn to cross the Pyrenees to safety.

This new system worked well, but when an American airman arrived who could not ride a bicycle it led to an incident which could have been disastrous if the quick-witted Nothomb had not reacted with his usual resourcefulness. The American was given a quick course in cycling and despite being very unsteady he was soon able to follow the others out of Dax. As the party rode along the dusty road to Bayonne they saw two German officers cycling stiffly towards them.

The sight of the Germans unnerved the American and he began to wobble. Nothomb shouted a warning but by now the American, zig-zagging from one side of the road to the other, had lost control of his machine. With horror Nothomb watched the airman as he was drawn towards the Germans like a magnet, and then there was a dreadful crash as the bicycles collided. All three riders fell in a heap and loud guttural swearing rent the air. Nothomb was off his bicycle in a flash and began helping the Germans to their feet, offering abject apologies for the behaviour of his colleague. Then he remembered the cognac bottle with which he bolstered the morale of those he was escorting, and produced it from his pocket. Luckily, it was almost empty and he held it up and said: 'Look what this fellow has drunk! All in one gulp!'

The Germans brushed the dust from their uniforms and glowered at the airman who stood rooted to the spot. 'You drunken fool,' Nothomb raved at him. 'Look what you have done. You deserve to be shot.' This seemed to have the desired effect on the Germans who laughed, remounted their bicycles and rode on.

Such narrow escapes were almost a daily occurrence and by September Nothomb was near to exhaustion. At the end of that month the British Consul at

Bilbao persuaded him that he must rest and it was agreed that he should go to Gibraltar for a conference with Airey Neave about the future of the Line. Neave tried to persuade Nothomb to go to England for a rest, but soon saw that this was a hopeless task.

'I studied this young Belgian aristocrat who had nearly rivalled Dédée in the number of men he had brought to freedom,' Neave later recorded, 'and whose conduct at the time of Frédéric de Jongh's arrest showed him to have nerves of steel. He was dark, rather Latin looking, and though pale and strained, very sure of himself. I knew that, like the others, he had an unshakeable faith in his mission and he would see it through to the bitter end.'

He told Nothomb that he was sending another wireless operator, Count Jacques Legrelle, alias 'Jérôme', to help the Line in Paris. Nothomb, remembering how strongly Dédée had felt about its independence, asked: 'It still remains a Belgian line? You are not trying to control it?' Neave assured him he was not. 'You must give the orders. We provide money and communications. We have always respected that since the days of Dédée.'

Next morning, when he shook hands with the brave Belgian, Neave instinctively knew that he would not see him again. He was right; after three more crossings which brought the number of men he had personally escorted to safety to 215 (only Dédée exceeded this number, taking across 218), Nothomb was arrested on 18 January 1944. By then Legrelle had also fallen into German hands. Both had been betrayed by Masson who was now masquerading as a genuine helper under the name Pierre Poulin, and only the courage of one of the Line's couriers, 20-year-old Micheline Dumon, alias 'Michou', stopped Masson from penetrating the southern part of the Line.

Michou – who looked and spoke like the 15-year-old schoolgirl her false identity card said she was – knew that there was a traitor in their midst, but who was he? Determined to find out she went to Fresnes prison where a friend of hers, a woman dentist named Martine, lay waiting to be interrogated by the Gestapo after being betrayed by Pierre Poulin. Michou approached the part of the prison that held women prisoners and shouted several times at the top of her voice: 'Martine! Who is the traitor? Who has betrayed you?' Her voice echoed against the grim prison walls. At first there was only silence, and then came Martine's reply, faint and ghostly: 'It is Pierre! It is Pierre!'

Michou turned and ran, but was caught by the prison guards. Arrested for communicating with a prisoner, she was taken before the prison governor. But her supposedly extreme youth saved her, and she was let off with a caution. She caught the next train to Bayonne and was able to warn Tante Go that Pierre was a traitor.

Despite the danger posed by Pierre, who knew her, Michou continued to serve as a courier, helping men across Paris, and between December 1943 and May 1944 she twice crossed the Pyrenees, taking with her ten airmen, before she was forced to flee to England. Altogether she was personally involved in the rescue of 150 air force personnel.

The intelligence file on Michou which is in the US National Archives shows how frequently she outwitted the Gestapo 'by suddenly enacting a tender, tearful love scene in a streetcar or on a station platform with some airman she had only known for an hour or two. Encountering such a scene, the embarrassed German agent would pass on and ask no questions ... At last the Gestapo did learn who the famous "Michou" really was ... but she brilliantly eluded their trap. She had been called to a rendezvous at the home of a COMET member, but Madame Ugeux [Michou] first placed a telephone call and discovered, as she expected, that it was the Gestapo waiting for her. On another occasion she suddenly became suspicious of an aviator she had gone to pick up. To test him before revealing herself, she used the latest slang she had learned from other aviators ... his bewilderment in the face of the slang words convinced Madame Ugeux that she was dealing with a German agent.'

During the months preceding the Normandy landings on 6 June 1944, it became too dangerous to bring men south by train because the Allies were bombing the railways. Instead, MI9 organised an operation code-named 'Marathon'. For this, airmen were to be gathered in groups in rural camps where they could be kept safely until sections of a specially formed escape and evasion unit called IS9(WEA), attached to Eisenhower's Supreme Headquarters, could locate and rescue them.

This operation apparently did not find favour with the Brussels end of the Line as the authors of *MI9* revealed. 'COMET had not approved of "Marathon". Neave searched the Ardennes in early September for his expected camp; it was not there. Instead, he found a fair number of evaders living it up in Brussels; where the resident IS9(WEA) field section had set up house in what its newsletter tactfully described as "two hotels of a type not met with in the UK" – that is, former brothels.'

Two 'Marathon' camps were successfully formed where escapers and evaders awaited the invading Allied armies. But parties were still taken across the Pyrenees by the COMET Line – organised by the irrepressible Tante Go and led by Florentino – right up to the time of the Allied landings in Normandy. The last consisted of two RAF sergeants who crossed on 4 June 1944.

Florentino crossed for the last time in July 1944 to take intelligence papers needed by the Allies. On his return journey this gallant Basque was ambushed and captured by the Germans when one of his legs had been shattered by automatic fire. He remained silent under interrogation and so severe were his injuries that the Germans sent him to a civilian hospital at Bayonne. Immediately Tante Go heard what had happened she arranged to have Florentino rescued and hidden.

Florentino survived the war but was left badly crippled by his injury. Tante Go and Fernand survived as well, but many did not. Of the hundreds of COMET Line helpers, 23 were shot including Dédée's father. Another 133 died in concentration camps, or shortly after they had been released, though Dédée, Legrelle,

Nothomb and Arnold de Pé all survived. Masson was tried at Lille under his real name of Jacques Desoubrie. He was found guilty and executed. Dédée, Tante Go, Michou and Florentino were all awarded the George Medal, the highest British decoration that can be awarded to a civilian for bravery, and the three women were also awarded the US Medal of Freedom, with Gold Palm, America's highest civilian decoration awarded during the Second World War.

12

MI9'S SEA ESCAPE LINES

M ost escapers and evaders were got out of enemy-occupied territory overland, but, as has been touched on in previous chapters, sea escape lines were also formed by the British secret services. The British escape and evasion organisation MI9 (see Chapter One) formed its first lines after the fall of Greece and Crete in the spring and summer of 1941 when it began operating a fleet of caiques from secret bases in neutral Turkey. Under the general supervision of Commander V. Wolfson, based in Istanbul – who was also helped by Major-General Arnold, the British military attaché in Ankara – these ferried escapers and evaders from the Greek mainland across the Aegean to Turkish ports for onward transportation by train to Egypt.

By March 1942 MI9 had five chartered caiques employed on this work, and in transporting stores from Cyprus for the secret bases, and shared another two employed by the British Secret Intelligence Service (MI6); the numbers rose rapidly thereafter. The Turks were generally helpful and considerate, according to one MI9 report, 'shutting their eyes (and opening their palms) as best they could to the flagrant breaches of neutrality committed by MI9 and the other secret departments'.

An early 'client' of these escape lines was Stoker Capes who in December 1941 was the sole survivor of a British submarine sunk by a mine in the Ionian Sea. He swam six miles to the island of Cephalonia and was hidden by the islanders. In due course this was reported to the secret base at Smyrna (Izmir) – the base MI9 shared with MI6 – by a Greek named Evangelatos who was MI9's 'most famous' skipper. Although the rescue attempt involved a voyage of several hundred miles across enemy-controlled waters, including the heavily fortified coastline of the Peloponnese, Evangelatos and a crew of picked volunteers carried out the rescue of Capes successfully.

In the words of the history of MI9 in the Mediterranean, 'They left our Turkish base in the MI9 caique, *Evangelistria*, on 20 May [1942], and after a hazardous journey involving numerous searches by Italian patrol boats and port officials, they reached Cephalonia on 23 May. After innumerable difficulties and subterfuges to get Stoker Capes out of the island without being detected, they left Cephalonia on 31 May and reached our secret base safely on 3 June.'

Even more remarkable was the evasion of an American pilot named Marting who belonged to the famous Eagle Squadron. It was extraordinary not so much for his rescue – though that was unusual enough – but for the absolute faith he showed in what he knew as 'A' Force (MI9's cover name in the Mediterranean

Theatre). He had been lectured about escape and evasion by 'A' Force personnel before being shot down in the Western Desert in October 1942. From the time he was captured by the Germans 'almost everything proceeded in accordance with what F/O Marting had been taught by MI9,' the MI9 history relates. 'He was taken to a POW camp. The German interrogation officer asked for his set of escape devices – which MI9 had told him they would do. He handed over his spare set to the Germans, which were clumsily concealed especially for that purpose, retaining his second set which was properly concealed.'

After he had been interrogated by the Germans Marting reported to the camp's senior British officer and discovered that, as MI9 had briefed him, there was an escape committee in the camp which, when he said he wished to escape, gave him all the help he needed, telling him the whereabouts of food dumps hidden in the desert, and supplying him with the necessary maps and other escape aids.

Before he could set about escaping, Marting was flown to Athens on 1 November for onward transmission to Germany. Again, MI9 had warned him this would happen, that he would have only 24 hours there, and that this would be his last good chance of escape before reaching Germany. He therefore lost no time in climbing out of a lavatory window in the hotel where he was being kept, having first stolen a German sentry's jacket which he put on. Such was his faith in MI9 that he walked down one of the main streets in Athens tapping on the shoulder each Greek he encountered and asking if he worked for 'A' Force!

'By one of those pieces of fortune, known rarely to MI9, the thirteenth person that he tapped on the shoulder did in fact work for 'A' Force. The previous twelve had shrugged their shoulders and hurried away on being accosted, but none betrayed him.'

Marting's luck held – or, as he saw it, 'A' Force was working with its normal efficiency – and he was hidden in a series of houses in Athens where he was, as MI9 had forewarned him, closely cross-questioned to establish his identity. One of his interrogators, a Greek girl working for MI9, asked Marting to tell her the names of all the Presidents of the USA, starting with Washington. 'She knew them – Marting didn't!'

Before he left, Marting was taken to the house of the head of MI9 in Athens, a senior Greek officer who had been educated at a famous British public school and spoke perfect English. He told Marting that he would be returned to Cairo next day via Turkey, and that he had just wanted to meet him before he left.

'Marting was evacuated in an MI9 caique from a point near Athens to Smyrna, caught a train through Turkey, and arrived back in Cairo in December,' the history concludes. 'The point of this story is that MI9 Middle East regarded this escape as a series of lucky incidents, whereas F/O Marting regarded it as the normal routine of MI9.' His faith apparently made him one of the most useful MI9 Preventive Training lecturers in the Western Desert.

In February 1942 three 'caique plans', as these sea escape lines were called, were operational, taking escapers and evaders from Greece to safety in Turkey, Cyprus or

Egypt (see Map 12). By May the number of 'caique plans' had grown to eight. Their routes included: Salonika to a Turkish island in the mouth of the Dardanelles and thence to Ankara; from the Chalcidice peninsula near Salonika to Smyrna; from Volos via the Sporades to Smyrna; from Athens via the Aegean islands to Smyrna and also direct to Cairo; and from Kalamata in the south-west Peloponnese to Smyrna.

Caique Plan No. 6, from Kalamata to Smyrna, 'proved particularly fruitful', according to the MI9 report. It also recorded that on 30 March one MI9 opera-

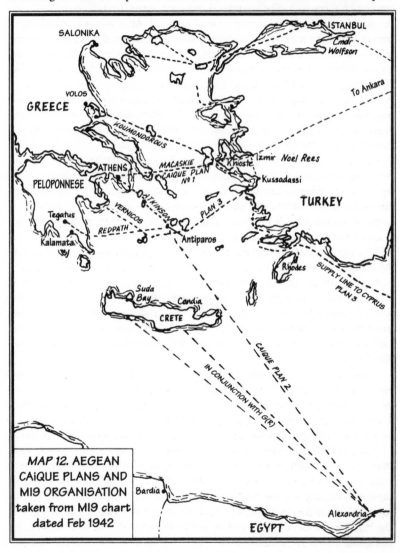

MAP 12. AEGEAN CAIQUE PLANS AND MI9 ORGANISATION taken from MI9 chart dated Feb 1942

tive reached Cyprus in his 15-ton caique, built to carry ten people, with 77 Greeks aboard. Later this record was beaten when a 20-ton MI9 caique transported 89 Greeks to Cyprus. Perhaps it is therefore no exaggeration when the same report stated that during 1942 'no less than two Greek combatant brigades were formed out of the material provided by MI9'.

Inevitably, there were casualties. When one MI9 party with escapers from Athens was marooned on the island of Antiparos – because the submarine which was to pick them up had been sunk – they were betrayed to the Italians occupying the island and, after a fight, they were all captured. After suffering terrible hardship in a civilian prison all the MI9 operatives were accepted as service personnel and transferred to a POW camp in Italy. But unfortunately their leader, a Lieutenant Atkinson, had also, without MI9's knowledge, been working for SOE, and had been caught red-handed, in civilian clothes, in possession of incriminating documents and a wireless set. He was taken to Athens where he and 27 Greeks were put on trial for espionage, and he and five of the Greeks were found guilty, condemned to death, and shot. Another MI9 operative was saved when his life was traded for three Italian spies who had been caught in Syria.

In the autumn of 1943, following the failure of the Dodecanese campaign, MI9 caiques were sent to the islands that had been overrun by the Germans. Agents were landed to hunt for British service personnel who had missed the official evacuations, and when these had been rounded up they were taken to the safety of Turkey. One letter in an SOE file credits MI9 with managing to clear Leros of British evaders almost single-handedly.

The success of MI9's sea escape lines in the Aegean no doubt encouraged the formation of sea escape routes elsewhere. After the PAT Line (see Chapter 3) had been virtually destroyed in early 1943, a dangerous log jam of air force personnel began to form in the Breton peninsula. These men had been shot down during raids on ports such as Brest, Cherbourg and Lorient, and they were urgently needed for further active service. So MI9 decided to form a new escape line which evacuated evaders by sea from Brittany instead of taking them over the Pyrenees.

Such a line had in fact been under discussion for some time. But the organisation's initial attempt to form one failed when it infiltrated two French naval officers into France by 'waltzing' – the term used by Room 900, MI9's operational centre, to describe sending in agents overland – one was recognised and betrayed by a former colleague and the other was shot by a German officer in a café brawl.

Then in February 1943, on the tenth attempt, two MI9 agents were dropped 'blind' – that is, without a reception committee to greet them – outside Paris to form one end of a new escape line code-named 'OAKTREE', which had at its other end Brittany and the English Channel. One of the agents, a White Russian named Vladimir Bouryschkine, who used the alias 'Val Williams', had worked for the PAT Line before escaping to England via Gibraltar the previous autumn; the other was a French-Canadian named Ray Labrosse who was to act as Williams' radio operator. In addition to the usual equipment they were given two folding bicycles, the first time these had been employed in an operation of this kind.

Williams went to Paris to contact a French lawyer named François Campinchi, who had been closely involved with the PAT Line and now agreed to organise the Paris end of the new one. Williams then travelled to Brittany to meet the local Resistance groups and to set up the Brittany end of the Line and to find where the evading airmen were hidden. At the Château de Bourblanc, the home of the comte and comtesse de Mauduit, near Paimpol, he discovered what he later described as a 'whole regiment' of American and British airmen hidden there. By May he had collected some 90 airmen in Brittany, of whom 39 were sheltering in the château.

Williams now needed to contact London to arrange the first pick-up by the Motor Gun Boats (MGB) which were stationed at Dartmouth. These came under the aegis of Captain F. A. Slocum, the Royal Navy's Deputy Director Operations Division (Irregular), who ran secret flotillas for the British intelligence services. But Labrosse, who had remained on a farm near where he and Williams had been parachuted, found that his wireless had been damaged during the drop and he was unable to contact London.

Desperate to get the line working, but contrary to all the rules of security, Williams resorted to using the radio communications of another organisation to establish contact with London. This was achieved but communications were too unreliable for Slocum to risk his MGBs on an operation and anyway the nights were becoming too short to be able to mount one under cover of darkness. Williams therefore arranged for guides to take the airmen over the Pyrenees and most of them eventually got away by this means.

By ignoring the security rules Williams compromised the escape line he was trying to start. He was arrested in Rennes and his organisation in Brittany was partially penetrated by Roger Le Neveu, known as Roger the Legionnaire, the same German agent who had helped break up the PAT Line. The comtesse de Mauduit was arrested and deported to a concentration camp, but when Le Neveu suggested the local Resistance group send evaders to him in Paris they became suspicious and broke off contact.

The Rennes Gestapo had a file on Williams from his days with the PAT Line and they were also in possession of a disconcerting amount of knowledge about MI9. They knew all about one of MI9's most senior officers, Major J. M. Langley, and even had a photograph of him. They were also well informed about MI9's system of training agents in parachuting, night-landing and wireless procedure. But Williams refused to talk under torture and he was subsequently given a medical examination which proved him 'fit to be shot', but he managed to escape and went into hiding in Paris.

The capture of Williams and the loss of the comtesse and other organisers in Brittany was a severe blow to the network. But some of the organisers in Paris, including Campinchi, had escaped arrest and the local Resistance, under a man named François Le Cornec, was still intact. Labrosse, who, on hearing that Williams had been arrested, made his way back to England via the Pyrenees, taking 27 evaders with him, reported that the ordinary people in Brittany were solidly behind helping any escape line. He pressed Langley to make a further attempt to set one up, and Langley agreed.

In place of Williams MI9 chose another French-Canadian, Lucien Dumais, a sergeant-major in the Fusiliers Mont-Royal, who had also been involved with the PAT Line when he had escaped from capture after the Dieppe raid. He was described by Airey Neave, the MI9 officer in charge of the new line, as 'short, articulate, and very tough'. The plan – and later the escape line – was code-named 'SHELBURNE' by Neave after the 18th-century Whig prime minister.

Dumais and Labrosse were flown by Lysander to Chauny, north-east of Compiègne in the *département* of the Aisne, in October 1943. Both their initial contacts were arrested soon after their arrival in Paris but they managed to make contact with Campinchi who was still in hiding.

At first Campinchi was unwilling to help, for Williams' lack of any sense of security had made him very wary of being involved in another escape line. But when Dumais convinced him that security would be tightened and that the line would be run efficiently, he agreed to take control in Paris and the surrounding suburbs. It was also agreed that he would appoint someone to organise guides whose task it would be to collect evaders and escort them to any destination designated by Dumais; and that he would also find the right people to supply lodgings, clothing and food for evaders in transit, and to print and supply false identity papers.

It was then agreed to follow strict security rules in order to impose a sense of professionalism among those they employed, and to avoid the Germans planting spies by infiltrating bogus airmen. The rules were: 1. All agents were to keep their addresses secret. 2. Chiefs were to meet their helpers only when necessary, and they were never to give them information that was not absolutely essential. 3. Everyone would work through accommodation addresses. 4. Agents were to avoid friendly meetings with one another. 5. Contacts between guides and evaders would be made by pre-arranged signals only. 6. Evaders had to be passed down the escape line without their guides meeting one another. 7. No one was to talk about his chief, or even admit to having one. 8. The head of the network was to remain totally unknown. 9. Evaders were not to be told of the existence of any network. 10. All evaders were to be interrogated as soon as they came under the network's control.

With the Paris end of the line organised, Dumais and Labrosse moved to Brittany where they met Le Cornec who ran a café and *charcuterie* at Plouha. After surveying several beaches, one protected by cliffs 60 metres high was chosen. Known locally as 'Sous-Kéruzeau', it was code-named 'Bonaparte', the name also given to the operations that used it (see Map 13). Although accessible at low tide, via a gully in the cliffs known as Anse Cochat, some 100 metres to the south of it, the beach could only be reached at high tide by sliding diagonally on one's bottom down the cliff face. But Dumais later remarked that as 'the people visualised using it would be young, fit and only too anxious to get away, this was not a serious objection'.

It had been agreed that on the day of an evacuation the BBC would broadcast a message *'Bonjour tout le monde à la maison d'Alphonse'* at 7.30 p.m., and again at 9 p.m. which would tell those waiting that the MGB had sailed. But in the interests of security, evaders from Paris were not to be brought to Brittany until three days before the MGB was due.

The first exodus was arranged for 29 January. The airmen from Paris were met off the overnight train to Brest at Saint-Brieuc by guides, and were held during the day at a reception centre in the town, before being taken under cover of darkness to a local train which ran to Plouha. The evaders were dropped off in small groups at successive stations and hidden in the vicinity of the beach. When the BBC message was heard, the airmen were taken to a stone farmhouse some 1.5 kilometres from the top of the cliffs from which they had to descend to the beach. The farmhouse, which became known as the 'maison d'Alphonse' because of the BBC message, belonged to a trusted friend of Le Cornec, a farmer named Gicquel, who lived there with his wife and baby. It had only two rooms, and a loft above, and was really no more than a hut.

On the night of 29 January there were thirteen USAAF airmen, four from the RAF, and two young Frenchman on the run from the Gestapo, crammed into one of the rooms of the farmhouse where Dumais gave them their instructions. They would be taken to the beach by three guides. One of them would lead the way; a

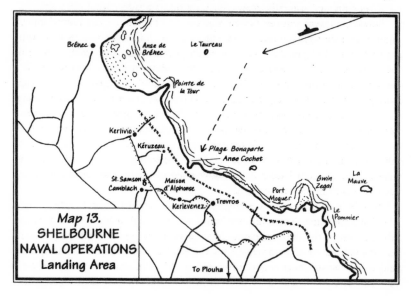

second, an 18-year-old girl named Marie-Thérèse Le Calvez, would follow directly behind him, and the evaders would follow her in single file. The first evader would hold on to the girl's coat tail and the others would hold on to the man in front of him. The third guide, Le Cornec, would follow behind. If any of the evaders lost contact with the man ahead he was to halt immediately and the guides would sort the problem out. When they reached the cliff they would have to lie on their backs and slide down. When they got to the bottom they would be told where to sit. When ordered to, and not before, they would wade out to the small boats that would be coming to pick them up. If, at any time during this procedure they were attacked, they were to fight back.

The party left the maison d'Alphonse at midnight and as the airmen began sliding down the cliff face one of the guides remained at the top to signal the MGB to send in its surf boats by flashing the letter 'B' in Morse with a torch masked by a cardboard tube. When the party had descended the cliff Marie-Thérèse signalled from the beach with a torch screened by blue plastic to show the incoming surf boats that everything was in order. If there had been any danger she would have changed the screen to red, switched the torch on and jammed it in the rocks to warn the incoming boats away.

'At about a quarter past one we saw three darks spots on the sea,' Dumais recorded later. 'We watched them intently. They were not an illusion, they were moving slowly towards the shore. I waded out to the centre one, flanked by Le Cornec and Huet, pistols drawn, ready to fire. A figure jumped off the bows and came closer.

'I called out the password: "Dinan".

'"Saint-Brieuc," came the reply. What a relief! It was the Royal Navy after all.'

Bonaparte I went without a hitch, and a second operation was arranged for the night of 26 February, and three more during the moonless period in March. Altogether at least 111 people – the records vary – were picked up in the course of these five operations, 74 of them in the space of seven days. There was then a pause because of the risk of the Germans increasing their defences and their vigilance prior to the Normandy landings, and Dumais and Labrosse returned to Paris.

The landings took place on 6 June and a few days later Dumais, his courier Louisette Lorre, and Labrosse set out for Plouha by bicycle, but before they arrived another operation ('Reflexion') was mounted on 17 June, not to the beach but to a small quay at Anse Cochat. This entailed landing three MI9 agents who were to collect aircrew hidden in central Brittany and arrange for them to be evacuated by sea from the Brittany coast.

As MI9 had no means of communicating with the Brittany end of the SHEL-BURNE Line, Airey Neave did not know if it were still intact. Despite Gestapo investigations, it had in fact survived, but without radio communications no reception committee could be arranged for the MI9 agents. They were successfully landed but the surf boat could not regain the MGB in time and its 3-man crew was left behind. Miraculously, both the agents and the surf boat crew, which included the future film director, Guy Hamilton, traversed a minefield that now guarded the beach, without treading on any of the mines.

Within days the crew were safely hidden by the local Resistance and when Dumais and Labrosse arrived the latter was able to transmit that they were safe and well. SHELBURNE was now re-activated as an escape line and in early July fifteen airmen were transported to the area, so that, with the surf boat crew, eighteen were awaiting transportation across the Channel. Bad weather stopped all sea operations for more than a week and it was not until 12 July that BBC messages confirmed that the MGB had sailed for what was known as Operation 'Crozier'.

The laying of the minefield had been closely observed by members of the local Resistance, including the remarkable Marie-Thérèse Le Calvez. That night the mines barring the approach down the Anse Cochat gully were clearly marked with white cloth tied to sticks before the eighteen evaders were taken down in Indian file to the Sous-Kéruzeau beach. The evacuation went without a hitch, and the reception party withdrew, removing the white flags from the minefield as they went.

By now the French Resistance in Brittany, supported by SAS groups and SOE teams, were openly fighting the Germans in the peninsula. One team of seven men, which had been dropped to contact an SAS unit in the area, was subsequently ordered to withdraw via the SHELBURNE Line after its mission had been completed. Only the team's leader, an SAS Major named Oswald Cary-Elwes, and his batman managed, with the help of the Resistance, to make their way to Plouha, but they accumulated on the way another SAS major and two evading airmen, one British and one American. The five men had just been installed in Gicquel's farmhouse near the cliff top when a patrol of drunken Vlasov Russians – Vlasov, a Soviet general, had defected to the Germans earlier in the war – appeared at the door. In the resulting confusion one of the patrol was shot and wounded by his comrades and the evaders took refuge in the loft.

The patrol did not to attempt to storm the loft – which was wise of them because Cary-Elwes's batman was waiting to greet them with a hand-grenade – but fired several rifle rounds into it from the floor below while demanding the evaders' surrender. When nothing came of this they returned outside where the wounded man lay writhing on the ground and ordered Gicquel to fetch a horse and cart from a nearby farm to take him away. They then departed, thanking Gicquel for his help, but the French farmer predicted that they would soon return in force, having told those in charge of them that the man had been wounded by those hiding in the loft. The house was immediately evacuated and the party, after spending the rest of the night in a ditch, were taken to a refuge some kilometres away.

In the meantime the Russians, accompanied this time by Germans, returned, as Gicquel had said they would. They ransacked the farmhouse before burning it to the ground. None of this deterred Dumais who declared that though the occupation forces in the area were now in a state of high alert, the evacuation would take place that night, 24 July. To protect them half a platoon of *Maquisards*, armed with Sten guns and a light machine-gun, were mustered to escort them to the beach from their hiding-place. When they reached the edge of the minefield, which had already been marked with white flags, the machine-gun was placed where its field of fire covered the coastal track to the narrow gully.

Once on the beach the party made the usual signals and at 0130 three surf boats appeared out of the dark. Fifteen suitcases full of arms were landed for the local *Maquis* and the evaders safely embarked. This was the last operation by the SHELBURNE Line in occupied territory, but a final one was carried out, in daylight, on 9 August, after the Germans in the area had surrendered. An MGB collected one MI6 and two French agents and any Allied evaders who remained.

Altogether the SHELBURNE Line, without losing one of its 'parcels', exfiltrated between 138 and 145 people, a number only exceeded by the PAT Line and the Gibraltar-based feluccas. To the Line's successes must also be added a further 98 men who were fed safely into Spain by SHELBURNE's system of guides.

'Thus ended', Airey Neave later commented, 'one of the most splendid exploits in which the Navy and agents of Room 900, aided by French patriots in Paris and Brittany, took part.'

13

DIE LIKE THE CARP!

The brutal treatment of Allied POW by the Japanese has rightly been condemned by the civilised world,* for it not only showed a remarkable lack of humanity but contravened the 1929 Geneva Convention which laid down certain rules about the treatment of prisoners.

Although Japan had been a signatory to the Convention, it did not ratify it (the USSR did not even sign it), and at least there was no hypocrisy about it because Japan's attitude towards its own POW was equally brutal. 'Don't survive shamefully as a prisoner; die, and thus escape ignominy,' were General Hideki Tojo's terse orders in *Instructions for the Military*.

In Japan the carp is considered an exceptionally courageous fish, and 'Die like the carp!' was a common rallying cry among the Japanese POW who, in the early hours of 5 August 1944, made a mass escape from Cowra camp, in New South Wales, 227 miles west of Sydney.

Erected in 1941, the camp consisted of four compounds: A–D, covering some 17 acres (see map 14). A and C Compounds held Italian other ranks, B held Japanese other ranks, and D held Formosans and Koreans, plus a dozen Japanese officers accommodated separately within D Compound. The camp was guarded by 22nd Garrison Battalion comprising an HQ and four companies, lettered A to D, each of which was responsible for guarding a compound. B Company, whose task it was to guard B Compound (see Map 15) containing 1,104 Japanese NCOs and other ranks, numbered 107 men, most of whom could hardly be regarded as combatant soldiers; many were over-age and were equipped with obsolete weapons.

Of the 1,104 prisoners in B Compound, 378 escaped from the camp. Other than the exodus of Allied POW after Italy's surrender in September 1943 (see Chapter Ten), this was the largest mass escape of POW ever recorded, but the Cowra camp episode is of primary interest today because it highlights the very different attitude the Japanese had *vis-à-vis* escape and evasion, and being POW.

When a Japanese was captured he ceased to be a soldier and was not entitled to wear badges of rank. At Cowra the inmates shed their military headgear and fashioned hats from blankets or linen, decorated with symbols. Many chose the cherry blossom or the chrysanthemum, these being national emblems. 'We had been taught', Masatoshi Kigawa wrote many years later, 'that a war prisoner

---

*In this context, however, Yuji Aida's humiliating experiences as a prisoner of war in British hands after the war are noteworthy; see his *Prisoner of the British*, London, 1966.

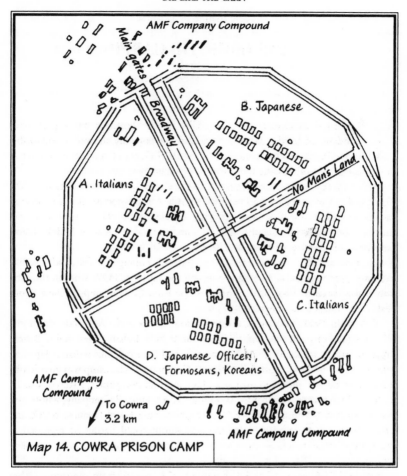

Map 14. COWRA PRISON CAMP

would be killed, but we were given no knowledge about what the life of a prisoner was like. Therefore we thought that a man, once a prisoner, had only a hopeless future before him even after the war. [We thought] that most [ex] prisoners [returning to Japan after the war] would be taken out to some deserted place like an uninhabited island and be shot dead by the Japanese army. In fact, according to the war history of Japan of the past, no Japanese had ever been a prisoner before. [We felt] that a prisoner could not hope to return to society even if he survived.'

Another survivor, who remembered the kindness of a farmer's wife who brought tea and cakes to the prison at Hay, said: 'She seemed like an angel, talking to us in a kindly way. We had been so apprehensive about what might happen to us ... You have to understand that we were so soaked with shame.'

This sense of shame was so acute that many Japanese gave false names to inter-rogators so that their families never knew what had happened to them and assumed they were dead. 'I would never have told them [the interrogators] my right name,' said Sergeant-Major Akira Kanazawa, who refused to talk about his prison experiences to anyone until 1977. 'The shame of being captured was too great. It would have brought dishonour to my family ... We were shocked when we learned [later] that American and Australian prisoners actually *asked* to have their names sent home, so that their families would know they were alive. We could never have inflicted that on our families. We received no mail as prisoners, and wanted none. We were dead men.'

That this sense of shame should continue for many ex-prisoners after the war may seem astonishing to the Western mind, but the fact is that many of those imprisoned at Cowra who have since died went to the grave without their families ever knowing that they had been captured, and many of those who are alive still refuse to acknowledge that they had been. The family of one man who died in the break-out had no idea of what had happened until told of it in 1970. Masaru Moriki, president of *Cowra Kai*, the society founded in Japan in 1964 for all those who were imprisoned at the camp, is not among those who remain ashamed, but he reckons that up to 50 per cent of the survivors of the Cowra escape refuse, even today, to admit to having been taken prisoner during the war.

'Most people didn't answer at all,' he told Harry Gordon, the author of *Voyage from Shame*, about the founding of the society. 'A lot of others sent back terse letters telling me never to get in touch with them again. I wasn't surprised.' Of those who did admit that they had been in Cowra camp, only 80 or so were prepared to join the society.

Moriki's experience when he returned home must have been coloured by his own determination not to allow his life to be overshadowed by his imprisonment, but at first he was received by his fellow villagers with some reserve. 'I came home on 8 April 1946,' he said, 'the only one from my village to return. The others had all died, and there was some discomfort, some suspicion towards me. My family believed that I had been killed on 11 November 1942, and I had a plaque in my ancestors' tomb.'

But when Moriki revealed that he had been a POW his family and neighbours responded positively. 'Someone said: "Don't worry. You fought like a soldier. You should not worry about being in a prison camp. All Japan is a prison camp now".'

Another of the alleged leaders of the break-out was a naval fighter pilot, Hajime Toyoshima, whose carrier-based Zero fighter was shot down during the Japanese raid on Darwin on 19 February 1942. Toyoshima's attitude to his capture was typical. He thought that he was going to be killed, and to avoid giving away any information told his initial interrogators in Darwin that he was the rear-gunner of an army bomber who had been forced to bale out. He then fabricated an untrue story of his background and gave his name as Tadao Minami.

But he did reply to one question truthfully. When asked if he wished to be returned to Japan he replied that he preferred to stay in Australia because 'He thought his friends would not want to have anything to do with him because he had been taken prisoner, and he would not be regarded as a good character, and would not be able to get back into the army.'

Toyoshima's reaction to his captivity was confirmed by an Australian flight-sergeant of the RAAF's service police special investigation unit who was in charge of the Japanese prisoner when the latter underwent further interrogation in Melbourne. Although Toyoshima gave every indication that he preferred being a prisoner to death – an attitude which later changed – the flight-sergeant confirmed that his prisoner 'spoke often about the impossibility of returning to Japan, whatever the outcome of the war, because he would be judged to have disgraced his country, emperor, and family by being captured. He said there would be no place for him in the future of his country or his family.'

Cowra is the best-known case of mutiny by Japanese POW, but it is not the only one. In February 1943 Japanese prisoners in a camp at Featherston, near Wellington in New Zealand, began a revolt which resulted in 48 of them being killed and 63 wounded, and one of the seven guards who were wounded also died. In Australian POW camps violence and escapes were unusual, but not unknown. Some German POW in the camp at Murchison, Victoria, were shot in September 1942, and an Italian officer did escape from the same camp. (He was recaptured when he made the mistake of ordering, in not very good English, red wine with his meal in an outback café!)

At Cowra the non-Japanese prisoners were docile, even openly co-operative, but the Japanese became increasingly troublesome as their numbers grew. One officer escaped in April 1943 but was quickly recaptured, and the following month Japanese prisoners refused to work on Japan's Navy Day, 27 May. One of them was seen making semaphore signals to the officers' compound and at the midday inspection an Australian guard was warned by Toyoshima – who was known to the camp authorities only by his assumed name of Minami – that if the Australians came to arrest those who had refused to work 'you will need to bring a machine-gun'. There were other minor incidents including an attempt by a Japanese prisoner to wrest a rifle from a guard. These manifestations were treated in a restrained manner by the garrison, but their tolerance was taken by the Japanese as a sign of weakness.

There was conflict, too, within B Compound between the airmen, some of whom had been captured at the beginning of 1942, while the soldiers only started to arrive at Cowra in February 1943. The airmen had used their longer time in captivity to accumulate belongings and influence, and some had learned at least a little English. One of Minami's friends, Marekuni Takahara, who had assumed the name Ichiro Takata, commented years later: 'The soldiers felt a real jealousy of us, and it was understandable, really. We had a bit of money, and we had possessions. When the wealthy civilians were repatriated from Hay to Japan in August 1942, they gave us all kinds of things ... money, clothes, watches, pens, wallets, so many things. Also, while we had been able to work outside the camp at Hay, we had been receiving payment. So in the environment of B Compound we were seen as rich people and Minami was probably the richest man inside the barbed wire. Maybe we did keep to ourselves too much ... it was a natural thing for us to do. By the time Kanazawa arrived, the soldiers were openly suspicious of us. To possess so much at such a time, they felt we must have done something bad, maybe betrayed our country. The feeling around the compound was one of distrust.'

Eventually a deputation told Minami that internal control of the compound could no longer be retained by the airmen simply because of their seniority as captives, and that an election must be held. This took place in July 1943 and resulted in Kanazawa being appointed camp leader. Another Army NCO, Sergeant Masao Kojima, was elected deputy leader, and Minami was made third in command in recognition of the length of time he had been a prisoner and because he was the only senior captive who spoke English.

Typically, the garrison commander, Lieutenant-Colonel Montague Brown, was not informed about the election and most of the Australians' communications with the prisoners continued to be through Minami. This meant that he, and the few other airmen who spoke English, retained the real power.

In the Australian autumn of 1944 the atmosphere in the Japanese compound changed, with the prisoners suddenly becoming docile and co-operative. This raised suspicions that they were probably planning a break-out. But the first real indication the authorities had that something might be amiss was on 3 June 1944 when a new inmate, a Korean soldier who had spent a short time in B before being moved to D Compound, reported that he had heard several Japanese plotting an uprising. The Korean warned that though the Japanese were overtly docile their thinking was: '... if we can hide our feelings we can put the enemy entirely off his guard, and thereby choose a moment when we shall be able to inflict heavy losses on him'.

The Korean's report was taken seriously – the break-out at Featherston saw to that – and the Camp Commandant requested and received extra Lewis guns and two old Vickers machine-guns, but was refused extra men. The Vickers were set up with fixed lines of fire along B Compound's boundaries, but both were left unmanned at night and there was no protection from attack. As a further precaution all the personnel of the garrison were issued with rifles which at night had to be kept beside their beds, and an alarm siren was installed. To ensure that everyone would turn out in an emergency, orders were issued on 18 July which stated that if a break-out were suspected the garrison would be alerted by two single rifle shots and/or a continuous sounding of the siren. Security was further tightened by the posting of a guard every night in the middle of what was called the Broadway – a brightly lit road some 50 yards wide by 750 yards long which ran in a north-south direction through the centre of the camp – with instructions to watch for any unusual movements within B Compound. Three Very lights would be fired to warn a nearby Infantry Training Centre of a break-out. This Centre was known to be a prime objective of the escaping Japanese because they hoped to obtain arms from the young, raw recruits.

In the event, all these measures proved hopelessly inadequate against the suicidal mass assault launched by the prisoners. Although daily inspection of the huts was routine, insufficient personnel prevented any full-scale searches of the compound for hidden weapons. Nor was any attempt made to restrict the circulation of tools and implements such as chisels and saws and baseball bats that could be – and were – turned into effective weapons. The garrison's officers conferred frequently in an endeavour to ensure that everyone was kept on a state of high alert. Major Ramsay, who was in charge of B Compound, expressed his worries about crossfire and ricochets if the machine-gunners were forced to open fire, and Major E. V. Timms, in charge of C Compound, declared: 'We've got to face the fact, the garrison is numerically inferior. If there is a break, and they do get out, the people of Cowra could be in real danger. It's only a mile and a half away.'

As the days passed, more POW arrived at the already overcrowded B Compound until there were about twice the number it had been designed to accommodate. Despite the good behaviour of the prisoners, tension remained high and early in August it was decided to remove the other ranks – about 700 of them – to another camp to deprive them of the NCOs who were rightly suspected as being the ringleaders of the incipient uprising.

This decision was kept secret because it was known that the Japanese would strongly resist the idea, and might well riot in an attempt to prevent the move. But on Thursday 3 August, 50 guards, who were to escort the 700 Japanese to Hay, arrived at the camp and by the following day the proposed move was generally known among the garrison. Although there was no obligation to do so under the Geneva Convention – to which, anyway, Japan did not adhere – it was decided to tell the B Compound prisoners that they were to be transferred on the following Monday. That afternoon Kanazawa, Kojima and Minami were ordered to report to Ramsay's office where the Major, according to the evidence he gave at the court of inquiry which followed the uprising, told them through the camp interpreter, Sergeant Oleg Negerevich, about the transfer and handed them a nominal roll of the men who were to be moved. He said that the roll included all those below the rank of lance-corporal, and that Minami, after examining it, said, 'very bad business ... why can't we all go?'

In 1977 Kanazawa maintained that Ramsay had not given them a nominal roll, nor had he mentioned that the purpose of the transfer was to separate the men from their NCOs. This was confirmed by interpreter Negerevich. 'We expressly did not tell them that they were to be split up according to rank. We knew that could be the fuse that could cause the whole thing to blow up.'

This assumption was correct. After an Australian guard had disclosed who was being transferred, and why, the three Japanese leaders immediately conferred with other senior POW as to what should be done. The idea of an uprising had frequently been discussed and weapons had been gathered, but, except for expressing the fervent wish to kill as many of the enemy as possible before dying an honourable death, no detailed plans had been made, and some at the conference doubted that much could be achieved without better preparation.

Curiously, the three leaders were not particularly enthusiastic about the proposed break-out, but most of the speakers were young fanatics. They pledged that the men were willing to die by following the *Bushido* code of honour under which all Japanese fought. 'Our comrades who died in battle are calling to us,' said one of them emotionally. 'Close your eyes tonight, and you will hear them dimly. This is the moment we have waited for so long.'

It was agreed that a consensus was needed and that a vote should be held in each hut, but this did not always happen. In one case the hut leader reported, quite untruthfully, that his men were against the break-out, and one or two huts were just ordered to join the outbreak without a vote being taken. Where a vote was held it showed that some were reluctant to take part. But in the end, everyone agreed to go along with what the hawks wanted, and in most huts it seems the men were overwhelmingly in favour of the break-out.

An *ad hoc* plan was now hastily agreed whereby the Japanese would attempt to seize control of the camp. If this were achieved, and firearms acquired, an attack on the nearby Infantry Training Centre would be launched. No one was in any doubt that any successes would only be temporary. The real aim was to die gloriously to obliterate the shame that haunted them all.

The 200 occupants of the four northernmost huts in the compound had the most important task, that of capturing the unmanned No. 2 Vickers machine-gun sited outside the wire at the northern end of the camp. If this could be taken and turned against B Company's quarters behind it, there seemed every chance that the entire camp could fall to the Japanese. At the same time a second group of about 300 from the six other huts closest to the perimeter wire were to break through the wire in the vicinity of Tower F and head for open country where they were to regroup before attacking the Infantry Training Centre.

The remaining ten huts in the compound were divided into two further groups totalling 250 men. One group would breach the compound's wire to gain access to the Broadway; the other would get into the Broadway by breaking out through the compound's gates. Once out of the compound the first group would turn right and make for the camp's main gates at the northern end of the Broadway, killing as many of the guards as possible in the process. The second group would turn left and head for the other camp gates at the southern end of the Broadway, and for D Compound containing the hut which held the Japanese officers whom the men were determined to rescue so that they could take part in the mutiny.

What happened after that would depend on how successful the escapers were in seizing the camp.

When these plans had been completed and agreed, Kanazawa told the hut leaders to make sure that everyone knew when the break-out was going to take place and to prepare their weapons, build fires under their huts, and gather as many blankets and baseball gloves as possible to be used when crossing the barbed wire. The following hours were spent making the preparations, in saying farewell to friends, in drinking the raw spirit that was brewed in the camp, and in composing themselves for what they knew was ultimately a suicidal assault. Warrant Officer Shichibei Matsushima, having thrown messages over the wire to warn the garrison, but without success, spent the time writing a poem:

> The wind stream flows on,
>   and knows not to what it flows,
> And on the surface float
>   the fallen leaves of autumn.
> They, too, are swept on,
>   unknowing.
> Even such is our life ...
>   At last I am again true to myself.
> If fate now decrees 'thou shalt die',
>   broken reed as I am, yet I shall not falter.

During this time one crippled inmate who could not take part in the uprising committed *seppaku* – the correct name for *hara-kiri* – by driving a knife into his belly. Others, who were also disabled, or chose not to take part in the break-out, hanged themselves. In the huts those who were to carry out the attacks were addressed by their leaders. One talked to them in an almost mystical tone about the carp, a fish for which the Japanese have a traditional reverence and which figures in their mythology. 'The whole thing, you must know,' he said, 'is more about dying than fighting. That is why it is so important for you to think tonight about the carp, its spirit, its bravery, the way it battles against onrushing currents, the way it can even swim up waterfalls. You know well that the carp is a symbol of a fine Japanese boy; that the true Japanese has to be able to fight and finally die like the carp. This whole thing could go wrong. The Australians may annihilate us all tonight. You have to be dignified at the last moment, like the carp.'

The signal to attack, planned for 0200 on the Saturday morning, was to be one strong bugle blast blown by Minami. But it is rare for any attack to go according to plan and the Japanese break-out was no exception. Fifteen minutes before the break-out was due to start, the nerves of one of the prisoners broke. Screaming incomprehensible warnings, he ran towards the double gates of the compound. He had already managed to climb the inner one when the sentry who had been positioned in the Broadway spotted him and responded by firing two warning shots in the air to alert the garrison.

Those inside the compound saw the defector at about the same time and realised what he was up to. Minami shouted to the others to get him and then sounded his bugle, and the group who were scheduled to break down the compound's gates to gain access to the Broadway ran from their huts. Lieutenant Thomas Aisbett and two soldiers ran to join the guard who had fired his rifle, while the prisoner, still shrieking incoherently, stood between the gates holding a blanket above his head and pointing behind him into the compound.

Aisbett heard a commotion in the compound and to his horror saw a solid mass of men screaming '*Banzai!*' surging towards the gate. He was unarmed and the other three had only their rifles, and he made his decision instantly. 'Run for your lives,' he yelled, and turned and raced down the Broadway towards the gates at the southern end. The gates were opened to let them through and Aisbett, glancing back, saw a solid block of men filling the Broadway in pursuit of them. They overran the defector and without seeming to stop clubbed and slashed him, and then cut his throat.

'By his warning', Aisbett wrote later, 'the prisoner saved many lives and, in my opinion, the whole garrison. We had no chance to rescue him because the [inner] gate was still locked, and time to release him had run out. As I was officer-in-charge I shepherded the sentries and escort back to the gates, went through last,

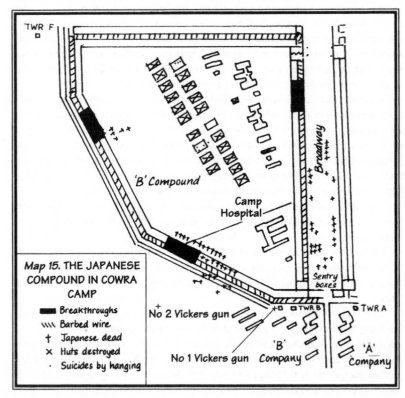

Map 15. THE JAPANESE COMPOUND IN COWRA CAMP

Breakthroughs
Barbed wire
† Japanese dead
✗ Huts destroyed
· Suicides by hanging

TWR F

'B' Compound

Camp Hospital

Broadway

Sentry boxes

No 2 Vickers gun

No 1 Vickers gun

TWR B   TWR A

'B' Company   'A' Company

and as I turned and looked back I saw Corporal McCormick fire at and shoot a Japanese POW brandishing some kind of weapon just behind us, right on the threshold of the gates.'

Minutes later the fires were started in the compound and soon all but two of the 20 huts were blazing and became the funeral pyres for the 20 or so Japanese who had chosen to kill themselves before the uprising began.

The POWs' principal objective, the No. 2 Vickers machine-gun, was mounted on a four-wheel trailer and positioned beneath a searchlight some 150 yards beyond the three-row fence of barbed wire (see Map 15). This fence presented a formidable obstacle: the rows were 30 feet apart and more than 6 feet high; each had seven strands, and the middle one had four coils of barbed wire around it. The area between the second and third fences was filled with a barbed wire entanglement 5 feet high.

Racing for the gun at the same time as the POW were scrambling their way over the barbed wire fences were two Australian privates, Ben Hardy and Ralph Jones, who six years later were both to receive a posthumous George Cross for their bravery. They reached it first and began firing into the heaving mass of Japanese who were struggling to overcome the barbed wire. Many were quickly mown down by the Vickers, but their bodies helped those behind to clamber over the wire. Then a stray bullet cut the power cable and all the camp's lights went out as did the searchlight for the Vickers. Nevertheless, the fires now blazing in the camp and the full moon gave the machine-gun's crew plenty of light, but as fast as they cut down the Japanese others appeared in their place.

Knowing that the Vickers would inevitably be overrun, Hardy almost certainly told Jones to run for it while he removed the breech-block to make the gun unworkable. Jones was clubbed and stabbed, and although he was able to stagger to B Company's quarters, he then collapsed and died. Hardy, too, was quickly killed, and the Japanese swarming over the trailer swung the gun round. But the Vickers would not fire so its barrel was swung into the air and its traversing clamp tightened to prevent the Australians firing it at those still scrambling over the wire.

Two of the alleged ringleaders had got out over the wire, but Kanazawa, who was partially crippled from battle wounds, had remained within the compound to direct operations. He saw the Vickers being overrun and could not understand why it had not been turned against B Company. He crawled out under the wire to discover what was happening and was told by one of the POW that as the gun would not work all those who had escaped were regrouping on a hill beyond the camp.

The firing was now growing heavier by the minute as the Australians began bringing what automatic weapons they had to bear on the compound and the escapees. They sealed off the escape route nearest B Company's quarters quite quickly and until it ran out of ammunition used the No. 1 Vickers to stop any further escapes from B Compound into the Broadway. The gun also kept those who had broken into the Broadway from trying to reach the main gates, and many were pinned down in the storm drains along each side of the Broadway. Nevertheless some managed to reach B Company's quarters and one Australian soldier was stabbed through the heart as he ran out of the guardroom. His killer was shot through the leg and promptly stabbed himself.

The third break-out point, near C Compound, was only covered by a single guard in F Tower and by a couple of guards positioned further towards B Company's quarters, and it was here that most of the 378 prisoners who did get clear of the camp escaped through the wire.

'I waited until they got over the first fence,' said one of the guards positioned outside B Compound, 'and then I opened up on them with the Owen gun. They threw blankets over the first, second and third wires, and those that didn't crawled underneath the wire. My mate and I got down in the trench and they threw batons at us, and we opened up again.'

At the southern end of the Broadway the officer commanding D Company lined his men up along the wire and ordered them to open fire on the prisoners who were breaking into the Japanese officers' quarters, and a Bren gun in a tower also opened up on them.

The scene was now one of utter chaos and confusion and was well described by Minami's friend, Takahara, who took part in the charge down the Broadway. 'I felt I could hear Minami's bugle again, telling me the enemy would all be killed. There were so many people running in front of me. At the beginning of the charge there was plenty of glare from the floodlights, then darkness, then the lights from the [Very] signal, red and yellow stripes across the sky, illuminating everything. The bullets from the tower were slanting down strongly, like heavy rain. In the middle many people fell down under the hail of bullets ... It was hard for me to go forward because there were so many bodies. Sometimes I walked across dead bodies, sometimes I pushed them aside. At last I reached the officers' gate, but here again there were many bodies. I huddled down prone.'

With Takahara was a close friend who tried desperately to get himself killed and eventually fell wounded. As he lay on the ground he stabbed himself. 'I shut my eyes quietly. The sounds of the guns were louder, and I was becoming satisfied that I would finally die. I could now avoid the shame of being a prisoner. Gradually I felt proud again to be a soldier of the Japanese Army.' His efforts proved in vain because he survived.

Many others decided they did not want to die and lay with their wounded and dead comrades by the wire, or in the storm drains along the Broadway. Those who had escaped into the countryside had no clear idea of what they should do next. Some were ready to surrender; others were still intent on creating as much mayhem as possible before getting themselves killed; a few decided to commit suicide.

By 0300 the situation in the camp had been contained. POW caught in the Broadway were still making occasional suicidal rushes for the gates at either end and were quickly cut down. Minami was shot near the entrance to the Japanese officers' quarters. He managed to crawl into a dry, storm-water drain and was found dead the next morning with his throat cut. Though no knife was found near him it seems likely that he either killed himself, or ordered someone to cut his throat. Certainly, some Japanese were murdered that night by their comrades. When word spread along the drain that Minami was dead, one POW decided it was time to surrender. The others with him did not agree and he was dragged out of the drain and stabbed to death.

The early light of dawn revealed an appalling scene of carnage. Bodies littered the Broadway and lay on and under the barbed wire. In B compound the burned huts smouldered as small groups of men huddled by them.

One of the Japanese officers had been killed, but during a conference early next morning the Camp Commandant was handed a note from the remainder which said that as all of them had been involved in the break-out 'we request death by shooting'. This of course was ignored by Brown who ordered a general cease-fire and for work to begin on clearing the Broadway. But firing did continue until at least 0900 because the camp interpreter saw a number of POW killed up to that time. 'They would jump out defiantly,' he said later, 'thump their chests and shout, "Go on, kill me!". Sometimes the guards obliged, even in front of me ... even when I asked them not to.'

Patrols from the camp, and later from the Infantry Training Centre, were dispatched to find those still at large. One clashed with a large party of escapees and a soldier was wounded and had his rifle taken from him. For some reason the rifle was not loaded and had no magazine, and when the Japanese who had taken it discovered this he committed suicide by plunging a knife into his stomach.

By midday the situation had to some extent been clarified. Of the 1,104 prisoners, 588 had escaped into the Broadway, 378 had made their getaway and 138 had remained in the compound. But it was too soon to know how many Japanese had been killed or wounded. Three Australians had lost their lives and four had been wounded. Another Australian, Lieutenant Harry Doncaster from the Infantry Training Centre, was killed that evening after his patrol of raw recruits, unarmed except for bayonets, turned and ran when faced by a group of Japanese who had escaped from the camp. They had converged on Doncaster with clubs, baseball bats and knives. He had tried to fend them off with his fists but was overpowered and battered to death.

When questioned afterwards about this incident, the Commandant of the Infantry Training Centre, Colonel John Mitchell, said that the patrol had not been issued with firearms on his express orders. The men under his command, he said, were untrained and he had been concerned about the possibility that the Japanese would take reprisals against Australian POW if more Japanese POW were killed.

'If I added one more to the big number lying on the wire and over the fields,' he remarked, 'I would probably be killing directly, on the other side of the world, perhaps up to ten of my own comrades in arms.'

In the event Mitchell's efforts to prevent further deaths were made meaningless by the actions of the Japanese themselves. An armed patrol combing the area where Doncaster had died found eight of the escapees hanging from nearby trees, and another was shot dead 'while attempting to escape'.

Two of a group of six Japanese were shot by a farmer who was out with his son after rabbits; he thought they were going to attack him – though in fact it had been agreed by all the POW that they would not harm civilians. A third was wounded when a patrol arrived to take the others back to the camp. On the Sunday morning a train beheaded two Japanese who had knelt down and laid their necks on the lines.

Altogether 25 Japanese died by one means or another beyond the confines of the camp and it took nine days to round up the rest. During this time a fifth Australian, a member of Blayney's Volunteer Defence Corps which had been asked to provide volunteers to help in the round-up, died after accidentally shooting himself. This brought the total to five Australians and 231 Japanese dead (188 from or partly from gunshot wounds), and four Australians and 108 Japanese wounded.

There was a great deal of apprehension that the Japanese would retaliate against Australian POW if they heard about the break-out, so the incident was shrouded in extreme secrecy which lasted for decades. But the bare facts had to be made public, which they were in September 1944 by the Australian prime minister, John Curtin. Although both the Germans and the Japanese predictably reacted to his announcement by accusing the Australians of committing an atrocity, the Japanese were in something of a dilemma because they could not possibly acknowledge that so many Japanese servicemen were being held in prison camps. Instead, they took the rather ingenious line that the Australians must have massacred civilian internees and an announcement to this effect was made over Batavia radio, but the break-out was not mentioned in Japan itself and was otherwise ignored.

In January 1945 Kanazawa, the only one of the three leaders in B Compound to survive, was put on trial for the murder of Hardy, one of the machine-gunners who had been killed, though it was made clear that Kanazawa was not accused of killing Hardy personally but was responsible for the events which led up to his death. The trial before a military court was held in secret and no official announcement that it had taken place was ever made. Kanazawa was found not guilty of murder but guilty of a subsidiary charge of 'conduct prejudicial to good order and military discipline'. He was given 15 months' 'hard labour' but served his sentence in solitary confinement in Cowra camp until March 1946 when he was repatriated.

14

THE VATICAN'S RATLINES

Frederick Forsyth's *Odessa File* was fictional – and no one has conclusively proved that the Odessa escape line ever existed – but at the end of the war real escape lines were used by Nazi war criminals and their sympathisers on the run from Allied justice.

Perhaps the most famous case was that of Adolf Eichmann, one of the prime instigators of the 'Final Solution' which the Nazis imposed on Europe's Jews. For four years Eichmann ran a chicken farm in the British zone of Germany after passing through several American interrogation centres without being detected. Then, in the summer of 1950, he was passed down an escape line – it is not known which one – and was hidden in a monastery in Genoa where he was given a false passport in the name of Ricardo Klement. On 14 July he obtained a visa for Argentina and reached Buenos Aires in October. Eventually the Israelis tracked him down, kidnapped him, and put him on trial in Israel. He was hanged in 1962.

Eichmann did not escape justice but there were plenty of others – Josef Mengele, 'the Angel of Death', was one of them – who did. This was because the crimes of some of the worst offenders were not immediately known to the Allies and in some cases it took years to accumulate the necessary evidence of guilt. The Allies did draw up lists of wanted war criminals, and special units were formed to hunt them down, but in the total confusion which followed the end of the war it was comparatively easy for a wanted war criminal to take on a new identity or cover his tracks by spreading the rumour that he was dead.

Also, by 1947 the Cold War was in full swing and most British and American intelligence agencies had become far more concerned with the communist threat, and how to counter it, than with bringing wanted war criminals – some of whom were now valued allies in the fight against communism – to justice. Priorities had changed, blind eyes were turned, and many shady deals must have been struck, the evidence for which is still buried deep in intelligence archives. Certainly some intelligence agencies, in working to protect their sources, kept their superiors in the dark.

The release of certain intelligence documents in the USA during the 1980s confirms allegations, which have been rife since the end of the war, that anti-communist priests in the Vatican, often with the collusion of the British and American authorities, helped war criminals escape justice. Involved were not only individual priests but a prominent Catholic lay group, known as Intermarium, which was strongly anti-communist. 'During its heyday in the 1940s and early 1950s,' wrote the author of *Blowback*, 'leading members of this organisation were deeply involved in smuggling Nazi fugitives out of eastern Europe to safety in the West.' Intermarium also became one of the single most important sources of recruits for the exile committees which were funded by the Central Intelligence Agency (CIA) to organise rebel groups behind the Iron Curtain.

The Vatican authorities certainly knew about the activities of pro-Allied priests such as Monsignor O'Flaherty (see Chapter Ten) who helped organise escape lines for Allied servicemen, so it is reasonable to assume that the activities of the pro-Axis ones were known as well. But that is a long way from proving that their activities had official approval, much less that anyone involved in running them knew the extent of the crimes that had been committed by those they were helping. The Vatican's attitude is that some priests set out to give aid to all those it could, without judging those who passed through their hands.

Yet one cannot help wondering at the lack of judgement, perhaps even of the naïvety, of some of the Vatican authorities to whom these pro-Fascist priests were responsible. When, for instance, the author Gitta Sereny asked the wartime director of the Vatican charity, Caritas International, if no one in the charity had thought to query those who must have had 'very serious things on their conscience', he replied: 'Do you really believe that there were more villains and thieves among them than among the British and Americans?'

'I am not really talking about stealing,' Sereny retorted. 'I am talking about murder.'

The name, ratline, was not a description of those who travelled down this escape network, appropriate though it sometimes was. Ratlines are the rope steps in the standing rigging of large sailing-ships and are used by the crew to go aloft to set or furl the sails. They extend to the top of the masts and when a ship foundered they were often the crew's last refuge before it sank. The name was apparently first used by the secret Second World War American organisation, the Office of Strategic Services (OSS), the forerunner of today's CIA, to describe the escape and evasion lines it set up in Italy from 1943 onwards to exfiltrate escaping POW and airmen. The name was obviously common parlance in the Italian combat theatre because the Allied escape and evasion organisation there, known as N Section, also used it and the term soon spread to the Far East too.

On 2 March 1939 Cardinal Pacelli was elected Pope, and chose the name Pius XII. The accusation that the Pope actively aided the Nazis during the war, or at least chose to ignore the worst of their excesses, has been rebutted to the satisfaction of most historians. But there is no doubt that there were a number of Fascist sympathisers – or perhaps it would be more accurate to describe them as ardent anti-communists – who aided the escape of suspected war criminals and were connected with the Vatican.

The first Vatican priest to become involved was Bishop Alois Hudal, the Austrian-born rector of one of the three seminaries for German priests in Rome. During the 1930s Hudal supported Hitler's anti-communist stance and apparently held a Golden Nazi Party membership badge. From 1930 he worked in the Holy

Office (now called the Congregation for the Doctrine of the Faith), a Vatican ministry of ancient origin whose task it was to censor books and educational aids.

In August 1944 the Pope's Secretary of State died, and a new one was not appointed. This left the handling of Pontifical Assistance to refugees in the hands of Monsignor Giovanni Montini, Under Secretary of State for Ordinary Affairs (the future Paul VI). According to the author Ladislas Farago, this gave Hudal the necessary entrée to arrange for Nazi refugees to be issued with identity documents which helped them emigrate.

Farago also claims that, thanks to Montini, Hudal was able to make contacts in the Vatican's Pontifical Commission for Assistance, which was involved in refugee work and was under Montini's control, and in Caritas International, the Catholic charity which funded refugees by paying their living and travelling expenses. And when in December 1944 the Allies acceded to the Vatican's request that a representative of the Holy See be permitted to visit German-speaking civilians interned in Italy, it was Hudal, as the Vatican's 'Spiritual Director of the German people resident in Italy', who was chosen for this mission.

'It is astonishing', wrote the authors of *Ratlines*, 'that the Holy See singled out the most notorious pro-Nazi bishop in Rome for this extremely sensitive mission. It was well known that these "civilian" camps were teeming with fugitive Nazis who had discarded their uniforms and were hiding among the legitimate refugees. The Americans were at least partly to blame for granting Hudal access to the internment camps. When a senior US diplomat at the Vatican forwarded the Secretariat of State's letter to Allied headquarters in Rome, he made no mention of Hudal's pro-Nazi sympathies ... for the Vatican to obtain an Allied travel pass for Hudal to visit the German internees was a bit like giving whisky to an alcoholic and telling him not to drink; the resulting corruption was inevitable.'

For his part Hudal remained quite unrepentant about his real mission. 'I thank God', he remarked many years later, 'that He [allowed me] to visit and comfort many victims in their prisons and concentration camps and [to help] them escape with false identity papers'. At the time he did not believe that the Allies' crusade against the Nazis was just. It was, he later wrote, merely a war of rival economic complexes which 'used catchwords like democracy, race, religious liberty and Christianity as a bait for the masses', which was why 'I felt duty-bound after 1945 to devote my whole charitable work mainly to former National Socialists and Fascists, especially to so-called "war criminals".'

One of the first Nazi criminals with whom Hudal made contact was Walter Rauff who had become head of the *Sicherheitsdienst* – the security service of the SS – in Milan following the Italian surrender in September 1943 which had precipitated the German occupation of the northern part of the country. Hudal had first met him in the spring of 1943 when Rauff had spent six months in the Vatican on some unspecified mission. When the German Army in Italy had begun negotiating secret surrender terms with the Americans, which led to its laying down its arms on 29 April 1945, Rauff had been very much involved in the negotiations. Subsequently, he obtained a false passport in the name of Carlo Comte and rented a flat in Milan, but was immediately arrested by the Americans. Within hours of his arrest a priest had arranged for his transfer from prison to an American Army hospital, and shortly after that he was released.

According to the famous Nazi hunter, Simon Wiesenthal, Rauff's release was arranged by Monsignor Don Giuseppe Bicchierai, Secretary to the Cardinal of Milan, who had been one of the Vatican's intermediaries in the secret surrender negotiations. He was released into the custody of 'S Force Verona', an OSS unit which was working with an Anglo-American counter-intelligence unit headed by James Jesus Angleton. They debriefed Rauff about communist activity in northern Italy and allowed him to return to his apartment in Milan. According to one source, Hudal contacted Rauff in July 1945 for a meeting in Rome. When this proved impossible Hudal suggested that Rauff go to Genoa to see the strongly anti-communist Archbishop Siri. Siri arranged for Rauff to be given money and a Red Cross passport with a valid visa for Syria.

Rauff returned to Milan and began working with Hudal to establish a ratline for Nazi refugees. To help him he had a former SS colleague, Frederico Schwendt, who during the war had counterfeited money for the SS which he had subsequently managed to launder through the banking system. It was this money, as well as the amount given to Rauff by one of Siri's private secretaries, that initially funded the organisation. It passed from Rauff in Milan, to Hudal in Rome, and thence to Siri in Genoa where Nazi escapers were able to board ships for the Middle East or South America. It is generally agreed that down the line, during the next four years, passed some of the most wanted war criminals, including the Commandant of Sobibor and Treblinka extermination camps, Franz Stangl.

Stangl's evidence about the ratline and Hudal's involvement in it is unequivocal. He escaped from Linz prison in May 1948 and made for Rome where, he had heard, Hudal helped Catholic SS officers. He eventually reached South America, but was extradited by the German authorities. In prison in Düsseldorf in 1971 he was interviewed by Gitta Sereny.

'It was strange, you know,' Stangl told her. 'I had no idea how one went about finding a bishop at the Vatican. I arrived in Rome and walked across a bridge over the Tiber and suddenly found myself face to face with a former comrade: there, in the middle of Rome where there were millions of people. He'd been in the security police in France and they wanted to put him on trial there. He'd been extradited from Glasenbach by the French and escaped in the Tyrol when on the way to France. Anyway, he said at once, "Are you on your way to see Hulda [Hudal]?" I said yes, but that I didn't know where to find him. So he told me ... The Bishop came into the room where I was waiting and he held out both his hands and said, "You must be Franz Stangl. I was expecting you."'

Sereny then asked Stangl what Hudal did for him.

'Well, first he got me quarters in Rome where I was to stay until my papers came through. And he gave me a bit more money – I had almost nothing left.

Then, after a couple of weeks, he called me in and gave me my new passport – a Red Cross passport.'

Sereny asked if the document actually stated that it was a Red Cross passport.

'Yes. It was a whitish booklet and there was a red cross on the cover – it was the same sort of thing, you know, as the old Nansen passports. They'd reversed my name by mistake; it was made out to Paul F. Stangl. I pointed it out to the Bishop. I said: "They made a mistake, this is incorrect. My name is Franz D. Paul Stangl." But he patted my shoulder and said, "Let's let sleeping dogs lie – never mind." He got me an entry visa to Syria and a job in a textile mill in Damascus, and he gave me a ticket for the ship. So I went to Syria. After a while my family joined me and three years later, in 1951, we emigrated to Brazil ...'

Money was essential for the ratline but so were the right documents and it was here that Hudal's influence was critical. Neither the Vatican identity card nor identity documents issued by the Vatican refugee organisations were sufficient to help a refugee emigrate – the former, for instance, was not valid outside Rome, much less Italy. But these documents were the first step for someone fleeing justice and Hudal had the contacts and the influence to have them issued. Vital to any escaper was a passport, issued by the International Red Cross (IRC). If an escaper could not obtain genuine IRC documents, there was a flourishing black market in stolen and forged IRC documents. That such documents were getting into the hands of war criminals was suspected by American intelligence at the end of 1945, and confirmed in mid-1946 when a number of German prisoners recaptured after breaking out of a camp at Rimini were found to have false IRC documents on them.

An American investigation was launched into this illegal emigration from Italy. Code-named Operation 'Circle', it sent its findings to Vincent La Vista, a member of the US State Department based in Rome, for further investigation. La Vista compiled his own report, entitled 'Illegal Emigration Movements In and Through Italy', which was forwarded to Washington in May 1947. Its central concern was communist infiltration into Latin America from Italy, but one of his principal conclusions was that the Vatican was aiding the escape of Nazi war criminals, a claim that was strongly denied by the official Vatican historian when the report was eventually made public in 1984.

La Vista, who was a Roman Catholic, also asserted that the Vatican had 'brought pressure to bear' on South American Catholic countries, especially Argentina, which resulted 'in the foreign missions of those countries taking an attitude almost favouring the entry into their country of former Nazi (*sic*) and former Fascists or other political groups, so long as they are anti-communist.'

La Vista's report also listed more than twenty Vatican relief and welfare organisations engaged in or suspected of engaging in illegal emigration, and pointed out that all of them were being generously financed by the Vatican. La Vista also named a number of priests involved in this illegal emigration, Hudal being one of the chief suspects.

But La Vista did not believe that all those working in these relief organisations were culpable. He called one of them, Father Josef Gallov, 'an honest, conscientious Catholic Priest, but he is likewise a sentimental old man' who did not trouble to ask too many questions. Gallov, who ran a Hungarian relief agency sponsored by the Vatican, gave refugees who applied to him a note to his contact in the International Red Cross (IRC) which bore an official stamp from the Vatican. This produced an IRC identity document which could then be used to acquire the necessary ration cards and temporary resident's permit from the Italian police. These allowed the refugee to remain in the country until he had obtained a passport and permission to emigrate, usually to a Central or South American country.

To prove how simple it was to obtain a passport and identity papers through Gallov, La Vista sent two of his Hungarian-speaking informants to the priest with the story that they had just fled from the Soviets and had no personal documents of any kind. 'Both men claimed to be natives of a small village in Hungary and to have lost their entire families in bombing raids during the war,' La Vista wrote in his report, and then went on to describe how Gallov drew up a sworn affidavit by one of the informants that corroborated the other's story. Gallov then gave the man a letter for the Red Cross which, within hours, presented him with a perfectly valid passport. The procedure was then simply reversed so that the other informant could also receive a passport. 'Needless to say,' La Vista commented about his informants, 'both men are Italian, neither ever having been outside Italy.'

One of the reports that La Vista appended to his own examined in detail the break-out from the Rimini camp. It transpired that two of those who had escaped had been told to go to Rome to contact a person who would help them emigrate to South America. Their contact was in fact an informant and the two men were put under surveillance. This revealed that they had joined two other fugitives who were in contact with local priests. One of these priests was 'aiding the escapees with food, lodging, and contacts with German and Vatican officials', and one of the men from Rimini was 'living in the apartment of a German woman who was formerly employed at the Germany Embassy in the Vatican'.

When two of the escapers went to Genoa to make arrangements to leave the country, the informant 'borrowed' their passports and found that they were issued by the International Red Cross. The informant was then instructed to try to obtain a false passport for himself which he did 'by paying 20,000 lire to a person known to have contacts with the International Red Cross'. This man took the informant's personal details and passed them to his IRC contact who looked through the IRC files to find 'the name of a missing or dead person who fitted the [informant's] description'. The informant was then told to apply for a Red Cross passport under the false name of Mirko Baucech. He did so and the informant's contact obtained two letters of identification from the Vatican and the Italian Red Cross so that the application would be approved.

La Vista also confirmed in his report that Milan was an important centre for Hudal's ratline. Although he did not name Rauff, he mentioned that Schwendt was involved in it and that 'there is a general movement of Germans ... who cross the border via Treviso and Milan for the sole purpose of obtaining ... fictitious identity documents, passports and visas, and leave almost immediately via Genoa and Barcelona for South America'.

The State Department's initial reaction was that La Vista's report required urgent attention, but it seems that on reflection it decided not to pursue the matter and the Vatican Secretariat of State was only advised that 'unscrupulous persons, often engaged in illicit and clandestine activities' had acquired travel documents 'through the unwitting assistance of charitable organisations', and left it at that.

Rumours about the Papal connection with the Nazis continued, however, and when Hudal's participation in helping wanted war criminals to escape threatened to become a public scandal, the Vatican deliberately strove to distance itself from him. He began to be shunned and in July 1952 he resigned his post, though he remained unrepentant. Vatican officials subsequently denied that he was in any way influential. 'He was,' one spokesman said, 'slightly suspect – not taken seriously. He desperately *wanted* to be taken seriously', but he was 'very much on the fringes'. More recently one of the official Vatican historians, Father Robert Graham, while strongly denying any official Vatican involvement in what Hudal was doing, has admitted that 'Hudal was rather notorious in Rome, being openly philo-Nazi. He had this idea that it was his divine call to settle relations between the Nazis and the Catholic Church.'

Another priest at the Vatican who ran a ratline was Father Krunoslav Draganović, a leading member of Intermarium and the secretary of a seminary in Rome called the Brotherhood of San Girolamo, which had produced a number of outstanding Croatian scholars, writers and priests. Croatia, a nation of Catholics, was one of the Vatican's most favoured, as a bulwark against the Orthodox church. After Hitler invaded Yugoslavia in April 1941, he made Croatia a puppet independent state. This was run by Ante Pavelić and members of his Fascist Ustashi Party whose massacres of Serbs, Jews and gypsies were among the war's most criminal acts. It is said that as many as half a million people were killed by them, and tens of thousands of others were compelled to change to the Catholic faith.

During the month that Pavelić came to power the Pope gave him an audience, which provoked the stiffest of protests by the British. The Foreign Office expressed astonishment that the Pope was willing to receive 'a notorious terrorist and murderer' such as Pavelić, and when the Vatican replied that he had been received as a private person, not as a head of state, and that it was not possible to ignore such an important Catholic 'statesman', the Foreign Office retorted that it was 'indeed astonished and pained that the Vatican should so consider him even for a moment'.

At this time Draganović was a professor of theology at Zagreb University. After the war the Yugoslav War Crimes Commission found that he had belonged to the committee which oversaw the forced conversion of Orthodox Serbs to Catholicism and that as Vice-President of the Ustashi's 'Office for Colonisation' he had been involved in the Nazis' 1942 anti-partisan campaign in western Bosnia before being sent to Rome as the Ustashi's representative to the Vatican in August 1943.

In Rome Draganović worked ostensibly for the Croatian Red Cross, an organisation of doubtful validity because it was not recognised by the International Red Cross. Even at that early date his plans for a ratline were apparently well advanced. Montini gave the Bosnian-born priest access to the Pope's Refugee Assistance Commission from whom he was able to obtain identity papers for refugees, and in late 1944 he was given permission by the Allies to visit the camps where Croatians were interned.

Draganović always denied helping to run a ratline for illegal refugees, but in November 1946 an American intelligence report concluded that he definitely was involved and that 'He is helped in this activity by his numerous contacts with the Embassies and Legations of South America in Italy and with the International Red Cross and by the fact that the Croatian Confraternity of the College of S. Girolamo degli Illirici, where he has his office, issues false identity cards to the Ustacha. With such documents and with the approval of the Pontifical Welfare Commission for Refugees, located in Via Piave 41, Rome, which is controlled almost exclusively by Ustacha, passports can be obtained from the International Red Cross, where Draganović has some way of ensuring their issue.'

One of Draganović's principal aides was Father Cecelja, who had been appointed a Deputy Military Vicar to the Ustashi militia by Pavelić in October 1941. He was the ratline's Austrian link to the Brotherhood of San Girolamo in Rome. Listed as war criminal number 7103 by Tito's government, he left Croatia in May 1944 and opened a branch of the Croatian Red Cross in Vienna to provide cover for the ratline. He was given the requisite papers to enable him to visit refugee camps without hindrance, and was able to issue false documents to those who wanted to acquire new identities, but in October 1945 he was arrested for doing this. The Assistant Chief of Staff of US Army Intelligence in Austria subsequently stated that Cecelja jeopardised 'the security of the occupational forces as well as the objectives of Military Government' and he was imprisoned for the next eighteen months.

During Cecelja's time in prison the Yugoslav authorities applied to have him extradited, but though the Americans had by now accumulated sufficient evidence to reasonably establish Cecelja's participation in collaborationist activities, extradition was refused, and after his release in March 1947 Cecelja returned to his task of sending wanted Nazis down his ratline.

Shortly before his death, according to the authors of *Ratlines*, 'Cecelja vividly recalled how the smuggling system worked. Up in Austria the fugitives would be cared for by his section of the organisation, which provided them with money, food, accommodation and the false papers they needed to travel from Austria to Italy. Down in Rome, Draganović was at the operation's nerve centre. He arranged the travel documents and through his high level contacts with South

American consulates, organised the necessary visas, especially to Argentina. Once a week Cecelja called Draganović who told him how many places were available that week. Cecelja then sent exactly that number to Rome.'

The Genoa end of the ratline was organised by another Croatian priest, Monsignor Karlo Petranović, who, the Yugoslav authorities alleged, had been involved in a number of wartime massacres in the mixed Croatian and Serbian district of Ogulin. Petranović arrived in Genoa at the end of 1945 via Graz and Trieste, where he had been sheltered by the local bishops, and Milan, where he had been helped by Cardinal Schuster.

In Genoa Petranović was recruited to help Draganović's ratline by Father Dragutin Kamber, another Croat priest with an unsavoury fascist reputation and one who was also wanted by the Yugoslav authorities for involvement in wartime massacres. Petranović agreed to help and became responsible for finding berths on ships for the people Draganović sent down the line to him. All Petranović needed to do was to find lodgings for those who arrived until their ships sailed for South America. In common with others working the ratline, Petranović did not only help illegal refugees; and when he was interviewed in 1989 he said proudly that one of the genuine refugees he had helped to reached the USA had been the Hungarian-born actress Zsa Zsa Gabor.

Mostly Petranović was allowed to work undisturbed, but on one occasion at least British Intelligence did intercept a wanted criminal before Petranović could get him to safety. This occurred in early 1947 when operatives from the British Special Screening Mission prevented sixteen refugees from boarding the SS *Philippa* which sailed regularly between Genoa and Buenos Aires. Ten of the sixteen were detained and one of them proved to be General Vladimir Kren, the head of Pavelić's wartime air force. He too was wanted by the Yugoslavs and was one of the few ever handed over to them.

Evidence exists that one of those Draganović helped was Pavelić himself. In May 1945, with many of his adherents, Pavelić fled from the advancing Red Army, and Tito's communist partisans, and made his way into Austria where he promptly disappeared. Tito's Yugoslav government demanded his return so that he could be put on trial, but the British and the Americans both stated that despite thorough searches they had not been able to find him in either of the zones which they now occupied in Austria. The Yugoslav kept up their demands and the British and Americans their denials, until eventually in December 1946 the Foreign Office decided that it seemed 'more and more likely that Pavelić is in Italy and that his whereabouts may be known to Dr Draganović ... and to no one else', and that Pavelić had probably not been in the British zone of occupation 'except possibly in transit'.

This, the Americans soon discovered when they began their own investigation into Pavelić's whereabouts in early 1947, was simply not true. One report stated that, 'according to reliable sources ... Pavelić was protected by the British in British-guarded and requisitioned quarters for a two (2) week period. Due to the insecurity of his position and due to the inevitable embarrassment of the British Command, he then left these quarters but remained in the British Occupation Zone for at least two (2) or three (3) months more still in contact with the British I[ntelligence] S[ervice].'

According to the Americans Pavelić had remained in Austria until April 1946 when he went to Italy where he was sheltered, among other places with Vatican connections, in the house of a former minister of the Nazi Romanian government at the Pope's summer retreat, Castelgandolfo, and that he was in constant touch with Draganović. It would seem that in mid-1946 he returned to Austria rather than leave Europe as he had originally planned, but in August 1947 it was reported that he had assumed the persona of an ex-Hungarian General named Giuseppe and was 'living in Church property under the protection of the Vatican, at Via Giacoma Venezian No. 17-C'. He shared the apartment with three other men, one of them a well-known Bulgarian terrorist, had a bodyguard of about a dozen men, and when he went out used a car with a Vatican number plate. Eventually he got away to Argentina, survived an assassination attempt there, and died in Madrid in 1959.

Two other Croats who escaped justice with the help of Draganović were Dragutin Toth and Vjekoslav Vrančić. Toth had been the Minister of Finance in Pavelić's government; Vrančić an Under Secretary of the Ustashi Interior Ministry, which controlled the police and the concentration camps in Croatia. Although the Yugoslav government was demanding their return, Toth made his way to Argentina in mid-1947 and a few months later Vrančić 'escaped' from British custody; in November 1947 US Intelligence recorded that he had arrived in Argentina using the name Ivo Rajičević.

Just a few months before Vrančić arrived in South America, Major James D. Milano, the commander of 430th Counter Intelligence Corps at Salzburg and *de facto* operations head of all US Army intelligence in Austria, decided to start his own ratline because at that time the unit had seventeen Red Army defectors who had been debriefed and were now in 'safe' houses. These defectors, who constituted an important source of Soviet military intelligence, had to be smuggled out of Europe before Soviet counter-intelligence hit squads caught up with them. Captain Paul Lyon, who headed operations for the CIC unit, knew immediately how to go about it. He had a friend in intelligence who knew Draganović. He called him the 'Good Father'.

'The deal is,' Lyon told Milano, 'various South American countries have allocated a bunch of visas to the Vatican for deserving Catholics, and Draganović hands them out. He's completely corrupt and will sell them for fifteen hundred cash, no questions asked. That's dollars. The only problem is, he's probably also selling visas to Nazis, SS men, Ustashes, and all the other lowlifes in Europe.'

This description did not deter Milano from proceeding any more than it deterred the unit's administrative and supply officer from accumulating goods to bribe officials who would otherwise have prevented the movement of what were illegal immigrants – the CIC called them 'visitors' – across their borders. He managed to steal six new jeeps and two were transferred to the ownership of officers in the Italian border police. The head of the border police and customs service, a general, was thought too senior to have his acquiescence bought with a jeep. Instead, he was given an even rarer gift, tickets for the Salzburg Festival! Lesser mortals were bribed with liquor, cartons of cigarettes, and that most precious commodity of all, nylon stockings.

At their first meeting Draganović told Lyon that he had six visas for Peru which he was willing to sell to the Americans. $9,000 was the price. The only condition Draganović made was that the visas were intended 'for good, serious Catholics' which Lyon hastily assured him they were.

Not surprisingly all the unit's files were destroyed by Milano before he left Austria in July 1950, but two memos outlining the history of the ratline have survived, both written by Lyon, and they clearly show how he ran the ratline for Milano.

The first is dated 15 July 1948 and its first three paragraphs read as follows: '1. In accordance with instructions from the Office of the Director of Intelligence, USFA, these agents [Lyon and Charles Crawford] have attempted to establish a safe means of resettlement of dependants of visitors and VIP personalities. 2. Through the Vatican connections of Father Draganović, Croat, DP Resettlement Chief of the Vatican Circle, a tentative agreement was reached to assist in this operation. The agreement consists of simply mutual assistance, i.e., these agents assist persons of interest to Father Draganović to leave Germany and, in turn, Father Draganović will assist these agents in obtaining the necessary visas to Argentina, South America, for persons of interest to this Command. 3. It may be stated that some of the persons of interest to Father Draganović may be of interest to the Denazification policy of the Allies; however, the persons assisted by Father Draganović are also of interest to our Russian ally. Therefore this operation cannot receive any official approval and must be handled with minimum amount of delay and with a minimum amount of general knowledge.'

The second memo is dated 10 April 1950 and is addressed to Milano who had obviously become concerned about controlling Draganović's activities. The first part, about the ratline's origins, reads as follows: 'a. During the summer of 1947 the undersigned received instructions from G-2 [Army Intelligence], USFA, through Chief CIC, to establish a means of disposition for visitors who had been in the custody of 430th CIC ... whose continued residence in Austria constituted a security threat as well as a source of possible embarrassment to the Commanding General USFA [United States Forces, Austria], since the Soviet Command had become aware of their presence in the US Zone of Austria and in some instances had requested the return of these persons to Soviet custody. b. The undersigned therefore proceeded to Rome where, through a mutual acquaintance, he conferred with a former Slovakian diplomat who in turn was able to recruit the services of a Croatian Roman Catholic Priest, Father Draganovich. Father Draganovich had by this time developed several clandestine evacuation channels to the various South American countries for various types of European refugees.'

There follows a section on the history of operations which states that during 1947 and 1948 all 'visitors' had to be escorted from Austria to Rome to ensure that no possible cause for embarrassment to the US government could arise from 'faulty documentation or unforeseen border or police incidents'. In Rome the 'visitors' were handed over to Draganović who placed them in 'safe' houses while he secured residence permits for them and permits to travel from Rome to Genoa or Naples, and permits from the Italian Foreign Office for visas. Later Draganović became so efficient at organising the necessary documentation that one of his agents could travel to Austria, pick up the 'visitors' and take them straight to Genoa where they were lodged in 'safe' houses until they could sail for South America.

There were, of course, difficulties which had to be overcome – frequent changes in valid travel documents and in immigration quotas, for example – and these were outlined in a third section which ends with a paragraph that leaves no doubt that Milano and his officers knew all about Draganović and that the unit had to be careful to cover its tracks.

'Although it might be advantageous to have absolute "control" of Father Dragonivich [sic] and his means of evacuation, it may be categorically stated that it is not possible and in the opinion of the undersigned not entirely desirable. Dragonivich is known and recorded as a Fascist, war criminal, etc., and his contacts with South American diplomats of a similar class are not generally approved by US State Department officials, plus the fact that in the light of security, it is better that we may be able to state, if forced, that the turning over of a DP [Displaced Person] to a welfare organisation falls in line with our democratic way of thinking and that we are not engaged in illegal disposition of war criminals, defectees and the like.'

Lyon goes on to say that although Draganović was reliable from the security point of view he 'is unscrupulous in his dealings concerning money, as he does a considerable amount of charity work for which he receives no compensation'. It was therefore not entirely impossible 'that he will delay one shipment for one organisation to benefit another organisation who pays higher prices' and he concludes by recommending that Draganović 'should be handled as a single operation by one agency and no attempt should be made to control him or his sources'.

In his book *Soldiers, Spies and the Rat Line*, Milano says that with one exception – a Nazi woman who had persuaded a Soviet officer to desert – his ratline was never used to exfiltrate Nazis on the run. But after Milano had left Austria the line was used to send the notorious Gestapo chief, Klaus Barbie, and his family to South America, and there is some indication that the CIA used it for the rest of the 1950s.

Barbie, who had been chief of the Gestapo in Lyons during the war, travelled down the line in early 1951 after being employed for a number of years by a US

Army Counter-Intelligence Corps (CIC) unit in Bavaria. Although it is improbable that that unit knew the full extent of his crimes, it certainly knew enough to warrant his arrest. Instead its commander used Barbie for espionage and sheltered him from those who were trying to trace him.

When official French demands for Barbie to be found and arrested became too strong to resist, those using his services (which were of negligible importance) passed him down the ratline. When Barbie reached Draganović the priest arranged the necessary documentation for him to go to Bolivia under the name of Klaus Altmann. There he was met by the line's local representative, another wanted war criminal, whose real name was Father Stjepan Osvaldi-Toth. Barbie remained in South America until he was extradited by the French in the 1980s, tried, and condemned to life imprisonment. He died in gaol in 1991.

Draganović had a happier fate. He returned to Yugoslavia in 1967 – perhaps under an amnesty, perhaps because he had always been a double agent – and died peacefully there in July 1983.

BIBLIOGRAPHY

Aarons, Mark, and Loftus, John. *Ratlines*. London, 1991
Absalom, Roger. *A Strange Alliance*. Florence, 1991
Barber, Noel. *Sinister Twilight*. London, 1968
Brome, Vincent. *The Way Back*. London, 1957
Brooke, Geoffrey. *Alarm Starboard!* Cambridge, 1982
Burt, K., and Leasor, J. *The One That Got Away*. London, 1956
Carew, Tim. *Hostages to Fortune*. London, 1971
Carr-Gregg, Charlotte. *Japanese Prisoners of War in Revolt*. Brisbane, 1978
Caskie, D. *The Scarlet Pimpernel*. London, 1957
Chadwick, O. *Britain and the Vatican During the Second World War*. London, 1986
Churchill, W. S., *My Early Life*. London, 1947
Darling, Donald. *Secret Sunday*. London, 1975
Derry, Sam. *The Rome Escape Line*. London, 1960
Dormer, Hugh. *Hugh Dormer's Diaries*. London, 1947
Duke, Madelaine. *No Passport*. London, 1957
Dumais, Lucien, with Hugh Popham. *The Man Who Went Back*. London, 1975
Endacott, G. B., and Birch, A. *Hong Kong Eclipse*. Oxford, 1978
Farago, Ladislas. *Aftermath*. London, 1976
Foot, M. R. D. *SOE in France*. London, 1968
Foot, M. R. D., and Langley, J. M. *MI9: Escape and Evasion 1939–45*. London, 1979, 1980
Furman, John. *Be Not Fearful*. London, 1959
Gallagher, J. P. *Scarlet Pimpernel of the Vatican*. London, 1967
Goodwin, R. B. *Hong Kong Escape*. London, 1953
– *Passport to Eternity*. London, 1956
Gordon, Harry. *Voyage from Shame*. Brisbane, 1994
Gough, Richard. *The Escape from Singapore*. London, 1987
Heaps, L. *The Grey Goose of Arnhem*. London, 1976
Hill, Richard. *My War With Imperial Japan*. New York, 1989
Hutton, C. Clayton. *Official Secret*. London, 1960
Kennedy, J. *When Singapore Fell*. London, 1989
Kirby, Woodburn S. *The War Against Japan*, vol. 1. London, 1957
Kochan, Miriam. *Prisoners in England*. London, 1980
Krammer, Arnold. *Nazi Prisoners of War in America*. New York, 1979
Langley, J. M. *Fight Another Day*. London, 1974

Lodwick, John. *Bid the Soldiers Shoot*. London, 1958

Long, Helen. *Safe Houses are Dangerous*. London, 1985

Milano, James D. *Soldiers, Spies, and the Rat Line*. London, 1995

Millar, George. *Horned Pigeon*. London, 1946

Miller, John. *Friends and Romans*. London, 1987

Moore, John Hammond. *The Faustball Tunnel*. New York, 1978

Neave, Airey. *The Little Cyclone*. London, 1954

– *Saturday at MI9*. London, 1969

Phillips, C. E. Lucas. *Cockleshell Heroes*. London, 1956

'Rémy'. *Réseau Comète*. Paris, 1966

Richards, Brooks. *The Secret Flotillas*. London, 1995

Ride, Edwin. *British Army Aid Group: Hong Kong Resistance 1942–1945*. Oxford, 1981

Scotland, A. P. *The London Cage*. London, 1957

Sereny, Gitta, *Into That Darkness: The Mind of a Mass Murderer*. London, 1977

Shoemaker, Lloyd R. *The Escape Factory*. New York, 1990

Simpson, C. *Blowback*. New York, 1988

Sparks, W. *The Last of the Cockleshell Heroes*. London, 1992

Sullivan, Matthew. *Thresholds of Peace*. London, 1979

Watt, G. *The Comet Connection*. Kentucky, USA, 1990

Wiesenthal, S. *The Murderers Amongst Us*. London, 1967

Winks, R. *Cloak and Gown*. New York, 1987

Wynne, Barry. *No Drums ... No Trumpets*. London, 1961

INDEX